READING REVELATION

READING REVELATION

A Comparison of

Four Interpretive Translations

of the Apocalypse

C. MARVIN PATE

Kregel
Academic & Professional

Reading Revelation: A Comparison of Four Interpretive Translations of the Apocalypse
© 2009 by C. Marvin Pate

Published by Kregel Publications, a division of Kregel, Inc., P.O. Box 2607, Grand Rapids, MI 49501.

The Greek texts used are Nestle-Aland, Novum Testamentum Graece, 27th Revised Edition and The Greek New Testament, Fourth Revised Edition.

Nestle-Aland, Novum Testamentum Graece, 27th Revised Edition, edited by Barbara Aland, Kurt Aland, Johannes Karavidopoulos, Carlo M. Martini, and Bruce M. Metzger in cooperation with the Institute for New Testament Textual Research, Münster/Westphalia, © 1993 Deutsche Bibelgesellschaft, Stuttgart. Used by permission.

The Greek New Testament, Fourth Revised Edition, edited by Barbara Aland, Kurt Aland, Johannes Karavidopoulos, Carlo M. Martini, and Bruce M. Metzger in cooperation with the Institute for New Testament Textual Research, Münster/Westphalia, © 1993 Deutsche Bibelgesellschaft, Stuttgart. Used by permission.

The Greek font used in this book is SymbolGreekTU and is available from www.linguistsoftware.com/lgku .htm, +1-425-775-1130.

ISBN 978-0-8254-3367-2

Printed in the United States of America
09 10 11 12 13 / 5 4 3 2 1

CONTENTS

INTRODUCTION

The "mark of the beast"; "666"; the "Antichrist"; seal, trumpet, and bowl judgments; the second coming of Christ; the Millennium; and much more! These intriguing, if not foreboding, topics all come together in one book—Revelation.

Apocalypse—even saying the name elicits a continuum of emotions ranging from fear to puzzlement to joy! Little wonder, then, that there is no consensus on the interpretation of the last book of the Bible. Rather, the interpretation of Revelation has customarily fallen along the lines of four major, essentially conflicting, hermeneutical approaches: preterist, historicist, futurist, and idealist.

Many excellent treatments championing these respective approaches to Revelation are found in introductions in the commentaries on Revelation and in the various study Bibles, in the counterpoint-type works, in the popular-level writings of the prophecy buffs, and even in novels. However, surprisingly missing in all of this is a parallel translation of Revelation showcasing the preceding four schools of interpretation,[1] somewhat like the synopsis columns in a harmony of the four Gospels. It will be helpful for readers of Revelation to have a work that converts the four major interpretations of that book into parallel translations, thereby highlighting both the similarities and differences characterizing those respective viewpoints. Thus, at a glance the reader can survey what these approaches say about this or that passage in the Apocalypse. This is what the present work attempts to do. Five columns are provided for each chapter of Revelation: a column containing the Greek text with interlinear English translation; and columns for the preterist, historicist, futurist, and idealist interpretations.

The Four Schools of Interpretation

Four major interpretations have been put forth in an attempt to unravel the mysteries of the Apocalypse: preterist, historicist, futurist, and idealist interpretations. The names of each capture the essence of the respective approaches.

The *preterist* (past) interpretation understands the events of Revelation to have been fulfilled in the first century of the Christian era—at the fall of Jerusalem in A.D. 70. In effect, the book was written to comfort Christians, who suffered persecution from both the Roman imperial cult and Judaism.

The *historicist* understanding of Revelation interprets the prophecies of Revelation as unfolding in church history. Indeed, the seven churches of Asia Minor (see Rev. 2–3) are thought to forecast seven stages of the church, beginning with the early church and continuing to the modern church at the end of time. Moreover, the historicist viewpoint focuses on the battle between Roman Catholicism and Protestantism (the "true" church), which is thought to form the subplot of the Apocalypse.

The *futurist* scheme argues that the events of Revelation remain largely unfulfilled, holding that chapters 4–22 await the end times for their realization. If the preterist interpretation has dominated among biblical scholars, the futurist reading is the preference of choice among the masses.

The *idealist* viewpoint, by way of contrast to the previous three theological constructs, is reticent to pinpoint the symbolism of Revelation historically. For this school of thought, Revelation sets forth timeless truths concerning the battle between good and evil that continues throughout the church age.

The Preterist Interpretation

The preterist viewpoint wants to take seriously the historical interpretation of Revelation by relating it to its original author and audience. That is, John addressed his book to real churches that faced dire problems in the first century A.D. Two quandaries in particular provided the impetus for the recording of the book. Kenneth L. Gentry Jr. writes of these:

> Revelation has two fundamental purposes relative to its original hearers. In the first place, it was designed to steel the first century Church against the gathering storm of persecution, which was reaching an unnerving crescendo of theretofore unknown proportions and intensity. A new and major feature of that persecution was the entrance of imperial Rome onto the scene. The first historical persecution of the Church by imperial Rome was by Nero Caesar from A.D. 64 to A.D. 68. In the second place, it was to brace the Church for a major and

---

1. Steve Gregg has provided a wonderful four-views parallel commentary (which I make much use of in this work, especially his treatment of the historicist viewpoint), *Revelation: Four Views—A Parallel Commentary* (Nashville: Nelson, 1997). A portion of the summary of the four interpretations of Revelation to follow in this introduction come from my edited book, *Four Views on the Book of Revelation* (Grand Rapids: Zondervan, 1998); and from J. Daniel Hays, J. Scott Duvall, and C. Marvin Pate, *Dictionary of Biblical Prophecy and End Times* (Grand Rapids: Zondervan, 2007).

fundamental re-orientation in the course of redemptive history, a re-orientation necessitating the destruction of Jerusalem (the center not only of Old Covenant Israel, but of Apostolic Christianity [cf. Ac. 1:8; 2:1ff.; 15:2] and the Temple [cf. Mt. 24:1–34 with Rev. 11]).[2]

Thus, the sustained attempt to root the fulfillment of the divine prophecies of Revelation in the first century A.D. constitutes the preterist's distinctive approach.

The origin of preterism can be traced to the theological system known as postmillennialism, which teaches that Christ will return after the Millennium, a period of bliss on earth brought about by the conversion of the nations because of the preaching of the gospel. The credit for formulating the postmillennial doctrine is usually given to Daniel Whitby (1638–1726), a Unitarian minister from England. Whitby's view of the Millennium was embraced by conservative and liberal theologians. John F. Walvoord observes,

> His views on the millennium would probably have never been perpetuated if they had not been so well keyed to the thinking of the times. The rising tide of intellectual freedom, science, and philosophy, coupled with humanism, had enlarged the concept of human progress and painted a bright picture of the future. Whitby's view of a coming golden age for the church was just what people wanted to hear. . . . It is not strange that theologians scrambling for readjustments in a changing world should find in Whitby just the key they needed. It was attractive to all kinds of theology. It provided for the conservative a seemingly more workable principle of interpreting Scripture. After all, the prophets of the Old Testament knew what they were talking about when they predicted an age of peace and righteousness. Man's increasing knowledge of the world and scientific improvements which were coming could fit into this picture. On the other hand, the concept was pleasing to the liberal and skeptic. If they did not believe the prophets, at least they believed that man was now able to improve himself and his environment. They, too, believed a golden age was ahead.[3]

Such an acceptance on the part of many resulted in two types of postmillennialism, as Paul N. Benware notes: "liberal postmillennialism" and "biblical postmillennialism."[4] The former had its heyday in the nineteenth century in association with the "social gospel," whose mission was the liberation of humanity from societal evil (poverty, racism, disease, war, and injustice). The presupposition of this school of thought was that humanity was basically good and that society ultimately would get better and better, resulting in a golden age on earth. Laudable as this attempt was, however, the social gospel suffered from two flaws: it abandoned the preaching of the gospel, and it naively based its view of history on the Darwinian evolutionary process. Time dealt a mortal blow to liberal postmillennialism—the catastrophic events of the twentieth and early twenty-first centuries rendered it an untenable position (e.g., two world wars; the Great Depression; the threat of nuclear destruction by the world's superpowers, terrorists, or both).

Alongside liberal postmillennialism was its evangelical counterpart. Those theologians of the eighteenth and nineteenth centuries who followed this approach maintained their commitment to the gospel and to its transforming power. Stanley J. Grenz writes of them,

> Their outlook differed fundamentally from both secular and liberal Christian utopianism. They were optimistic concerning the future to be sure. But their optimism was born out of a belief in the triumph of the gospel in the world and of the work of the Holy Spirit in bringing in the kingdom, not out of any misconception concerning the innate goodness of humankind or of the ability of the church to convert the world by its own power.[5]

Today, biblical postmillennialism has rebounded from the catastrophes of history and is currently experiencing a resurgence of influence, especially through Christian reconstructionism. This movement's conviction is admirable—as the church preaches the gospel and performs its role as the salt of the earth, the kingdom of God will advance until the whole world will one day gladly bow to the authority of

---

2. Kenneth L. Gentry Jr., *Before Jerusalem Fell: Dating the Book of Revelation* (Tyler, TX: Institute for Christian Economics, 1989), 15–16. It should be remembered, however, that preterism is comprised of two camps—one that locates the fulfillment of Revelation largely in the first century relative to the fall of Jerusalem, and another that sees the fulfillment of Revelation in both the first century (the fall of Jerusalem) and in the fifth century (the fall of Rome). This discussion on the schools of interpretation comes in part from Pate, *Four Views on the Book of Revelation*, 19–34.

3. John F. Walvoord, *The Millennial Kingdom* (Findlay, OH: Dunham, 1963), 22–23. In a recent correspondence, Ken Gentry helpfully provides two clarifications of the presentation we have been providing here regarding the connection between preterism and postmillennialism. First, it is simplistic to restrict the preterist view to postmillennialism. Many amillennialists also align themselves with this interpretation (e.g., Jay Adams, Cornelis Vanderwaal). Second, although Whitby is credited as popularizing postmillennialism, actually it is Thomas Brightman (1562–1607) who deserves that credit. Moreover, there is a nascent postmillennialism/preterism in some of the church fathers (e.g., Origen, Eusebius, Athanasius, Augustine).

4. The following synopsis is taken from Paul N. Benware, *Understanding End Times Prophecy: A Comprehensive Approach* (Chicago: Moody, 1995), 120–22.

5. Stanley J. Grenz, *The Millennial Maze: Sorting Out Evangelical Options* (Downers Grove, IL: InterVarsity Press, 1992), 66.

Christ. The means for accomplishing this goal will be the law of God, which impacts the church and, in turn, the world.[6]

Preterists locate the timing of the fulfillment of the prophecies of Revelation in the first century A.D., specifically just before the fall of Jerusalem in A.D. 70 (though some also see its fulfillment in the fall of both Jerusalem [first century] and Rome [fifth century]). Despite the opinion of many that Revelation was written in the 90s during the reign of Domitian (81–96), much of evangelical preterism holds the date of the book to be Neronian (54–68).

Three basic arguments are put forth to defend that period. First, there are allusions throughout Revelation to Nero as the current emperor (e.g., 6:2; 13:1–18; 17:1–13).

Second, the condition of the churches in Asia Minor to which John writes his letters (chaps. 2–3) best correlates with pre-70 Jewish Christianity, a time that witnessed the rupture between Christianity and Judaism. In effect, Revelation attests to the twofold persecution of Jewish Christianity—by the Jews and by the Romans. The former persecuted Jewish believers because of their faith in Jesus as the Messiah, so that they were consequently expelled from the synagogues, thus exposing them to Caesar worship.[7] The latter, subsequently, tried to force Jewish Christians to revere Caesar. John predicts that in retaliation on first-century Jews for persecuting Christians, Christ will come in power to destroy Jerusalem, using the Roman Empire to do so (e.g., 1:7–8; 22:20; chaps. 2–3; 11; 17–18)—a warning that came true with Jerusalem's fall in A.D. 70.

Third, according to Revelation 11, the temple seems still to be standing (that is, at the time of the writing of the book).

Based on the preceding arguments, we might outline Revelation as follows:

Chapter 1:	John's vision of the risen Jesus
Chapters 2–3:	The situation of early Jewish Christianity
Chapters 4–5:	The heavenly scene of Christ's reign
Chapters 6–18:	Parallel judgments on Jerusalem
Chapter 19:	The coming of Christ to complete the judgment of Jerusalem
Chapters 20–22:	Christ's rule on earth[8]

With regard to the philosophy of history presumed by most preterists, as noted before, it is a positive one. The world will get better and better because of the triumph of the gospel. In that sense, postmillennialism aligns itself more with the role of the Old Testament prophet, whose message proclaimed the intervention of God in history, than with the apocalypticist's doom-and-gloom forecasts of the future.

The Historicist Interpretation

The historicist approach argues that Revelation supplies a prophetic overview of church history from the first century until the return of Christ. Indeed, one could imagine proponents of the historicist interpretation using Revelation to teach a course in church history! Although there have been many esteemed advocates of the historicist approach in the past (e.g., Wycliffe, Knox, Tyndale, Luther, Calvin, Zwingli, Wesley, Edwards, Finney, Spurgeon), there are very few today. Historicism was extremely popular during the Protestant Reformation as reformers identified the Antichrist and Babylon with the pope and Roman Catholicism of their day.

The primary strength of this view lies in its attempt to make sense of Revelation for the interpreter by correlating the prophecies directed to the seven churches of Asia Minor with the stages comprising church history. The vast majority of scholars agree, however, that this single strength is far outweighed by its many weaknesses. The historicist outline applies only to the history of the Western church, ignoring the spread of Christianity throughout the rest of the world. Since images such as the beast of Revelation 13 are always identified with people and events contemporary to the interpreter, the historicist reading of Revelation is constantly being revised as new events occur and new figures emerge. Most problematic for historicism is the complete lack of agreement about the various outlines of church history. History is like a moving target for those who want to read Revelation in this way, and there is no consensus about what the book means, even among interpreters within the same school of interpretation.

The historicist interpretation follows closely the amillennialism of the idealist reading of Revelation and subscribes to that viewpoint's realistic philosophy of history (for these two ideas, see our discussion below of the idealist interpretation).

The Futurist Interpretation

While the futurist view tends to interpret Revelation 4–22 as still unfulfilled (awaiting the events surrounding

---

6. Authors who identify themselves with the preterist interpretation of Revelation include David Chilton, *The Days of Vengeance: An Exposition of the Book of Revelation* (Fort Worth: Dominion, 1987); and Gary DeMar, *Last Days Madness: Obsession of the Modern Church* (Atlanta: American Vision, 1994).

7. Judaism was permitted freedom of worship by Rome. To be separated from Judaism, therefore, was to lose that privileged status.

8. A more logical division of chapters 21 and 22 is 21:1–22:9 and 22:10–21. This division is clear in the Greek but not in our English translations.

the second coming of Christ), it is not completely unified. There are two camps of interpretation: dispensationalism and historic premillennialism.

Dispensationalism

The most popular interpretation of Revelation among American audiences during the twentieth century has been dispensationalism, one of the varieties of premillennialism. The name of the movement is derived from the biblical word "dispensation" (KJV), a term referring to the administration of God's earthly household (1 Cor. 9:17; Eph. 1:10; 3:2; Col. 1:25). Dispensationalists divide salvation history into historical eras or epochs in order to distinguish the different administrations of God's involvement in the world. C. I. Scofield, after whom the enormously popular *Scofield Reference Bible* was named, defined a dispensation as "a period of time during which man is tested in respect of obedience to some specific revelation of the will of God."[9] During each dispensation, humankind fails to live in obedience to the divine test, consequently bringing that period under God's judgment and thus creating the need for a new dispensation. Read this way, the Bible can be divided into the following eight dispensations (though the number and names vary in this school of thought): innocence, conscience, civil government, promise, Mosaic law, age of grace, and kingdom.[10]

The hallmark of dispensationalism has been its commitment to a literal interpretation of prophetic Scripture. This has resulted in three well-known tenets cherished by adherents of the movement.

First, a distinction between the prophecies made about Israel in the Old Testament and the church in the New Testament must be maintained. In other words, the church has not replaced Israel in the plan of God. The promises he made to the nation about its future restoration will occur. The church, therefore, is a parenthesis in the outworking of that plan. The dispensational distinction between Israel and the church was solidified in the minds of many as a result of two major events in this century: the Holocaust (which has rightly elicited from many deep compassion for the Jewish people) and the rebirth of the State of Israel in 1948. Second, dispensationalists are premillennialists; that is, they believe Christ will come again and establish a temporary, one-thousand-year reign on earth from Jerusalem.

Third, dispensationalists believe in the pretribulation rapture; that is, Christ's return will occur in two stages: in the first stage he comes for his church, which will be spared the Tribulation; in the second stage he comes in power and glory to conquer his enemies.

Dispensationalism seems to have been articulated first by John Nelson Darby, an influential leader in the Plymouth Brethren movement in England during the nineteenth century. The movement was imported to the United States, receiving notoriety with the publication in 1909 of the *Scofield Reference Bible*. At least three developments have unfolded within the movement during the twentieth century. The earliest stage was propounded by Darby and Scofield, a period that emphasized the dispensations themselves. A second stage emerged in the 1960s, thanks to the work by Charles C. Ryrie, *Dispensationalism Today*. With this second development two noticeable changes transpired: Faith was highlighted as the means of salvation in any of the dispensations (contra the old *Scofield Reference Bible*'s statement about works being the means of salvation in the Old Testament; see its footnote on John 1:17), and the individual dispensations were no longer the focal point; rather, the emphasis now lay on the literal hermeneutic of dispensationalism.

In the 1980s a third development arose, commonly called progressive dispensationalism. This variant of dispensationalism adheres to the already/not yet eschatological tension. This approach allows it to root Revelation in the first century A.D. (especially the early church's struggle with the imperial cult) while still holding to the futurity of the Great Tribulation, the Parousia, and the Millennium. As such, progressive dispensationalism is hospitable to the eclectic approach.[11]

The classical dispensationalist's understanding of the time frame of Revelation and its structure go hand in hand. Because this school of thought interprets the prophecies of the book literally, their fulfillment, therefore, is perceived as still future (esp. chaps. 4–22). Moreover, the magnitude of the prophecies (e.g., one-third of the earth destroyed; the sun darkened) suggests that they have not yet occurred in history. The key verse in this discussion is 1:19, particularly its three tenses, which are thought to provide an outline for Revelation: "what you have seen" (the past, John's vision of Jesus in chap. 1); "what is now" (the present, the letters to the seven churches in chaps. 2–3); "what will take place later" (chaps. 4–22). In addition, the classical dispensationalist believes that the lack of mention of the church from chapter 4 on indicates that it has been raptured to heaven by Christ before the advent of the Tribulation (chaps. 6–18).

Intimately associated with premillennialism as dis-

---

9. *The Scofield Reference Bible* (New York: Oxford, 1909), note to Genesis 1:28, heading. For an updated definition that emphasizes faith as the means for receiving the revelations in the various dispensations, see Charles C. Ryrie, *Dispensationalism Today* (Chicago: Moody, 1965), 74.

10. C. I. Scofield, *Rightly Dividing the Word of Truth* (New York: Loizeaux Brothers, 1896). Many modern dispensationalists, however, have grown uncomfortable with these periodizations, preferring rather to talk about the Bible in terms of its two divisions—the old and new covenants.

11. Proponents of this approach include Craig A. Blaising and Darrell L. Bock, *Progressive Dispensationalism* (Wheaton, IL: Victor, 1993); and Robert L. Saucy, *The Case for Progressive Dispensationalism: The Interface Between Dispensational and Non-Dispensational Theology* (Grand Rapids: Zondervan, 1993); see Pate, *Four Views on the Book of Revelation*.

pensationalism is, one is not surprised that this perspective views the history of the world pessimistically. Grenz summarizes this interpretation:

> In contrast to the optimism of postmillennialism, premillennialism displays a basic pessimism concerning history and the role we play in its culmination. Despite all our attempts to convert or reform the world, prior to the end antichrist will emerge and gain control of human affairs, premillennialism reluctantly predicts. Only the catastrophic action of the returning Lord will bring about the reign of God and the glorious age of blessedness and peace.
>
> In keeping with this basic pessimism concerning world history, premillennial theologies emphasize the discontinuity, or even the contradiction between, the present order and the kingdom of God, and they elevate the divine future over the evil present. The kingdom is the radically new thing God will do. However it may be conceived, the "golden age"—the divine future—comes as God's gracious gift and solely through God's action.[12]

Historic Premillennialism

The historic premillennial interpretation agrees with its sibling viewpoint—dispensationalism—that Christ will return to establish a thousand-year reign on earth at his Parousia. But sibling rivalry ensues between the two approaches on the issue of the relationship of the church to the Tribulation (Rev. 6–18). According to historic premillennialism,[13] the church will undergo the messianic woes, the Tribulation. This is so because the church has replaced Old Testament Israel as the people of God (Rom. 2:26–28; 11; Gal. 6:16; Eph. 2:11–22; 1 Peter 2:9–10; Rev. 1:5–6; 7:1–8; etc.). Like amillennialism and progressive dispensationalism, the historic premillennial view is based on the already/not yet eschatological hermeneutic: the kingdom of God dawned with the first coming of Christ, but it will not be completed until the second coming of Christ (compare also the eclectic viewpoint). And in the between period the church encounters the messianic woes, which will intensify and culminate in the return of Christ.

In this volume, we focus on the dispensational interpretation of Revelation since that is the most popular reading of the Apocalypse among the masses. Furthermore, because the posttribulational viewpoint of historic premillennialism

is assumed by preterists, historicists, and idealists (though interpreted in their own respective ways), the uniqueness of the historic premillennal approach is diluted.

The Idealist Interpretation

The idealist approach to Revelation has sometimes been called the "spiritualist" view in that it interprets the book spiritually, or symbolically. Accordingly, Revelation is seen from this perspective as representing the ongoing conflict of good and evil, with no immediate historical connection to any social or political events. Raymond Calkins well describes this interpretation:

> If we understand the emergency which caused the book to be written, the interpretation of it for its time, for our time, and for all time, it becomes as clear as daylight. In the light of this explanation, how far from the truth becomes that use of it which finds the chief meaning of the book in the hints it gives us about the wind-up of creation, the end of the world, and the nature of the Last Judgment. . . . To use Revelation in this way is to abuse it, for the book itself makes no claim to be a key to the future.[14]

Consequently, Calkins captures the chief message of Revelation in terms of five propositions:

1. It is an irresistible summons to heroic living.

2. It contains matchless appeals to endurance.

3. It tells us that evil is marked for overthrow *in the end.*

4. It gives us a new and wonderful picture of Christ.

5. It reveals to us the fact that history is in the mind of God and in the hand of Christ as the author and reviewer of the moral destinies of men.[15]

While all four schools of interpretation surveyed here resonate with these affirmations, the idealist view distinguishes itself by refusing to assign the preceding statements to any historical correspondence and thereby denies that the prophecies in Revelation are predictive except in the most general sense of the promise of the ultimate triumph of good at the return of Christ.[16]

---

12. Grenz, *The Millennial Maze*, 185.
13. The name "historic premillennialism" comes from the conviction that this was the earliest view of the church fathers. For a helpful, detailed investigation of the four schools of interpretation relative to Revelation, see Gregg, *Revelation: Four Views.*
14. Raymond Calkins, *The Social Message of the Book of Revelation* (New York: Womans Press, 1920), 3–4.
15. Ibid., 7–9.
16. Merrill C. Tenney provides a helpful summary of the idealist interpretation of Revelation, as well as the other viewpoints, in *Interpreting Revelation* (Grand Rapids: Eerdmans, 1957), 143–44.

The origin of the idealist school of thought can be traced back to the allegorical or symbolic hermeneutic espoused by the Alexandrian church fathers, especially Clement (second century) and Origen (third century). R. H. Charles writes that these Alexandrians

> under the influence of Hellenism and the traditional allegorical school of interpretation which came to a head in Philo, rejected the literal sense of the Apocalypse, and attached to it a spiritual significance only. This theory dominates many schools of exegetes down to the present day. Thus Clement saw in the four and twenty elders a symbol of the equality of Jew and Gentile within the Church, and in the tails of the locusts the destructive influences of immoral teachers. Origen as well as his opponent Methodius rejects as Jewish the literal interpretation of chap. XX and in the hands of his followers the entire historical contents of the Apocalypse were lost sight of.[17]

Akin to the Alexandrian interpretation of Revelation was the amillennial view propounded by Dionysius, Augustine, and Jerome (third to fifth centuries). Thus the Alexandrian school, armed with the amillennial method, became the dominant approach to Revelation until the Reformation.

As mentioned above, the idealist does not restrict the contents of Revelation to a particular historical period but rather sees it as an apocalyptic dramatization of the continuous battle between God and evil. Because the symbols are multivalent in meaning and without specific historical referent, the application of the book's message is limitless. Each interpreter therefore can find significance for his or her respective situation.

Two recent commentaries on Revelation nicely illustrate this method. The first is the work by Paul S. Minear, whose interpretation of the symbols of Revelation is stimulating.[18] For him the purpose of Revelation is to warn Christians of the enemy within—"the false Christian." The whole of the book is viewed from that perspective. The seven letters provide the context of the book—it is a divine challenge to the church to be faithful to Christ. The judgments thereafter are designed not to effect the ruination of those outside of Christendom, but of the unfaithful within it. But those who persevere in righteousness receive the promise of the new heaven and new earth. Read in this way, Revelation is to be taken not as an apocalyptic invective against the non-Christian but rather as a prophetic warning to the Christian.

A second work on Revelation illustrating the idealist interpretation is the challenging commentary by Elisabeth Schüssler Fiorenza, whose purpose in writing it is to "liberate the text from its historical captivity and rescue the message of Revelation for today."[19] In other words, the meaning of Revelation is not to be sought in the first century or in the remote events of the end time, but rather in the ongoing struggle between those disadvantaged sociopolitically and their oppressors. Thus understood, Revelation is a powerful tool in the hands of liberation and feminist theologians for throwing off the yoke of capitalism and chauvinism, respectively.

The best way to appreciate Fiorenza's approach is to see her method at work. For example, she approvingly quotes from the poem "Thanksgiving Day in the United States" by Julia Esquivel, which reworks Revelation 17–18 by applying it to her own third-world experience:

> In the third year of the massacres
> by Lucas and the other coyotes
> against the poor of Guatemala
> I was led by the Spirit into the desert.
>
> And on the eve
> of Thanksgiving Day
> I had a vision of Babylon:
> The city sprang forth arrogantly
> from an enormous platform
> of dirty smoke produced
> by motor vehicles, machinery
> and contamination from smokestacks.
>
> It was as if all the petroleum
> from a violated earth was being consumed by the Lords
>   of capital
> and was slowly rising
> obscuring the face
> of the Sun of Justice
> and the Ancient of Days. . . .
>
> Each day false prophets
> invited the inhabitants
> of the Unchaste City
> to kneel before the idols
> of gluttony,
> money,
> and death:
> Idolators from all nations
> were being converted to the American
>   Way of Life. . . .
>
> The Spirit told me
> in the River of death
> flows the blood of many peoples

---

17. R. H. Charles, *Studies in the Apocalypse* (Edinburgh: T & T Clark, 1913), 11–12.
18. Paul S. Minear, *I Saw a New Earth: An Introduction to the Visions of the Apocalypse* (Cleveland: Corpus, 1968).
19. Elisabeth Schüssler Fiorenza, *Revelation: Vision of a Just World*, Proclamation Commentaries (Minneapolis: Fortress, 1991), 2.

sacrificed without mercy
and removed a thousand times from their lands,
the blood of Kekchis, of Panzos,
of blacks from Haiti, of Guaranis from Paraguay,
of the peoples sacrificed for "development"
in the Trans-Amazonic strip,
the blood of the Indians' ancestors
who lived on these lands, of those who
even now are kept hostage in the Great
   Mountain
and on the Black Hills of Dakota
by the guardians of the beast. . . .

My soul was tortured like this
for three and a half days
and a great weariness weighed upon my breast.
I felt the suffering of my people very deeply!

Then in tears, I prostrated myself
and cried out: "Lord, what can we do? . . .
Come to me, Lord, I wish to die among my
   people!"
Without strength, I waited for the answer.
After a long silence
and a heavy obscurity
The One who sits on the throne
to judge the nations
spoke in a soft whisper
in the secret recesses of my heart:

You have to denounce their idolatry
in good times and in bad.
Force them to hear the truth
for what is impossible to humans
is possible for God.[20]

Whether or not one agrees with the ideology informing this poem or, for that matter, with Fiorenza's radical feminist persuasion, the attempt here to capture and apply the symbolism of Revelation is engaging, if not arresting.

There does not seem to be a hard-and-fast rule for the idealist in delineating the structure of Revelation. For Minear, the key to outlining the book is to be aware that the running contrasts between the visions of heaven and earth are symbolic of the struggle within Christians between faithfulness to Christ (heaven) and unfaithfulness (earth). For Fiorenza, Revelation is chiastically structured such that the key to the book is to be found in 10:1–15:4, with its description of the struggle and liberation of the oppressed communities of the world.[21] The only notable structural feature in the idealist interpretive agenda is its disavowal of a literal and chronological reading of Revelation 20. Rather in good amillennial fashion, that chapter is to be viewed as a symbolic description of the church's potential to reign with Christ in this age.

As to the worldview of the idealist school of thought, "realism" is its preferred perspective. Stanley Grenz encapsulates this mind-set of the idealist, amillennial position:

> The result is a world view characterized by realism. Victory and defeat, success and failure, good and evil will coexist until the end, amillennialism asserts. The future is neither a heightened continuation of the present nor an abrupt contradiction to it. The kingdom of God does not come by human cooperation with the divine power currently at work in the world, but neither is it simply the divine gift for which we can only wait expectantly.[22]

Consequently, both unbridled optimism and despairing pessimism are inappropriate, amillennialism declares. Rather, the amillennialist worldview calls the church to "realistic activity" in the world. Under the guidance and empowerment of the Holy Spirit, the church will be successful in its mandate; yet ultimate success will come only through God's grace. The kingdom of God arrives as the divine action breaking into the world; yet human cooperation brings important, albeit penultimate, results. Therefore, God's people must expect great things in the present, but knowing that the kingdom will never arrive in its fullness in history, they must always remain realistic in their expectations.

Using This Book

In using this book, the reader should keep in mind several points. First, in my translation of Revelation, I use the Nestle-Aland 27th edition/UBS 4th edition made available through BibleWorks; and I have sought to provide a strict word-for-word translation because this approach seemed to be the most neutral way of translating Revelation. This procedure seems to be a fair policy to follow, even though the reader-friendly approach of the "sense-for-sense" (dynamic equivalence) translation is preferred by most translators today. Moreover, the word-for-word translation gives a delightfully archaic, even arcane, tone to the text, which is appropriate for the last book of the Bible—one filled with mysterious prophecies.

Second, while one should enjoy and respect all four of the schools of interpretation presented in this volume, one also should lament the polemics often associated with each of these approaches. Thus preterism's attack on ancient Judaism comes dangerously close to espousing an anti-Semitic attitude (though it should be noted that ancient Jewish sects

---

20. Quoted in ibid., 27–28.
21. Ibid., 35–36.
22. Grenz, *The Millennial Maze*, 187.

issued similar vitriolic language against those Jews who did not agree with them [see, for example, the Dead Sea Scrolls] and this was certainly not to be confused with anti-Semitism). The anti-Catholic sentiment so obvious in the historicist reading of Revelation is equally unfortunate (though it must be said that the annals of Catholicism are hardly exempt from anti-Protestant polemic). Die-hard dispensationalists seem to think they have a corner on how one is supposed to interpret Revelation, and it is not the poetics of the idealist viewpoint! Conversely, idealists have had a heyday mocking the literal hermeneutic of dispensationalism. Hopefully, one of the lessons we can learn from this tendency of the major schools of thought to exalt their respective opinions over all others is that today as much as ever before, humility is needed in interpreting biblical prophecy. And maybe this volume can aid that process.

Finally, it is important to remember that most biblical scholars today interpret Revelation through an eclectic lens. That is, they embrace what they perceive as the strong points of each of the previously delineated four views of Revelation while leaving aside the perceived weaknesses associated with each approach. Thus, there is much to be said for rooting the prophecies of the Apocalypse in the first-century struggle between Christians and the Roman imperial cult, as the preterist does. And, yet, with the futurist school of thought it does seem that the Parousia is still forthcoming. Interpreting church history with the historicist as the fulfillment of the prophecies originally given to the seven churches of Asia Minor does indeed add zest to what otherwise could be viewed as a dull subject. And the ever-relevant approach of the idealist camp of interpretation toward the last book of the Bible is welcomed. At the end of the day, however, readers no doubt will come to their own decisions regarding the four views presented here, whether they align with this or that perspective or to a certain measure all of or, maybe, none of them! Be that as it may, the reader can be assured of at least one point: reading Revelation and taking it to heart carries with it the blessing of God (see Rev. 1:3; 22:7)!

A Comparison of
Four Interpretive Translations
of the Apocalypse

Greek Text and English Translation	Preterist View	Historicist View	Futurist View	Idealist View
1:1 Ἀποκάλυψις Ἰησοῦ Χριστοῦ ἣν ἔδοκεν αὐτῷ ὁ θεὸς The revelation of Jesus Christ which God gave to him δεῖξαι τοῖς δούλοις αὐτοῦ ἃ δεῖ γενέσθαι ἐν τάχει, to show to his servants what things must happen quickly καὶ ἐσήμανεν ἀποστείλας διὰ τοῦ ἀγγέλου αὐτοῦ τῷ δούλῳ αὐτοῦ Ἰοάννῃ, and he signified having sent [it] through his angel to his servant John	1 The revelation of Jesus Christ which God gave to him to show to his servants what things must happen quickly (immediately, at or right before A.D. 70 and the fall of Jerusalem to the Romans), and he signified (which indicates that Revelation is to be interpreted figuratively), having sent through his angel to his servant John,	1 The revelation of Jesus Christ which God gave to him to show to his servants what things must begin to take place now and throughout church history, and he signified (which indicates that Revelation is to be interpreted figuratively), having sent through his angel to his servant John,	1 The revelation of Jesus Christ which God gave to him to show to his servants what is imminent (can happen at any time), and he signified (to be interpreted literally not figuratively), having sent through his angel to his servant John,	1 The revelation of Jesus Christ which God gave to him to show to his servants what has begun and will continue, and he signified (which indicates Revelation is to be interpreted figuratively), having sent through his angel to his servant John,
1:2 ὃς ἐμαρτύρησεν τὸν λόγον τοῦ θεοῦ who witnessed the word of God καὶ τὴν μαρτυρίαν Ἰησοῦ Χριστοῦ ὅσα εἶδεν. and the testimony of Jesus Christ whatever he saw.	2 who witnessed the word of God and the witness of Jesus Christ whatever he saw.	2 who witnessed the word of God and the witness of Jesus Christ whatever he saw.	2 who witnessed the word of God and the witness of Jesus Christ whatever he saw.	2 who witnessed the word of God and the witness of Jesus Christ whatever he saw.
1:3 Μακάριος ὁ ἀναγινώσκον Blessed [is] the one who reads καὶ οἱ ἀκούοντες τοὺς λόγους τῆς προφητείας and the ones who hear the words of the prophecy καὶ τηροῦντες τὰ ἐν αὐτῇ γεγραμμένα, ὁ γὰρ καιρὸς ἐγγύς. and who keep the things in it having been written, for the time is near.	3 Blessed is the one who reads and who hears the words of this prophecy (of the replacement of Israel by the church) and who keeps the things having been written in it, for the time has begun.	3 Blessed is the one who reads and who hears the words of this prophecy (of the triumph of the Protestant Reformation over Roman Catholicism and the papacy) and who keeps the things having been written in it, for the time of fulfillment is beginning now and will continue throughout the church age.	3 Blessed is the one who reads and who hears the words of this prophecy (of the end times) and who keeps the things having been written in it, for the time is near, because the rapture of the church can happen at any moment.	3 Blessed is the one who reads and who hears the words of this prophecy (of the spiritual war between the true church and the ungodly, anti-Christian world that unfolds throughout history) and who keeps the things having been written in it, for the time is always near.

4 John to the seven churches which are in Asia (that is, only in the first century A.D.): Grace to you and peace from the one who is and who was and who is coming and from the seven Spirits (the Holy Spirit) which are before his throne	4 John to the seven churches which are in Asia (which symbolically correspond with church history: Ephesus until A.D. 100; Smyrna, from 64 to 313; Pergamum, from 313 to 606; Thyatira, from 606 to 1517; Sardis, from 1517 to 1793; Philadelphia, from 1793 to the 1900s; Laodicea, from the 1900s to the present): Grace to you and peace from the one who is and who was and who is coming and from the seven Spirits (the Holy Spirit) which are before his throne	4 John to the seven churches which are in Asia and to any church in time that finds itself in situations like the first-century seven churches of Asia Minor/modern Turkey: Grace to you and peace from the one who is and who was and who is coming and from the seven Spirits (the Holy Spirit) which [are] before his throne (**Editor's note**: Some futurists take the historicist approach to the seven churches)	4 John to the seven churches which are in Asia and to any church in time that finds itself in situations like the first-century seven churches of Asia Minor/modern Turkey: Grace to you and peace from the one who is and who was and who is coming and from the seven Spirits (the Holy Spirit) which are before his throne	4 John to the seven churches which are in Asia and to any church in time that finds itself in situations like the first-century seven churches of Asia Minor/modern Turkey: Grace to you and peace from the one who is and who was and who is coming and from the seven Spirits (the Holy Spirit) which are before his throne
5 and from Jesus Christ, the faithful witness, the firstborn from the dead and the ruler of the kingdoms of the earth. To the one who loves us and loosed us from our sins by his blood,	5 and from Jesus Christ, the faithful witness, the firstborn from the dead and the ruler of the kingdoms of the earth. To the one who loves us and loosed us from our sins by his blood,	5 and from Jesus Christ, the faithful witness, the firstborn from the dead and the ruler of the kingdoms of the earth. To the one who loves us and loosed us from our sins by his blood,	5 and from Jesus Christ, the faithful witness, the firstborn from the dead and the ruler of the kingdoms of the earth. To the one who loves us and loosed us from our sins by his blood,	5 and from Jesus Christ, the faithful witness, the firstborn from the dead and the ruler of the kingdoms of the earth. To the one who loves us and loosed us from our sins by his blood,
6 and he made us (the church) a kingdom, priests (the New Israel) to God and to his Father; to him be the glory and the power forever. Amen!	6 and he made us a kingdom, priests (the priesthood of all believers, one of the great truths of the Reformation) to God	6 and he made us a kingdom, priests (in heaven but not yet on earth) to God and to his Father; to him	6 and he made us a kingdom, priests (the New Israel) to God and to his Father; to him be the glory and the power forever. Amen!	6 and he made us (the church) a kingdom, priests (the New Israel) to God and to his Father; to him be the glory and the power forever. Amen!

1:4 Ἰωάννης ταῖς ἑπτὰ ἐκκλησίαις ταῖς ἐν τῇ Ἀσίᾳ·
John to the seven churches which are in Asia:

χάρις ὑμῖν καὶ εἰρήνη ἀπὸ ὁ ὢν
grace to you and peace from the one who is

καὶ ὁ ἦν καὶ ὁ ἐρχόμενος
and the one who was and the one who is coming

καὶ ἀπὸ τῶν ἑπτὰ πνευμάτων ἃ ἐνώπιον τοῦ θρόνου αὐτοῦ
and from the seven Spirits which [are] before his throne

1:5 καὶ ἀπὸ Ἰησοῦ Χριστοῦ, ὁ μάρτυς,
and from Jesus Christ, the witness,

ὁ πιστός, ὁ πρωτότοκος τῶν νεκρῶν
the faithful, the firstborn from the dead

καὶ ὁ ἄρχων τῶν βασιλέων τῆς γῆς.
and the ruler of the kingdoms of the earth.

Τῷ ἀγαπῶντι ἡμᾶς καὶ λύσαντι ἡμᾶς ἐκ τῶν ἁμαρτιῶν ἡμῶν ἐν τῷ αἵματι αὐτοῦ,
To the one loving us and having loosed us out of our sins by his blood,

1:6 καὶ ἐποίησεν ἡμᾶς βασιλείαν, ἱερεῖς τῷ θεῷ
And he made us a kingdom, priests to God

καὶ πατρὶ αὐτοῦ, αὐτῷ ἡ δόξα
and to his father, to him [be] the glory

Greek Text and English Translation	Preterist View	Historicist View	Futurist View	Idealist View
καὶ τὸ κράτος εἰς τοὺς αἰῶνας [τῶν αἰώνον]· ἀμήν. and the power forever. Amen!		and to his Father; to him be the glory and the power forever. Amen!	be the glory and the power forever. Amen!	
1:7 Ἰδοὺ ἔρχεται μετὰ τῶν νεφελῶν, Behold, he comes with the clouds,	7 Behold, he comes with the clouds to judge Jerusalem (which happened in A.D. 70 when Jerusalem fell to the Romans), and every eye will see him and the Jews in Israel who crucified Jesus, and all the tribes of the earth will mourn because of him. Yes! Amen!	7 Behold, he comes with the clouds at his second coming, at the end of history, and every eye will see him and those who pierced him (especially the papacy with its teaching of the Mass—that Christ is crucified over and over again rather than was crucified once for our sins), and all the tribes of the earth will mourn over him. Yes! Amen!	7 Behold, he comes with the clouds at his second coming, at the end of history (to be distinguished from the rapture of the church before the end-time Tribulation on earth), and every eye will see him and those who pierced him, and all the tribes of the earth will mourn over him. Yes! Amen!	7 Behold, he comes with the clouds in judgment throughout history and culminating at his second coming, at the end of history to bring final judgment, and every eye will see him and those who pierced him, and all the tribes of the earth will mourn over him. Yes! Amen!
καὶ ὄψεται αὐτὸν πᾶς ὀφθαλμὸς καὶ οἵτινες αὐτὸν ἐξεκέντησαν, and every eye will see him and those who pierced him				
καὶ κόψονται ἐπ᾽ αὐτὸν πᾶσαι αἱ φυλαὶ τῆς γῆς. ναί, ἀμήν. and all the tribes of the earth will mourn over him. Yes! Amen!				
1:8 Ἐγώ εἰμι τὸ ἄλφα καὶ τὸ ὦ, λέγει κύριος ὁ θεός, "I am the Alpha and the Omega," says the Lord God,	8 "I am the Alpha and the Omega," says the Lord God, "the one who is and who was and who is coming, the Almighty."	8 "I am the Alpha and the Omega," says the Lord God, "the one who is and who was and who is coming, the Almighty."	8 "I am the Alpha and the Omega," says the Lord God, "the one who is and who was and who is coming, the Almighty."	8 "I am the Alpha and the Omega," says the Lord God, "the one who is and who was and who is coming, the Almighty."
ὁ ὢν καὶ ὁ ἦν καὶ ὁ ἐρχόμενος, ὁ παντοκράτωρ. "the one who is and who was and who is coming, the Almighty"				
1:9 Ἐγὼ Ἰωάννης, ὁ ἀδελφὸς ὑμῶν καὶ συγκοινωνὸς I, John, your brother and co-sharer	9 I John, your brother and co-sharer in the tribulation (the end-time Tribulation/messianic woes) and the present spiritual "millennial" kingdom of God and the perseverance in Jesus,	9 I, John, your brother and co-sharer in the tribulation (of the end-time Tribulation/messianic woes) and in the soon-to-arrive millennial kingdom (to be brought to earth by the triumph	9 I, John, your brother and co-sharer in the present tribulation of this age (but not the end-time Tribulation, at the end of history) and in hope of the future, literal one-thousand-year reign	9 I, John, your brother and co-sharer in the end-time Tribulation/messianic woes and in the present, spiritual "millennial" kingdom of God and the perseverance in Jesus, came to be on the
ἐν τῇ θλίψει καὶ βασιλείᾳ καὶ ὑπομονῇ in the tribulation and kingdom and the perseverance				

ἐν Ἰησοῦ, ἐγενόμην ἐν τῇ νήσῳ in Jesus, came to be on the island	came to be on the island called Patmos because of the word of God and the witness of Jesus.	of the gospel of justification by faith alone) and the perseverance in Jesus, came to be on the island called Patmos because of the word of God and the witness of Jesus.	of Christ on earth, i.e., the millennium, and the perseverance in Jesus, came to be on the island called Patmos because of the word of God and the witness of Jesus.	island called Patmos because of the word of God and the witness of Jesus.
τῇ καλουμένῃ Πάτμῳ διὰ τὸν λόγον τοῦ θεοῦ καὶ τὴν μαρτυρίαν Ἰησοῦ. being called Patmos because of the word of God and the witness of Jesus.				
1:10 ἐγενόμην ἐν πνεύματι ἐν τῇ κυριακῇ ἡμέρᾳ I came to be in the Spirit on the Lord's Day	10 I came to be in the Spirit on the Lord's Day and heard behind me a great voice like a trumpet,	10 I came to be in the Spirit on the Lord's Day and heard behind me a great voice like a trumpet,	10 I came to be in the Spirit on the Lord's Day and heard behind me a great voice like a trumpet,	10 I came to be in the Spirit on the Lord's Day and heard behind me a great voice like a trumpet,
καὶ ἤκουσα ὀπίσω μου φωνὴν μεγάλην ὡς σάλπιγγος· and I heard behind me a great voice like a trumpet,				
1:11 λεγούσης ὁ βλέπεις γράψον εἰς βιβλίον saying, "What you see write into a scroll	11 saying, "What you see, write onto a scroll and send it to the seven churches, unto Ephesus and unto Smyrna and unto Pergamum and unto Thyatira and unto Sardis and unto Philadelphia and unto Laodicea."	11 saying, "What you see, write onto a scroll and send it to the seven churches, unto Ephesus and unto Smyrna and unto Pergamum and unto Thyatira and unto Sardis and unto Philadelphia and unto Laodicea."	11 saying, "What you see, write onto a scroll and send it to the seven churches, unto Ephesus and unto Smyrna and unto Pergamum and unto Thyatira and unto Sardis and unto Philadelphia and unto Laodicea."	11 saying, "What you see, write onto a scroll and send it to the seven churches, unto Ephesus and unto Smyrna and unto Pergamum and unto Thyatira and unto Sardis and unto Philadelphia and unto Laodicea."
καὶ πέμψον ταῖς ἑπτὰ ἐκκλησίαις, and send [it] to the seven churches,				
εἰς Ἔφεσον καὶ εἰς Σμύρναν unto Ephesus and unto Smyrna				
καὶ εἰς Πέργαμον καὶ εἰς Θυάτειρα and unto Pergamum and unto Thyatira				
καὶ εἰς Σάρδεις καὶ εἰς Φιλαδέλφειαν καὶ εἰς Λαοδίκειαν. and unto Sardis and unto Philadelphia and unto Laodicea."				
1:12 Καὶ ἐπέστρεψα βλέπειν τὴν φωνὴν ἥτις ἐλάλει μετ' ἐμοῦ, And I turned to see the voice which was speaking with me,	12 And I turned to see the voice which was speaking with me, and after turning I saw seven golden lampstands	12 And I turned to see the voice which was speaking with me, and after turning I saw seven golden lampstands	12 And I turned to see the voice which was speaking with me, and after turning I saw seven golden lampstands	12 And I turned to see the voice which was speaking with me, and after turning I saw seven golden lampstands
καὶ ἐπιστρέψας εἶδον ἑπτὰ λυχνίας χρυσᾶς and having turned, I saw seven golden lampstands				

Greek Text and English Translation	Preterist View	Historicist View	Futurist View	Idealist View
1:13 καὶ ἐν μέσῳ τῶν λυχνιῶν ὅμοιον υἱὸν ἀνθρώπου and in the middle of the lampstands one like a son of man	13 and, in the middle of the lampstands, one like a son of man being clothed to the feet and having been girded around the breasts with a golden girdle.	13 and, in the middle of the lampstands, one like a son of man being clothed to the feet and having been girded around the breasts with a golden girdle.	13 and, in the middle of the lampstands, one like a son of man being clothed to the feet and having been girded around the breasts with a golden girdle.	13 and, in the middle of the lampstands, one like a son of man being clothed to the feet and having been girded around the breasts with a golden girdle.
ἐνδεδυμένον ποδήρη καὶ περιεζωσμένον having been clothed to the feet and having been girded				
πρὸς τοῖς μαστοῖς ζώνην χρυσᾶν. about the breasts with a golden girdle.				
1:14 ἡ δὲ κεφαλὴ αὐτοῦ καὶ αἱ τρίχες λευκαὶ ὡς ἔριον λευκόν ὡς χιὼν And his head and hairs [were] white as wool, white as snow	14 And his head and hair were white as wool as snow, and his eyes like flaming fire	14 And his head and hair were white as wool as snow, and his eyes like flaming fire	14 And his head and the hair were white as wool as snow, and his eyes like flaming fire	14 And his head and the hair were white as wool as snow, and his eyes like flaming fire
καὶ οἱ ὀφθαλμοὶ αὐτοῦ ὡς φλὸξ πυρός and his eyes like flaming fire				
1:15 καὶ οἱ πόδες αὐτοῦ ὅμοιοι χαλκολιβάνῳ and his feet like burnished brass	15 and his feet like burnished brass as in a furnace having been fired and his voice like a voice of many waters,	15 and his feet like burnished brass as in a furnace having been fired and his voice like a voice of many waters,	15 and his feet like burnished brass as in a furnace having been fired and his voice like a voice of many waters,	15 and his feet like burnished brass as in a furnace having been fired and his voice like a voice of many waters,
ὡς ἐν καμίνῳ πεπυρωμένης like as in a furnace having been fired				
καὶ ἡ φωνὴ αὐτοῦ ὡς φωνὴ ὑδάτων πολλῶν, and his voice like a voice of many waters,				
1:16 καὶ ἔχων ἐν τῇ δεξιᾷ χειρὶ αὐτοῦ ἀστέρας ἑπτὰ and having in his right hand seven stars	16 and having in his right hand seven stars and out of his mouth proceeding a double-edged sword, and his face shines like the sun in its power.	16 and having in his right hand seven stars and out of his mouth proceeding a double-edged sword, and his face shines like the sun in its power.	16 and having in his right hand seven stars and out of his mouth proceeding a double-edged sword, and his face shines like the sun in its power.	16 and having in his right hand seven stars and out of his mouth proceeding a double-edged sword, and his face shines like the sun in its power.

καὶ ἐκ τοῦ στόματος αὐτοῦ ῥομφαία δίστομος ὀξεῖα ἐκπορευομένη and out of his mouth a double-edged sword proceeding καὶ ἡ ὄψις αὐτοῦ ὡς ὁ ἥλιος φαίνει ἐν τῇ δυνάμει αὐτοῦ. and his face like the sun shines in its power.				
1:17 Καὶ ὅτε εἶδον αὐτόν, ἔπεσα πρὸς τοὺς πόδας αὐτοῦ ὡς νεκρός, And when I saw him, I fell before his feet as dead, καὶ ἔθηκεν τὴν δεξιὰν αὐτοῦ ἐπ᾽ ἐμὲ λέγων· and he placed his right[hand] upon me saying, μὴ φοβοῦ· ἐγώ εἰμι ὁ πρῶτος καὶ ὁ ἔσχατος "Do not fear! I am the first and the last	17 And when I saw him, I fell before his feet as dead, and he placed his right hand upon me, saying, "Do not fear! I am the first and the last	17 And when I saw him, I fell before his feet as dead, and he placed his right hand upon me, saying, "Do not fear! I am the first and the last	17 And when I saw him, I fell before his feet as dead, and he placed his right hand upon me, saying, "Do not fear! I am the first and the last	17 And when I saw him, I fell before his feet as dead, and he placed his right hand upon me, saying, "Do not fear! I am the first and the last
1:18 καὶ ὁ ζῶν, καὶ ἐγενόμην νεκρός, and the one who lives, and I became dead καὶ ἰδοὺ ζῶν εἰμι εἰς τοὺς αἰῶνας τῶν αἰώνων and behold, I am alive forever καὶ ἔχω τὰς κλεῖς τοῦ θανάτου καὶ τοῦ ᾅδου. and I have the keys of death and of hades.	18 and the one who lives, and I became dead and behold, I am alive forever and I have the keys of death and hades.	18 and the one who lives, and I became dead and behold, I am alive forever and I have the keys of death and hades.	18 and the one who lives, and I became dead and behold, I am alive forever and I have the keys of death and hades.	18 and the one who lives, and I became dead and behold, I am alive forever and I have the keys of death and hades.
1:19 γράψον οὖν ἃ εἶδες καὶ ἃ εἰσὶν Write therefore what you saw, and the things that are καὶ ἃ μέλλει γενέσθαι μετὰ ταῦτα. and the things that are about to be after these things.	19 Write therefore what you have seen (Rev. 1), and what is now (Rev. 2–3), and what will take place soon after these things (Rev. 4–22 = the fall of Jerusalem in A.D. 70 as a result of Christ's coming to destroy it).	19 Write therefore what you saw, both the things that are (Rev. 1–3) and the things that are about to become after these things (Rev. 4–22 = the seven periods of church history culminating in the triumph of the gospel).	19 Write therefore what you saw (Rev. 1), and the things that are (Rev. 2–3) and the things that are about to become after these things (Rev. 4–22 and the signs of the times that will begin after the rapture of the church into heaven).	19 Write therefore what you saw (the whole vision of Rev. 1–22), both the things that are (the "already" aspect of the kingdom of God) and the things that are about to become after these things (the "not yet" aspect of the kingdom of God, which awaits the return of Christ).

Greek Text and English Translation	Preterist View	Historicist View	Futurist View	Idealist View
1:20 τὸ μυστήριον τῶν ἑπτὰ ἀστέρων οὓς εἶδες The mystery of the seven stars which you saw ἐπὶ τῆς δεξιᾶς μου καὶ τὰς ἑπτὰ λυχνίας τὰς χρυσᾶς· upon my right [hand] and the seven golden lampstands. οἱ ἑπτὰ ἀστέρες ἄγγελοι τῶν ἑπτὰ ἐκκλησιῶν εἰσιν The seven stars are angels of the seven churches καὶ αἱ λυχνίαι αἱ ἑπτὰ ἑπτὰ ἐκκλησίαι εἰσίν." and the seven lampstands are the seven churches.	20 The mystery of the seven stars which you saw upon my right hand and the seven golden lampstands: the seven stars are angels (if humans are intended, then they are the pastors, but if they are supernatural, then they are the guardian angels of the churches; if both, then the angels are the heavenly counterparts of the pastors) of the seven churches, and the seven lampstands are the seven churches."	20 The mystery of the seven stars which you saw upon my right hand and the seven golden lampstands: the seven stars are angels (if humans are intended, then they are the pastors of the churches, but if they are supernatural, then they are the guardian angels of the churches, or both with the latter being the heavenly counterpart of the former) of the seven churches, and the seven lampstands are the seven churches."	20 The mystery of the seven stars which you saw upon my right hand and the seven golden lampstands: the seven stars are angels (either pastors or guardian angels or both, the latter being the heavenly counterpoint of the former) of the seven churches, and the seven lampstands are the seven churches."	20 The mystery of the seven stars which you saw upon my right hand and the seven golden lampstands: the seven stars are angels (pastors or guardian angels or both, the latter being the heavenly counterpart to the former) of the seven churches, and the seven lampstands are the seven churches."
2:1 Τῷ ἀγγέλῳ τῆς ἐν Ἐφέσῳ ἐκκλησίας γράψον· To the angel of the church in Ephesus write: Τάδε λέγει ὁ κρατῶν τοὺς ἑπτὰ ἀστέρας These things says the one holding the seven stars ἐν τῇ δεξιᾷ αὐτοῦ, ὁ περιπατῶν in his right [hand] the one who walks ἐν μέσῳ τῶν ἑπτὰ λυχνιῶν τῶν χρυσῶν· in the middle of the seven golden lampstands.	1 To the angel of the church in Ephesus, write: Thus says the one holding the seven stars in his right hand, the one who walks in the middle of the seven golden lampstands.	1 To the angel of the church in Ephesus (which corresponds to the apostolic church, A.D. 33–100), write: Thus says the one holding the seven stars in his right hand, the one who walks in the middle of the seven golden lampstands.	1 To the angel of the church in Ephesus, write: Thus says the one holding the seven stars in his right hand, the one who walks in the middle of the seven golden lampstands.	1 To the angel of the church in Ephesus, write: Thus says the one holding the seven stars in his right hand, the one who walks in the middle of the seven golden lampstands.
2:2 οἶδα τὰ ἔργα σου καὶ τὸν κόπον I know your works and labor	2 I know your works and labor and your perseverance and that you are not able to bear evil men, and having tried those saying	2 I know your works and labor and your perseverance and that you are not able to bear evil men, and having tried those saying	2 I know your works and labor and your perseverance and that you are not able to bear evil men, and having tried those saying	2 I know your works and labor and your perseverance and that you are not able to bear evil men, and having tried those saying

that they themselves are apostles (the Nicolaitans) and are not and you found them to be liars,	that they themselves are apostles (the Nicolaitans) and are not and you found them to be liars,	that they themselves are apostles (the Nicolaitans) and are not and you found them to be liars,	that they themselves are apostles (the Nicolaitans) and are not and you found them to be liars,	**καὶ τὴν ὑπομονήν σου καὶ ὅτι οὐ δύνῃ βαστάσαι κακούς,** and your perseverance and that you are not able to bear evil men,
				καὶ ἐπείρασας τοὺς λέγοντας ἑαυτοὺς ἀποστόλους and having tried those saying they themselves [are] apostles
				καὶ οὐκ εἰσὶν καὶ εὗρες αὐτοὺς ψευδεῖς, and are not and you found them [to be] liars,
3 and you have perseverance also, having borne my name and having not grown weary.	3 and you have perseverance also, having borne my name and having not grown weary.	3 and you have perseverance also, having borne my name and having not grown weary.	3 and you have perseverance also, having borne my name and having not grown weary.	**2:3 καὶ ὑπομονὴν ἔχεις καὶ ἐβάστασας διὰ τὸ ὄνομά μου καὶ οὐ κεκοπίακες.** and you have perseverance also having borne my name and not having grown weary.
4 But I have against you that you have left your first love.	4 But I have against you that you have left your first love.	4 But I have against you that you have left your first love.	4 But I have against you that you have left your first love.	**2:4 ἀλλὰ ἔχω κατὰ σοῦ ὅτι τὴν ἀγάπην σου τὴν πρώτην ἀφῆκες.** But I have against you that your first love you have left.
5 Remember therefore from where you have fallen, and repent and do the first works! But if not, I will come to you and will remove your lampstand from its place, unless you repent.	5 Remember therefore from where you have fallen, and repent and do the first works! But if not, I will come to you and will remove your lampstand from its place, unless you repent.	5 Remember therefore from where you have fallen, and repent and do the first works! But if not, I will come to you and will remove your lampstand from its place, unless you repent.	5 Remember therefore from where you have fallen, and repent and do the first works! But if not, I will come to you and will remove your lampstand from its place, unless you repent.	**2:5 μνημόνευε οὖν πόθεν πέπτωκας** Remember therefore from where you have fallen **καὶ μετανόησον καὶ τὰ πρῶτα ἔργα ποίησον·** and repent and the first works do! **εἰ δὲ μή, ἔρχομαί σοι καὶ κινήσω τὴν λυχνίαν σου** But if not, I will come to you and will remove your lampstand **ἐκ τοῦ τόπου αὐτῆς, ἐὰν μὴ μετανοήσῃς.** from its place, unless you repent.
6 But you have this, that you hate the works of the Nicolaitans, which also I hate (the ones who "overcome the people"	6 But you have this, that you hate the works of the Nicolaitans, which also I hate (the ones who "overcome the people"	6 But you have this, that you hate the works of the Nicolaitans, which also I hate (the ones who "overcome the people"	6 But you have this, that you hate the works of the Nicolaitans, which also I hate (the ones who "overcome the people"	**2:6 ἀλλὰ τοῦτο ἔχεις, ὅτι μισεῖς τὰ ἔργα** But you have this, that you hate the works **τῶν Νικολαϊτῶν ἃ κἀγὼ μισῶ.** of the Nicolaitans which also I hate.

Greek Text and English Translation	Preterist View	Historicist View	Futurist View	Idealist View
	by saying it is okay to worship Caesar).	by saying it is okay to worship Caesar).	by saying it is okay to worship Caesar).	by leading the church into moral compromise with the world).
2:7 Ὁ ἔχων οὖς ἀκουσάτω The one having ears, let him hear	7 The one having ears, let him hear what the Spirit says to the churches! To the one overcoming I will give to him to eat from the tree of life, which is in the paradise of God.	7 The one having ears, let him hear what the Spirit says to the churches! To the one overcoming I will give to him to eat from the tree of life, which is in the paradise of God.	7 The one having ears, let him hear what the Spirit says to the churches! To the one overcoming I will give to him to eat from the tree of life, which is in the paradise of God.	7 The one having ears, let him hear what the Spirit says to the churches! To the one overcoming I will give to him to eat from the tree of life, which is in the paradise of God.
τί τὸ πνεῦμα λέγει ταῖς ἐκκλησίαις, what the Spirit says to the churches!				
Τῷ νικῶντι δώσω αὐτῷ φαγεῖν ἐκ τοῦ ξύλου τῆς ζωῆς, To the one overcoming I will give to him to eat from the tree of life,				
ὅ ἐστιν ἐν τῷ παραδείσῳ τοῦ θεοῦ. which is in the paradise of God.				
2:8 Καὶ τῷ ἀγγέλῳ τῆς ἐν Σμύρνῃ ἐκκλησίας γράψον· And to the angel of the church in Smyrna write:	8 And to the angel of the church in Smyrna write: Thus says the first and the last, who became dead and came alive.	8 And to the angel of the church in Smyrna (which corresponds to the persecuted church, A.D. 64–313) write: Thus says the first and the last, who became dead and came alive.	8 And to the angel of the church in Smyrna write: Thus says the first and the last, who became dead and came alive.	8 And to the angel of the church in Smyrna write: Thus says the first and the last, who became dead and came alive.
Τάδε λέγει ὁ πρῶτος καὶ ὁ ἔσχατος, ὃς ἐγένετο νεκρὸς καὶ ἔζησεν· These things says the first and the last, who became dead and came alive.				
2:9 οἶδά σου τὴν θλῖψιν καὶ τὴν πτωχείαν, I know your tribulation and poverty,	9 I know your tribulation and your poverty, but you are rich, and the blasphemy of the ones saying that they themselves are Jews and are not but are a synagogue of Satan (non-Christian Jews who expel Jewish	9 I know your tribulation and your poverty, but you are rich, and the blasphemy of the ones saying that they themselves are Jews and are not but are a synagogue of Satan (non-Christian Jews who expel Jewish	9 I know your tribulation and your poverty, but you are rich, and the blasphemy of the ones saying that they themselves are Jews and are not but are a synagogue of Satan (non-Christian Jews who expel Jewish	9 I know your tribulation and your poverty, but you are rich, and the blasphemy of the ones saying that they themselves are Jews (mere outward Jews, not true Jews, the church) and are not but are a synagogue of Satan.
ἀλλὰ πλούσιος εἶ, καὶ τὴν βλασφημίαν but you are rich, and the blasphemy				
ἐκ τῶν λεγόντων Ἰουδαίους εἶναι ἑαυτοὺς of the ones saying [that] they themselves are Jews				

Greek / Interlinear	Translation 1	Translation 2	Translation 3	Translation 4
καὶ οὐκ εἰσὶν ἀλλὰ συναγωγὴ τοῦ σατανᾶ. and they are not but [are] a synagogue of Satan.	Christians from the synagogues and thereby expose them to Caesar worship, since Jews in the synagogues are exempt from the imperial cult).	Christians from the synagogues and thereby expose them to Caesar worship, since Jews in the synagogues are exempt from the imperial cult).	Christians from the synagogues and thereby expose them to Caesar worship, since Jews in the synagogues are exempt from the imperial cult).	
2:10 μηδὲν φοβοῦ ἃ μέλλεις πάσχειν. Do not fear what you are about to suffer.	10 Do not fear what you are about to suffer.	10 Do not fear what you are about to suffer.	10 Do not fear what you are about to suffer.	10 Do not fear what you are about to suffer.
ἰδοὺ μέλλει βάλλειν ὁ διάβολος ἐξ ὑμῶν εἰς φυλακὴν Behold, the devil is about to cast some of you into prison	Behold, the devil is about to cast some of you into prison in order that you might be tested, and you	Behold, the devil is about to cast some of you into prison in order that you might be tested, and you	Behold, the devil is about to cast some of you into prison in order that you might be tested, and you	Behold, the devil is about to cast some of you into prison in order that you might be tested, and you
ἵνα πειρασθῆτε καὶ ἕξετε θλῖψιν ἡμερῶν δέκα. in order that you might be tested and you will have tribulation ten days.	will have tribulation for ten days (that is, a brief time). Be faithful until death, and I will give to you the crown of life.	will have tribulation for ten days (symbolic for the ten years of Emperor Diocletian's persecution of the church, A.D. 303–313). Be faithful until death, and I will give to you the crown of life.	you will have tribulation for ten days (a brief time). Be faithful until death, and I will give to you the crown of life.	you will have tribulation for ten days (a brief time). Be faithful until death, and I will give to you the crown of life.
γίνου πιστὸς ἄχρι θανάτου, καὶ δώσω σοι τὸν στέφανον τῆς ζωῆς. Be faithful until death, and I will give to you the crown of life.				
2:11 Ὁ ἔχων οὖς ἀκουσάτω τί τὸ πνεῦμα λέγει ταῖς ἐκκλησίαις. The one having ears, let him hear what the Spirit says to the churches!	11 The one having ears, let him hear what the Spirit says to the churches! The one overcoming will never ever be hurt by the second death.	11 The one having ears, let him hear what the Spirit says to the churches! The one overcoming will never ever be hurt by the second death.	11 The one having ears, let him hear what the Spirit says to the churches! The one overcoming will never ever be hurt by the second death.	11 The one having ears, let him hear what the Spirit says to the churches! The one overcoming will never ever be hurt by the second death.
Ὁ νικῶν οὐ μὴ ἀδικηθῇ ἐκ τοῦ θανάτου τοῦ δευτέρου. The one overcoming will never ever be hurt by the second death.				
2:12 Καὶ τῷ ἀγγέλῳ τῆς ἐν Περγάμῳ ἐκκλησίας γράψον And to the angel of the church in Pergamum write:	12 And to the angel of the church in Pergamum write: Thus says the one having the sharp double-edged sword.	12 And to the angel of the church in Pergamum (which is the church from 313–606; which means "one married" to the politics of the state) write: Thus says	12 And to the angel of the church in Pergamum write: Thus says the one having the sharp double-edged sword.	12 And to the angel of the church in Pergamum write: Thus says the one having the sharp double-edged sword.

Greek Text and English Translation	Preterist View	Historicist View	Futurist View	Idealist View
Τάδε λέγει ὁ ἔχων τὴν ῥομφαίαν τὴν δίστομον τὴν ὀξεῖαν· These things says the one having the sharp double-edged sword.		the one having the sharp double-edged sword.		
2:13 οἶδα ποῦ κατοικεῖς, ὅπου ὁ θρόνος τοῦ σατανᾶ, I know where you dwell, where the throne of Satan [is], καὶ κρατεῖς τὸ ὄνομά μου καὶ οὐκ ἠρνήσω τὴν πίστιν μου and you hold my name and did not deny my faith καὶ ἐν ταῖς ἡμέραις Ἀντιπᾶς even in the days of Antipas, ὁ μάρτυς μου ὁ πιστός μου, ὃς ἀπεκτάνθη παρ᾽ ὑμῖν, my faithful witness, who was killed among you ὅπου ὁ σατανᾶς κατοικεῖ. where Satan dwells.	13 I know where you dwell, where the throne of Satan is (the capital of the Roman imperial cult), and you hold my name and did not deny my faith even in the days of Antipas, my faithful witness, who was killed among you, where Satan dwells.	13 I know where you dwell, where the throne of Satan is (representative of those who oppose the Roman papacy), where Satan dwells (that is, Rome, the center of Christendom and home of the pope).	13 I know where you dwell, where the throne of Satan is, and you hold my name and did not deny my faith even in the days of Antipas, my faithful witness, who was killed among you, where Satan dwells.	13 I know where you dwell, where the throne of Satan is (which is any idolatrous system), and you hold my name and did not deny my faith even in the days of Antipas, my faithful witness, who was killed among you, where Satan dwells.
2:14 ἀλλ᾽ ἔχω κατὰ σοῦ ὀλίγα But I have against you a few things ὅτι ἔχεις ἐκεῖ κρατοῦντας τὴν διδαχὴν Βαλαάμ, that you have there the ones holding the teaching of Balaam, ὃς ἐδίδασκεν τῷ Βαλὰκ βαλεῖν σκάνδαλον ἐνώπιον τῶν υἱῶν Ἰσραὴλ who taught Balak to cast a stumbling block before the sons of Israel	14 But I have against you a few things: that you have there ones holding the teaching of Balaam, who taught Balak to cast a stumbling block before the sons of Israel: to eat idol sacrifices and to commit immorality. These Balaamites ("overcomers of the people") teach Christians that they	14 But I have against you a few things: that you have there ones holding the teaching of Balaam, who taught Balak to cast a stumbling block before the sons of Israel: to eat idol sacrifices and to commit immorality.	14 But I have against you a few things: that you have there ones holding the teaching of Balaam, who taught Balak to cast a stumbling block before the sons of Israel: to eat idol sacrifices and to commit immorality. These Balaamites ("overcomers of the people") teach it is okay	14 But I have against you a few things: that you have there ones holding the teaching of Balaam, who taught Balak to cast a stumbling block before the sons of Israel: to eat idol sacrifices and to commit immorality.

Greek / Literal	Version	Version	Version	Version
2:14 φαγεῖν εἰδωλόθυτα καὶ πορνεῦσαι. / to eat idol sacrifices and to commit immorality.				
2:15 οὕτως ἔχεις καὶ σὺ κρατοῦντας τὴν διδαχὴν [τῶν] Νικολαϊτῶν ὁμοίως. / Thus you yourself have also the ones holding the teaching like [that] of the Nicolaitans.	can worship Caesar and Christ at the same time. 15 Thus you yourself have also the ones holding the teaching like that of the Nicolaitans.	15 Thus you yourself have holding the teaching like that of the Nicolaitans. These two—Balaamites and Nicolaitans—influence the church at Rome to bow down before the idolatry of Roman Catholicism.	for Christians to worship Caesar and Christ. 15 Thus you yourself have also the ones holding the teaching like that of the Nicolaitans.	15 Thus you yourself have also the ones holding the teaching like that of the Nicolaitans. Balaamites and Nicolaitans represent all those who seduce the church to succumb to idolatry.
2:16 μετανόησον οὖν· εἰ δὲ μή, ἔρχομαί σοι ταχὺ / Repent therefore! But if not, I will come to you quickly / καὶ πολεμήσω μετʼ αὐτῶν ἐν τῇ ῥομφαίᾳ τοῦ στόματός μου. / and will make war with them with the sword of my mouth.	16 Repent therefore! But if not, I will come to you quickly and will make war with them with the sword of my mouth.	16 Repent therefore! But if not, I will come to you quickly and will make war with them with the sword of my mouth.	16 Repent therefore! But if not, I will come to you quickly and will make war with them with the sword of my mouth.	16 Repent therefore! But if not, I will come to you quickly and will make war with them with the sword of my mouth.
2:17 Ὁ ἔχων οὖς ἀκουσάτω τί τὸ πνεῦμα λέγει ταῖς ἐκκλησίαις· / The one having ears, let him hear what the Spirit says to the churches! / Τῷ νικῶντι δώσω αὐτῷ τοῦ μάννα τοῦ κεκρυμμένου / To the one overcoming I will give to him the manna having been hidden / καὶ δώσω αὐτῷ ψῆφον λευκήν, / and I will give to him a white stone, / καὶ ἐπὶ τὴν ψῆφον ὄνομα καινὸν γεγραμμένον / and upon the stone a new name having been written / ὃ οὐδεὶς οἶδεν εἰ μὴ ὁ λαμβάνον. / which no one knows except the one receiving [it].	17 The one having ears, let him hear what the Spirit says to the churches! To the one overcoming I will give to him the manna having been hidden and I will give to him a white stone, and upon the stone a new name having been written, which no one knows except the one receiving it.	17 The one having ears, let him hear what the Spirit says to the churches! To the one overcoming I will give to him the manna having been hidden and I will give to him a white stone, and upon the stone a new name having been written, which no one knows except the one receiving it.	17 The one having ears, let him hear what the Spirit says to the churches! To the one overcoming I will give to him the manna having been hidden and I will give to him a white stone, and upon the stone a new name having been written, which no one knows except the one receiving it.	17 The one having ears, let him hear what the Spirit says to the churches! To the one overcoming I will give to him the manna having been hidden and I will give to him a white stone, and upon the stone a new name having been written, which no one knows except the one receiving it.

Greek Text and English Translation	Preterist View	Historicist View	Futurist View	Idealist View
2:18 Καὶ τῷ ἀγγέλῳ τῆς ἐν Θυατείροις ἐκκλησίας γράψον· And to the angel of the church in Thyatira write:	18 And to the angel of the church in Thyatira write: Thus says the Son of God, the one having eyes like flaming fire and his feet like burnished brass.	18 And to the angel of the church in Thyatira (which means "to be ruled by a woman"; a fitting description of the church from 606–1517, which was dominated by Mariology) write: Thus says the Son of God, the one having eyes like flaming fire and his feet like burnished brass.	18 And to the angel of the church in Thyatira write: Thus says the Son of God, the one having eyes like flaming fire and his feet like burnished brass.	18 And to the angel of the church in Thyatira write: Thus says the Son of God, the one having eyes like flaming fire and his feet like burnished brass.
Τάδε λέγει ὁ υἱὸς τοῦ θεοῦ, These things says the Son of God,				
ὁ ἔχων τοὺς ὀφθαλμοὺς αὐτοῦ ὡς φλόγα πυρὸς the one having his eyes like flaming fire				
καὶ οἱ πόδες αὐτοῦ ὅμοιοι χαλκολιβάνῳ· and his feet like burnished brass.				
2:19 οἶδά σου τὰ ἔργα καὶ τὴν ἀγάπην I know your works and love	19 I know your works and love and faith and service and your perseverance, and your last works more than the first.	19 I know your works and love and faith (faith produces works and love, not the reverse) and service and your perseverance, and your last works more than the first.	19 I know your works and love and faith and service and your perseverance, and your last works more than the first.	19 I know your works and love and faith and service and your perseverance, and your last works more than the first.
καὶ τὴν πίστιν καὶ τὴν διακονίαν καὶ τὴν ὑπομονήν σου, and faith and service and your perseverance,				
καὶ τὰ ἔργα σου τὰ ἔσχατα πλείονα τῶν πρώτων. and your last works more than the first.				
2:20 ἀλλὰ ἔχω κατὰ σοῦ ὅτι ἀφεῖς τὴν γυναῖκα Ἰεζάβελ, But I have against you that you permit the woman Jezebel,	20 But I have against you that you permit the woman Jezebel, the one who calls herself a prophetess and she teaches and deceives my servants to commit immorality and to eat idol sacrifices. She does this by saying it is okay to join the guilds and celebrate their meals offered to Caesar and to the pagan gods.	20 But I have against you that you permit the woman Jezebel, the one who calls herself a prophetess and she teaches and deceives my servants to commit immorality and to eat idol sacrifices. Like Jezebel in the OT, who led Israel into idolatry by worshipping the mother goddess Ashtaroth, the Queen of Heaven (Jer.	20 But I have against you that you permit the woman Jezebel, the one who calls herself a prophetess and she teaches and deceives my servants to commit immorality and to eat idol sacrifices. She does this by saying it is okay to join the guilds and celebrate their meals to Caesar and to the pagan gods.	20 But I have against you that you permit the woman Jezebel, the one who calls herself a prophetess and she teaches and deceives my servants to commit immorality and to eat idol sacrifices. She does this by leading the church into compromise with the world.
ἡ λέγουσα ἑαυτὴν προφῆτιν the one who calls herself a prophetess				
καὶ διδάσκει καὶ πλανᾷ τοὺς ἐμοὺς δούλους and teaches and deceives my servants				
πορνεῦσαι καὶ φαγεῖν εἰδωλόθυτα. to commit immorality and to eat idol sacrifices.				

Greek / Interlinear (2:20)	Translation	Translation	Translation	Translation
2:21 καὶ ἔδωκα αὐτῇ χρόνον ἵνα μετανοήσῃ, / And I gave her time in order that she might repent, / καὶ οὐ θέλει μετανοῆσαι ἐκ τῆς πορνείας αὐτῆς. / and she did not choose to repent of her immorality.	21 And I gave her time in order that she might repent, and she did not choose to repent of her immorality.	44:17–18, 25), so the papacy led the church into the idolatrous worship of Mary, mother of Jesus, instead of only Jesus. 21 And I gave her time in order that she might repent, and she did not choose to repent of her immorality.	21 And I gave her time in order that she might repent, and she did not choose to repent of her immorality.	21 And I gave her time in order that she might repent, and did not choose to repent of her immorality.
2:22 ἰδοὺ βάλλω αὐτὴν εἰς κλίνην / Behold, I am casting her into a bed / καὶ τοὺς μοιχεύοντας μετ᾽ αὐτῆς εἰς θλῖψιν μεγάλην, / and the ones who commit adultery with her into great tribulation,	22 Behold, I am casting her into a bed and those who commit adultery with her into great tribulation, unless they repent from her works,	22 Behold, I am casting her into a bed and those who commit adultery with her into great tribulation, unless they repent from her works,	22 Behold, I am casting her into a bed and those who commit adultery with her into great tribulation, unless they repent from her works,	22 Behold, I am casting her into a bed and those who commit adultery with her into great tribulation, unless they repent from her works,
ἐὰν μὴ μετανοήσωσιν ἐκ τῶν ἔργων αὐτῆς, / unless they repent of her works,				
2:23 καὶ τὰ τέκνα αὐτῆς ἀποκτενῶ ἐν θανάτῳ. / and her children I will kill by death. / καὶ γνώσονται πᾶσαι αἱ ἐκκλησίαι / And all the churches will know / ὅτι ἐγώ εἰμι ὁ ἐραυνῶν νεφροὺς καὶ καρδίας, / that I myself am the one who searches [the] kidneys and [the] hearts / καὶ δώσω ὑμῖν ἑκάστῳ κατὰ τὰ ἔργα ὑμῶν. / and I will give to each one of you according to your works.	23 and her children I will kill by death. Thus her followers will meet with God's judgment. And all the churches will know that I am the one who searches the mind and the heart, and I will give to each one according to their works.	23 and her children I will kill by death (which Jesus did through the Black Plague, ca. 1347). And all the churches will know that I am the one who searches the mind and the heart, and I will give to each one according to their works.	23 and her children I will kill by death. Her followers will meet with divine judgment. And all the churches will know that I am the one who searches the mind and the heart, and I will give to each one according to their works.	23 and her children I will kill by death. The eventual demise of the seven churches in Asia Minor repeats itself in all compromising churches. And all the churches will know that I am the one who searches the mind and the heart, and I will give to each one according to their works.
2:24 ὑμῖν δὲ λέγω τοῖς λοιποῖς τοῖς ἐν Θυατείροις, / But I say to the rest of you who are in Thyatira,	24 But I say to the rest of you who are in Thyatira, as many as are not having this teaching, the ones	24 But I say to the rest of you who are in Thyatira, as many as are not having this teaching, the ones	24 But I say to the rest of you who are in Thyatira, as many as are not having this teaching, the ones	24 But I say to the rest of you who are in Thyatira, as many as are not having this teaching, the ones

Greek Text and English Translation	Preterist View	Historicist View	Futurist View	Idealist View
ὅσοι οὐκ ἔχουσιν τὴν διδαχὴν ταύτην, as many as are not having this teaching, οἵτινες οὐκ ἔγνωσαν τὰ βαθέα τοῦ σατανᾶ ὡς λέγουσιν· the ones who have not known the deep things of Satan as they are saying. οὐ βάλλω ἐφ᾽ ὑμᾶς ἄλλο βάρος, I am not casting upon you another burden;	who have not known the deep things of Satan as they are saying—the idea that it is okay to serve both Caesar and Christ. I am not casting upon you another burden;	who have not known the deep things of Satan (the idolatry of the papacy) as they are saying. I am not casting upon you another burden;	who have not known the deep things of Satan as they are saying—the idea that it is okay to serve both Caesar and Christ. I am not casting upon you another burden;	who have not known the deep things of Satan as they are saying—the error that the church can worship Christ and the world. I am not casting upon you another burden;
2:25 πλὴν ὃ ἔχετε κρατήσατε ἄχρι[ς] οὗ ἂν ἥξω. nevertheless, what you have, hold until I shall come.	25 nevertheless, what you have, hold until I shall come.	25 nevertheless, what you have, hold until I shall come.	25 nevertheless, what you have, hold until I shall come.	25 nevertheless, what you have, hold until I shall come.
2:26 Καὶ ὁ νικῶν καὶ ὁ τηρῶν ἄχρι τέλους τὰ ἔργα μου, And the one overcoming and the one keeping my works until the end, δώσω αὐτῷ ἐξουσίαν ἐπὶ τῶν ἐθνῶν I will give to him authority over the nations	26 And the one overcoming and the one keeping my works until the end, I will give to him authority over the nations	26 And the one overcoming and the one keeping my works until the end, I will give to him authority over the nations	26 And the one overcoming and the one keeping my works until the end, I will give to him authority over the nations	26 And the one overcoming and the one keeping my works until the end, I will give to him authority over the nations
2:27 καὶ ποιμανεῖ αὐτοὺς ἐν ῥάβδῳ σιδηρᾷ ὡς τὰ σκεύη τὰ κεραμικὰ συντρίβεται, and he will shepherd them with a rod of iron as vessels of clay are broken,	27 and he will shepherd them with a rod of iron, as vessels of clay are broken,	27and he will shepherd them with a rod of iron, as vessels of clay are broken,	27 and he will shepherd them with a rod of iron, as vessels of clay are broken,	27 and he will shepherd them with a rod of iron, as vessels of clay are broken,
2:28 ὡς κἀγὼ εἴληφα παρὰ τοῦ πατρός μου, as also I have received from my Father, καὶ δώσω αὐτῷ τὸν ἀστέρα τὸν πρωϊνόν. and I will give to him the morning star.	28 as also I have received from my Father, and I will give to him the morning star.	28 as also I have received from my Father, and I will give to him the morning star.	28 as also I have received from my Father, and I will give to him the morning star.	28 as also I have received from my Father, and I will give to him the morning star.

2:29 Ὁ ἔχων οὖς ἀκουσάτω τί τὸ πνεῦμα λέγει ταῖς ἐκκλησίαις. The one having ears, let him hear what the Spirit says to the churches!	29 The one having ears, let him hear what the Spirit says to the churches!	29 The one having ears, let him hear what the Spirit says to the churches!	29 The one having ears, let him hear what the Spirit says to the churches!	29 The one having ears, let him hear what the Spirit says to the churches!
3:1 Καὶ τῷ ἀγγέλῳ τῆς ἐν Σάρδεσιν ἐκκλησίας γράψον· And to the angel of the church in Sardis write:	1 And to the angel of the church in Sardis write: Thus says the one having the seven Spirits of God and the seven stars. I know your works, that you have a name, that you live, and you are dead.	1 And to the angel of the church in Sardis, which corresponds to the Reformation church (1517–1793), from Martin Luther to John Wesley), write: Thus says the one having the seven Spirits of God and the seven stars. I know your works, that you have a name, that you live, and you are dead.	1 And to the angel of the church in Sardis write: Thus says the one having the seven Spirits of God and the seven stars. I know your works, that you have a name, that you live, and you are dead.	1 And to the angel of the church in Sardis write: Thus says the one having the seven Spirits of God and the seven stars. I know your works, that you have a name, that you live, and you are dead.
Τάδε λέγει ὁ ἔχων τὰ ἑπτὰ πνεύματα τοῦ θεοῦ These things says the one having the seven Spirits of God				
καὶ τοὺς ἑπτὰ ἀστέρας· and the seven stars.				
οἶδά σου τὰ ἔργα ὅτι ὄνομα ἔχεις ὅτι ζῇς, καὶ νεκρὸς εἶ. I know your works that you have a name that you live, and you are dead.				
3:2 γίνου γρηγορῶν καὶ στήρισον τὰ λοιπὰ Become alert and establish the remainder	2 Become alert and establish the remainder, which were about to die, for I have not found your works to have been completed before my God!	2 Become alert and establish the remainder which were about to die, for I have not found your works to have been completed before my God! These are the Protestant Reformers—Luther, Calvin, Zwingli, Wesley, and their followers—who restored the church to God, in part by discarding unscriptural traditions and reinstituting biblical authority. But they did not go far enough; that was left to the Anabaptists.	2 Become alert and establish the remainder, which were about to die, for I have not found your works to have been completed before my God!	2 Become alert and establish the remainder, which were about to die, for I have not found your works to have been completed before my God!
ἃ ἔμελλον ἀποθανεῖν, οὐ γὰρ εὕρηκά σου τὰ ἔργα which were about to die, for I have not found your works				
πεπληρωμένα ἐνώπιον τοῦ θεοῦ μου. having been completed before my God.				

REVELATION

Greek Text and English Translation	Preterist View	Historicist View	Futurist View	Idealist View
3:3 μνημόνευε οὖν πῶς εἴληφας καὶ ἤκουσας Remember therefore how you have received and heard	3 Remember therefore how you have received and heard, and keep and repent. If you do not, therefore, become alert, I will come as a thief to destroy Jerusalem, and you never ever will know what hour I will come unto you to judge you for compromising with the imperial cult and with the Jews.	3 Remember therefore how you have received and heard, and keep and repent. If you do not, therefore, become alert, I will come as a thief at the second coming, at the end of history, and you never ever will know what hour I will come unto you and judge you.	3 Remember therefore how you have received and heard, and keep and repent. If you do not, therefore, become alert, I will come as a thief at the Rapture, and you never ever will know what hour I will come unto you (though you can discern what season it will be; cf. Mark 13:28–37) and judge you because you have compromised your faith with the imperial cult and with the Jews.	3 Remember therefore how you have received and heard, and keep and repent. If you do not, therefore, become alert, I will come as a thief at the second coming at the end of history, and you never ever will know what hour I will come unto you to judge you.
καὶ τήρει καὶ μετανόησον. and keep and repent.				
ἐὰν οὖν μὴ γρηγορήσῃς, ἥξω ὡς κλέπτης, If therefore you do not become alert, I will come as a thief,				
καὶ οὐ μὴ γνῷς ποίαν ὥραν ἥξω ἐπὶ σέ. and you never ever will know what hour I will come unto you.				
3:4 ἀλλὰ ἔχεις ὀλίγα ὀνόματα ἐν Σάρδεσιν But you have a few names in Sardis	4 But you do have a few names in Sardis which did not defile their garments, and they shall walk with me in white, because they are holy by not bowing down to worship Caesar.	4 But you do have a few names in Sardis which did not defile their garments, and they shall walk with me in white, because they are holy. These are the Anabaptists, who taught believers' baptism, repudiated sacramentalism, espoused congregational polity, and emphasized personal piety.	4 But you do have a few names in Sardis which did not defile their garments, and they shall walk with me in white, because they are holy in that they did not bow before Caesar but rather worshipped Christ.	4 But you do have a few names in Sardis which did not defile their garments, and they shall walk with me in white, because they are holy. These are the faithful ones who have not submitted to idolatry but have been faithful to Christ.
ἃ οὐκ ἐμόλυναν τὰ ἱμάτια αὐτῶν, which did not defile their garments				
καὶ περιπατήσουσιν μετ᾽ ἐμοῦ ἐν λευκοῖς, ὅτι ἄξιοί εἰσιν. and they shall walk with me in white, because they are holy.				
3:5 Ὁ νικῶν οὕτως περιβαλεῖται ἐν ἱματίοις λευκοῖς The one who overcomes thus will be clothed in white garments	5 The one who overcomes thus will be clothed in white garments, and even though the synagogue expelled him, I	5 The one who overcomes thus will be clothed in white garments, and I will never cast his name out of the book of life,	5 The one who overcomes thus will be clothed in white garments, and even though the synagogue expelled him, I	5 The one who overcomes thus will be clothed in white garments, and even though the synagogue expelled him, I

Greek / Interlinear	Translation A	Translation B	Translation C	Translation D
καὶ οὐ μὴ ἐξαλείψω τὸ ὄνομα αὐτοῦ / and I will never cast out his name	will never cast his name out of the book of life, and I will confess his name before my Father and before his angels.	and I will confess his name before my Father and before his angels.	will never cast his name out of the book of life. and I will confess his name before my Father and before his angels.	will never cast his name out of the book of life, and I will confess his name before my Father and before his angels.
ἐκ τῆς βίβλου τῆς ζωῆς καὶ ὁμολογήσω τὸ ὄνομα αὐτοῦ / out of the book of life and I will confess his name				
ἐνώπιον τοῦ πατρός μου καὶ ἐνώπιον τῶν ἀγγέλων αὐτοῦ. / before my Father and before his angels.				
3:6 Ὁ ἔχων οὖς ἀκουσάτω / The one having ears, let him hear	6 The one having ears, let him hear what the Spirit says to the churches!	6 The one having ears, let him hear what the Spirit says to the churches!	6 The one having ears, let him hear what the Spirit says to the churches!	6 The one having ears, let him hear what the Spirit says to the churches!
τί τὸ πνεῦμα λέγει ταῖς ἐκκλησίαις. / what the Spirit says to the churches!				
3:7 Καὶ τῷ ἀγγέλῳ τῆς ἐν Φιλαδελφείᾳ ἐκκλησίας γράψον· / And to the angel of the church in Philadelphia write:	7 And to the angel of the church in Philadelphia write: Thus says the holy one, the true one, the one who opens the key of David, the one who opens (the kingdom of God) and no one will close (not even those Jews who oppose the gospel): and the one who closes and no one opens.	7 And to the angel of the church in Philadelphia which corresponds to the church of the Great Awakening that resulted in the modern missions movement (1793 to the 1900s), write: Thus says the holy one, the true one, the one having the key of David, the one who opens the door(s) of revival (the revivals of Wesley, Whitefield, Edwards, Finney, and Graham) and missions (the modern missions movement begun by Carey) and no one will close, and the one who closes and no one opens.	7 And to the angel of the church in Philadelphia write: Thus says the holy one, the true one, the one having the key of David (the millennial kingdom that will come to earth after the second coming of Christ), the one who opens and no one will close, and the one who closes and no one opens.	7 And to the angel of the church in Philadelphia write: Thus says the holy one, the true one, the one having the key of David (the gospel of the kingdom of God, to be entered into now through faith in Jesus), the one who opens and no one will close, and the one who closes and no one opens.
Τάδε λέγει ὁ ἅγιος, ὁ ἀληθινός, / These things says the holy one, the true one,				
ὁ ἔχων τὴν κλεῖν Δαυίδ, ὁ ἀνοίγων / the one having the key of David, the one who opens				
καὶ οὐδεὶς κλείσει καὶ κλείων καὶ οὐδεὶς ἀνοίγει· / and no one will close and the one who closes and no one opens.				

Greek Text and English Translation	Preterist View	Historicist View	Futurist View	Idealist View
3:8 οἶδά σου τὰ ἔργα, ἰδοὺ δέδωκα I know your works, behold I have given	8 I know your works; be-hold, I have given before you a door having been opened, which no one is able to close, because you have a little power and you kept my word and did not deny my name.	8 I know your works; be-hold, I have given before you a door having been opened, which no one is able to close, because you have a little power and you kept my word and did not deny my name.	8 I know your works; be-hold, I have given before you a door having been opened, which no one is able to close, because you have a little power and you kept my word and did not deny my name.	8 I know your works; be-hold, I have given before you a door having been opened, which no one is able to close, because you have a little power and you kept my word and did not deny my name.
ἐνώπιόν σου θύραν ἠνεῳγμένην, before you a door having been opened,				
ἣν οὐδεὶς δύναται κλεῖσαι αὐτήν, which no one is able to close it,				
ὅτι μικρὰν ἔχεις δύναμιν because you have a little power				
καὶ ἐτήρησάς μου τὸν λόγον καὶ οὐκ ἠρνήσω τὸ ὄνομά μου. and you kept my word and did not deny my name.				
3:9 ἰδοὺ διδῶ ἐκ τῆς συναγωγῆς τοῦ σατανᾶ Behold I will give out of the synagogue of Satan	9 Behold I will give out of the synagogue of Satan of the ones saying that they themselves are Jews (who expelled true Jews—Jewish Christians—from their synagogues, thus exposing them to Caesar worship) and they are not but are lying. Behold, I will make them in order that they will come and worship before your feet and they will know that I loved you.	9 Behold I will give out of the synagogue of Satan of the ones saying that they themselves are Jews, and they are not but are lying (that is, any part of mere Christendom, not true Christianity, which opposes the gospel). Behold, I will make them in order that they will come and worship before your feet and they will know that I loved you.	9 Behold I will give out of the synagogue of Satan (who cast you out of their synagogues) of the ones saying that they themselves are Jews, and they are not but are lying. Behold, I will make them in order that they will come and worship before your feet and they will know that I loved you.	9 Behold I will give out of the synagogue of Satan (who cast you out of their synagogues) of the ones saying that they themselves are Jews, and they are not but are lying. Behold, I will make them in order that they will come and worship before your feet and they will know that I loved you. Thus the gospel and the world system will collide.
τῶν λεγόντων ἑαυτοὺς Ἰουδαίους εἶναι, the ones saying that they themselves are Jews,				
καὶ οὐκ εἰσὶν ἀλλὰ ψεύδονται. and are not but lie.				
ἰδοὺ ποιήσω αὐτοὺς ἵνα ἥξουσιν Behold, I will make them in order that they will come				
καὶ προσκυνήσουσιν ἐνώπιον τῶν ποδῶν σου and worship before your feet				
καὶ γνῶσιν ὅτι ἐγὼ ἠγάπησά σε. and they will know that I loved you.				

3:10				
3:10 ὅτι ἐτήρησας τὸν λόγον τῆς ὑπομονῆς μου, Because you kept the word of my perseverance, κἀγώ σε τηρήσω ἐκ τῆς ὥρας τοῦ πειρασμοῦ I also will keep you from the hour of trial τῆς μελλούσης ἔρχεσθαι ἐπὶ τῆς οἰκουμένης ὅλης which is about to come upon the entire dispensation πειράσαι τοὺς κατοικοῦντας ἐπὶ τῆς γῆς. to try the inhabitants upon the earth.	10 Because you kept the word of my perseverance, by worshipping Christ, not Caesar, I also will keep you from the hour of trial which is about to come upon the entire dispensation to try the inhabitants upon the earth. (That is to say, Emperor Nero's death brought about a world-wide crisis to the Roman Empire, threatening to undo it with civil wars. As a result, even the Jews, who revolted against Rome, would meet their defeat at the hands of the Romans at the destruction of Jerusalem. But the church, the true Israel, which parted company with Judaism, lived to fight Rome another day in a spiritual battle—one in which it confessed Christ, not Caesar, to be Lord.)	10 Because you kept the word of my perseverance, I also will keep you from the hour of trial which is about to come upon the entire dispensation to try the inhabitants upon the earth at the second coming. (That is, Christ will protect the church even though it suffers on earth from the persecution of false religion, which is a part of the Tribulation of the end times. But the preaching of the gospel will prevail and thereby establish the kingdom of God on earth, after which Christ will come again.)	10 Because you kept the word of my perseverance, I also will keep you from the hour of trial which is about to come upon the entire dispensation to try the inhabitants upon the earth. (That is, the church will be raptured out of the earth before the start of the end-time Tribulation. After the seven-year Tribulation, Christ will return to earth to establish his thousand-year reign on earth with Jerusalem as his capital.)	10 Because you kept the word of my perseverance, I also will keep you from the hour of trial which is about to come upon the entire dispensation to try the inhabitants upon the earth. (Those who are faithful to Christ and his kingdom, opposing the idolatry of the kingdoms of this world, will prevail after "a little while" [the hour of trial] and persevere through the "Great Tribulation" [which is symbolic for the current struggle of the church against the world].)
3:11 ἔρχομαι ταχύ· κράτει ὃ ἔχεις, I come quickly; hold what you have, ἵνα μηδεὶς λάβῃ τὸν στέφανόν σου. in order that no one may take your crown.	11 I come quickly to destroy Jerusalem (which indeed happened in A.D. 70); hold what you have, in order that no one may take your crown.	11 I come quickly; in the meantime, hold what you have, in order that no one may take your crown.	11 I come quickly in the form of the Rapture, since there are no signs that have to be fulfilled before that event; hold what you have, in order that no one may take your crown.	11 I will come quickly at the second coming; hold what you have in order that no one may take your crown.

Greek Text and English Translation	Preterist View	Historicist View	Futurist View	Idealist View
3:12 Ὁ νικῶν ποιήσω αὐτὸν στῦλον ἐν τῷ ναῷ τοῦ θεοῦ μου The one who overcomes I will make him a pillar in the temple of my God καὶ ἔξω οὐ μὴ ἐξέλθῃ ἔτι and never ever will he be cast outside καὶ γράψω ἐπ᾿ αὐτὸν τὸ ὄνομα τοῦ θεοῦ μου and I will write upon him the name of my God καὶ τὸ ὄνομα τῆς πόλεως τοῦ θεοῦ μου, τῆς καινῆς Ἰερουσαλὴμ and the name of the city of my God, the New Jerusalem ἡ καταβαίνουσα ἐκ τοῦ οὐρανοῦ ἀπὸ τοῦ θεοῦ μου, καὶ τὸ ὄνομά μου τὸ καινόν. which is descending out of heaven from my God and my new name.	12 I will make the one who overcomes a pillar in the temple of my God, and never ever will he be cast outside, and I will write upon him the name of my God and the name of the city of my God, the new Jerusalem, the church, which is descending out of heaven from my God to replace the old covenant and the old Jerusalem, and my new name.	12 I will make the one who overcomes a pillar in the temple of my God, and never ever will he be cast outside, and I will write upon him the name of my God and the name of the city of my God, the new Jerusalem, which is descending out of heaven from my God (the kingdom of God which will be brought to the earth by the church's victorious preaching of the gospel), and my new name.	12 I will make the one who overcomes a pillar in the temple of my God, and never ever will he be cast outside, and I will write upon him the name of my God and the name of the city of my God, the new Jerusalem, which is descending out of heaven from my God at the end of the Millennium, which begins the eternal state, and my new name.	12 I will make the one who overcomes a pillar in the temple of my God, and never ever will he be cast outside, and I will write upon him the name of my God and the name of the city of my God, the new Jerusalem, which is descending out of heaven from my God (the visible manifestation of the true status of the church, the kingdom of God, at the second coming of Christ).
3:13 Ὁ ἔχων οὖς ἀκουσάτω The one having ears, let him hear τί τὸ πνεῦμα λέγει ταῖς ἐκκλησίαις. what the Spirit says to the churches!	13 The one having ears, let him hear what the Spirit says to the churches!	13 The one having ears, let him hear what the Spirit says to the churches!	13 The one having ears, let him hear what the Spirit says to the churches!	13 The one having ears, let him hear what the Spirit says to the churches!
3:14 Καὶ τῷ ἀγγέλῳ τῆς ἐν Λαοδικείᾳ ἐκκλησίας γράψον· And to the angel of the church in Laodicea write: Τάδε λέγει ὁ ἀμήν, ὁ μάρτυς ὁ πιστὸς καὶ ἀληθινός, These things says the Amen, the faithful and true witness	14 And to the angel of the church in Laodicea write: Thus says the Amen, the faithful and true witness, the beginning of the creation of God.	14 And to the angel of the church in Laodicea, which corresponds to the apostate church from the 1900s to the present (the counterfeit church to the true church of Philadelphia with which it overlaps in time), write:	14 And to the angel of the church in Laodicea, which existed in John's day but also corresponds to the apostate church of the end times, write: Thus says the Amen, the faithful and true	14 And to the angel of the church in Laodicea, write: Thus says the Amen, the faithful and true witness, the beginning of the creation of God.

(Greek / literal)	(paraphrase)			
3:14 ἡ ἀρχὴ τῆς κτίσεως τοῦ θεοῦ· the beginning of the creation of God.		Thus says the Amen, the faithful and true witness, the beginning of the creation of God.	witness, the beginning of the creation of God.	
3:15 οἶδά σου τὰ ἔργα ὅτι οὔτε ψυχρὸς εἶ οὔτε ζεστός, I know your works, that you are neither cold nor hot. ὄφελον ψυχρὸς ἦς ἢ ζεστός, I wish [that] you were cold or hot.	15 I know your works, that you are neither cold nor hot. (The church at Laodicea is compromising with Judaism and with Rome; therefore it is a lukewarm church, which has watered down Christianity.) I wish you were cold or hot.	15 I know your works, that you are neither cold nor hot. I wish you were cold or hot.	15 I know your works, that you are neither cold nor hot. I wish you were cold or hot.	15 I know your works, that you are neither cold nor hot. I wish you were cold or hot.
3:16 οὕτως ὅτι χλιαρὸς εἶ καὶ οὔτε ζεστός οὔτε ψυχρός, Thus because you are lukewarm and neither hot nor cold μέλλω σε ἐμέσαι ἐκ τοῦ στόματός μου. I am about to vomit you out of my mouth.	16 Thus, because you are lukewarm and neither hot nor cold, I am about to vomit you out of my mouth. (That is, Christ will cast out the Laodicean church from his kingdom).	16 Thus, because you are lukewarm and neither hot nor cold, I am about to vomit you out of my mouth.	16 Thus, because you are lukewarm and neither hot nor cold, I am about to vomit you out of my mouth.	16 Thus, because you are lukewarm and neither hot nor cold, I am about to vomit you out of my mouth.
3:17 ὅτι λέγεις ὅτι πλούσιός εἰμι Because you say that "I am rich καὶ πεπλούτηκα καὶ οὐδὲν χρείαν ἔχω," and I have become rich and I have no need," καὶ οὐκ οἶδας ὅτι σὺ εἶ ὁ ταλαίπωρος and you do not know that you yourself are the wretched one καὶ ἐλεεινὸς καὶ πτωχὸς καὶ τυφλὸς καὶ γυμνός, and pitiable and poor and blind and naked,	17 Because you say, 'I am rich and I have become rich' (the Laodicean church is rich because it is unpersecuted because it compromised its faith by worshipping Caesar and kowtowing to the synagogues) 'and I have no need'; and you do not know that you yourself are the wretched one and pitiable and poor and blind and naked,	17 Because you say, 'I am rich and I have become rich and I have no need'; and you do not know that you yourself are the wretched one and pitiable and poor and blind and naked,	17 Because you say, 'I am rich and I have become rich and I have no need'; and you do not know that you yourself are the wretched one and pitiable and poor and blind and naked,	17 Because you say, 'I am rich and I have become rich and I have no need'; and you do not know that you yourself are the wretched one and pitiable and poor and blind and naked,

REVELATION

Greek Text and English Translation	Preterist View	Historicist View	Futurist View	Idealist View
3:18 συμβουλεύω σοι ἀγοράσαι παρ᾽ ἐμοῦ χρυσίον I counsel you to buy from me gold πεπυρωμένον ἐκ πυρὸς ἵνα πλουτήσῃς, having been tested by fire in order that you may be rich καὶ ἱμάτια λευκὰ ἵνα περιβάλῃ and white garments in order that you may be clothed καὶ μὴ φανερωθῇ ἡ αἰσχύνη τῆς γυμνότητός σου, and the shame of your nakedness not be manifested, καὶ κολλ[ο]ύριον ἐγχρῖσαι τοὺς ὀφθαλμούς σου ἵνα βλέπῃς. and eye salve to anoint your eyes in order that you might see.	18 I counsel you to buy from me gold having been tested by fire in order that you may be rich, and white garments in order that you may be clothed and the shame of your nakedness not be manifested, and eye salve to anoint your eyes in order that you might see. (In other words, the Laodicean "Christians" are spiritually bankrupt and sick.)	18 I counsel you to buy from me gold having been tested by fire in order that you may be rich, and white garments in order that you may be clothed and the shame of your nakedness not be manifested, and eye salve to anoint your eyes in order that you might see. (The Laodicean church is the modern liberal church, which has exchanged the orthodox Christian faith for an anti-supernatural biased "faith," due to the evil influence of the historical-critical method of interpreting the Bible wedded to Darwinianism. The church of Laodicea therefore represents the apostate church of the end times. It has a form of religion but without godliness. Consequently, Christ is about to judge it by destroying that "church" unless it repents and returns to the biblical Christ.)	18 I counsel you to buy from me gold having been tested by fire in order that you may be rich, and white garments in order that you may be clothed and the shame of your nakedness not be manifested, and eye salve to anoint your eyes in order that you might see.	18 I counsel you to buy from me gold having been tested by fire in order that you may be rich, and white garments in order that you may be clothed and the shame of your nakedness not be manifested, and eye salve to anoint your eyes in order that you might see.

3:19 ἐγὼ ὅσους ἐὰν φιλῶ ἐλέγχω καὶ παιδεύω· As many as I myself love I rebuke and I chasten. ζήλευε οὖν καὶ μετανόησον. Be hot therefore and repent!	19 As many as I love, I rebuke and I chasten. Be hot therefore and repent!	19 As many as I love, I rebuke and I chasten. Be hot therefore and repent!	19 As many as I love, I rebuke and I chasten. Be hot therefore and repent! You need to repent because you have compromised the true, orthodox faith in Christ and become apostate.	19 As many as I love, I rebuke and I chasten. Be hot therefore and repent!
3:20 Ἰδοὺ ἕστηκα ἐπὶ τὴν θύραν καὶ κρούω· Behold, I stand at the door and I knock. ἐάν τις ἀκούσῃ τῆς φωνῆς μου καὶ ἀνοίξῃ τὴν θύραν, If any one hears my voice and opens the door, [καὶ] εἰσελεύσομαι πρὸς αὐτὸν καὶ δειπνήσω μετ᾽ αὐτοῦ καὶ αὐτὸς μετ᾽ ἐμοῦ. and I will enter into him and I will dine with him and he with me.	20 Behold, I have been standing at the door and knock. If any one hears my voice and opens the door, I will enter into him and I will dine with him and him with me. (Thus, Christ is outside the church there, looking in and seeking entrance into the hearts of the professing Christians at Laodicea.)	20 Behold, I have been standing at the door and knock. If any one hears my voice and opens the door, I will enter into him and I will dine with him and him with me. (Thus there is still a window of opportunity for the Laodicean church to repent.)	20 Behold, I have been standing at the door and knock. If any one hears my voice and opens the door, I will enter into him and I will dine with him and he with me. But the time to repent is fleeting.	20 Behold, I have been standing at the door and knock. If any one hears my voice and opens the door, I will enter into him and I will dine with him and he with me. Repent or I will remove you from my kingdom.
3:21 Ὁ νικῶν δώσω αὐτῷ καθίσαι μετ᾽ ἐμοῦ ἐν τῷ θρόνῳ μου, The one who overcomes I will give to him to sit with me in my throne, ὡς κἀγὼ ἐνίκησα καὶ ἐκάθισα μετὰ τοῦ πατρός μου ἐν τῷ θρόνῳ αὐτοῦ. as I also overcame and sat with my Father in his throne.	21 The one who overcomes I will give to him to sit with me in my throne, as I also overcame and sat with my Father in his throne.	21 The one who overcomes (those who embrace conservative, orthodox Christianity) I will give to him to sit with me in my throne, as I also overcame and sat with my Father in his throne.	21 The one who overcomes I will give to him to sit with me in my throne in the millennial kingdom after the second coming of Christ, as I also overcame and sat with my Father in his throne.	21 The one who overcomes I will give to him to sit with me in my throne, as I also came and sat with my Father in his throne, which is my present reign through the true church.
3:22 Ὁ ἔχων οὖς ἀκουσάτω The one having ears, let him hear τί τὸ πνεῦμα λέγει ταῖς ἐκκλησίαις. what the Spirit says to the churches!	22 The one having ears, let him hear what the Spirit says to the churches!"	22 The one having ears, let him hear what the Spirit says to the churches!"	22 The one having ears, let him hear what the Spirit says to the churches!"	22 The one having ears, let him hear what the Spirit says to the churches!"

REVELATION

Greek Text and English Translation	Preterist View	Historicist View	Futurist View	Idealist View
4:1 Μετὰ ταῦτα εἶδον, καὶ ἰδοὺ θύρα After these things I looked, and behold, a door ἠνεῳγμένη ἐν τῷ οὐρανῷ, καὶ ἡ φωνὴ ἡ πρώτη having been opened in heaven, and the first voice ἣν ἤκουσα ὡς σάλπιγγος λαλούσης μετ᾿ ἐμοῦ λέγων· which I heard like a trumpet speaking with me saying, ἀνάβα ὧδε, καὶ δείξω σοι "Come up here, and I will show you ἃ δεῖ γενέσθαι μετὰ ταῦτα. what things must happen after these things."	1 After these things I looked, and behold, there was a door having been opened in heaven, and the first voice which I heard like a trumpet spoke with me saying, "Come up here, and I will show you what things must happen after these things"; that is, the fall of Jerusalem in A.D. 70 to the Romans in three majors stages corresponding with the seal, trumpet, and bowl judgments (seals = Roman campaign against Galilee and Samaria; trumpets = Roman campaign against Judea; bowls = Roman siege and destruction of Jerusalem).	1 After these things I looked, and behold, there was a door having been opened in heaven, and the first voice which I heard like a trumpet spoke with me saying, "Come up here, and I will show you what things must happen after these things." (Revelation 4 and 5 present God as the Lord of history and Christ as on par with God, respectively. These unfold the divine plan in the three sets of judgments to follow: The seal judgments—Revelation 6–7—give a glimpse of the conquests of imperial Rome, along with the waxing and waning of the church, culminating in Constantine's establishment of Christianity as the religion of the empire. The trumpet judgments—Revelation 8–11—foretell the fall of the Western and then the Eastern Roman Empires. The bowl judgments—Revelation 15–18—predict the rise of the Protestant	1 After these things (Rev. 1–3 refers to John's past vision, while Rev. 4–22 pertains exclusively to the future) I looked, and behold, there was a door having been opened in heaven, and the first voice which I heard like a trumpet spoke with me saying, "Come up here (the rapture of the church is here visualized as John's rapture to heaven, for the church does not appear in Revelation after this verse until Revelation 19, when it will descend from heaven with Christ), and I will show you what things must happen after these things" (the end-time Tribulation, the Parousia, the Millennium, and the eternal state).	1 After these things I looked, and behold, there was a door having been opened in heaven, and the first voice which I heard like a trumpet spoke with me saying, "Come up here, and I will show you what things must happen after these things"; that is, the struggles and triumphs of the church throughout history.

4:2 Εὐθέως ἐγενόμην ἐν πνεύματι, Immediately I came to be in the Spirit καὶ ἰδοὺ θρόνος ἔκειτο ἐν τῷ οὐρανῷ, καὶ ἐπὶ τὸν θρόνον καθήμενος, and behold, a throne was set in heaven and upon the throne one sitting,	2 Immediately I became in the Spirit, and behold, a throne was set in heaven, and upon the throne one sitting, ready to make judgment against Jerusalem,	Reformation and its divinely ordained defeat of Roman Catholicism.) 2 Immediately I became in the Spirit, and behold, a throne was set in heaven, and upon the throne one sitting,	2 Immediately I became in the Spirit, and behold, a throne was set in heaven, and upon the throne one sitting,	2 Immediately I became in the Spirit, and behold, a throne was set in heaven, and upon the throne one sitting,
4:3 καὶ ὁ καθήμενος ὅμοιος ὁράσει λίθῳ ἰάσπιδι and the one sitting [was] like in appearance a jasper stone καὶ σαρδίῳ, καὶ ἶρις κυκλόθεν τοῦ θρόνου ὅμοιος ὁράσει σμαραγδίνῳ. and a sardis and a rainbow around the throne like in appearance an emerald.	3 and the one sitting was like a jasper stone and a sardis in appearance, and a rainbow was around the throne, like an emerald in appearance. This symbolizes that God has inaugurated the new covenant through the church.	3 and the one sitting was like a jasper stone and a sardis in appearance, and a rainbow was around the throne, like an emerald in appearance.	3 and the one sitting was like a jasper stone and a sardis in appearance, and a rainbow was around the throne, like an emerald in appearance.	3 and the one sitting was like a jasper stone and a sardis in appearance, and a rainbow was around the throne, like an emerald in appearance. (The word "throne" occurs forty times in Revelation and signifies that God is sovereign, judging the world and vindicating the saints.)
4:4 Καὶ κυκλόθεν τοῦ θρόνου θρόνους εἴκοσι τέσσαρες, And around the throne [were]twenty-four thrones, καὶ ἐπὶ τοὺς θρόνους εἴκοσι τέσσαρας πρεσβυτέρους καθημένους and upon the thrones twenty-four elders sitting περιβεβλημένους ἐν ἱματίοις λευκοῖς having been clothed in white garments καὶ ἐπὶ τὰς κεφαλὰς αὐτῶν στεφάνους χρυσοῦς. and upon their heads golden crowns.	4 And around the throne were twenty-four thrones, and upon the thrones twenty-four elders (the replacement of Israel; hence the imagery of 12 tribes and 12 apostles; 12 + 12 = 24) sitting, having been clothed in white garments, and upon their heads golden crowns.	4 And around the throne were twenty-four thrones, and upon the thrones twenty-four elders (the true church) sitting having been clothed in white garments (justification by faith), and upon their heads golden crowns.	4 And around the throne twenty-four thrones, and upon the thrones twenty-four elders (the NT church which is in heaven during the end-time Tribulation; it is Israel with whom God deals at that time to win her to Jesus the Messiah) sitting, having been clothed in white garments, and upon their heads golden crowns.	4 And around the throne twenty-four thrones, and upon the thrones twenty-four elders sitting, having been clothed in white garments, and upon their heads golden crowns. The twenty-four elders represent the true church, which is the replacement of Israel; thus 12 (tribes of Israel) + 12 (apostles) = 24 elders = the church.

Greek Text and English Translation	Preterist View	Historicist View	Futurist View	Idealist View
4:5 Καὶ ἐκ τοῦ θρόνου ἐκπορεύονται ἀστραπαὶ And out of the throne proceed lightnings καὶ φωναὶ καὶ βρονταί, καὶ ἑπτὰ λαμπάδες and voices and thunders and seven lamps πυρὸς καιόμεναι ἐνώπιον τοῦ θρόνου, of fire burning before the throne, ἅ εἰσιν τὰ ἑπτὰ πνεύματα τοῦ θεοῦ, which are the seven Spirits of God	5 And out of the throne proceed lightnings and voices and thunders, and seven lamps of fire burn before the throne, which are the seven Spirits of God,	5 And out of the throne proceed lightnings and voices and thunders, and seven lamps of fire burn before the throne, which are the seven Spirits of God,	5 And out of the throne proceed lightnings and voices and thunders, and seven lamps of fire burn before the throne, which are the seven Spirits of God,	5 And out of the throne proceed lightnings and voices and thunders, and seven lamps of fire burn before the throne, which are the seven Spirits of God,
4:6 καὶ ἐνώπιον τοῦ θρόνου ὡς θάλασσα ὑαλίνη ὁμοία κρυστάλλῳ. and before the throne [was] like a glassy sea, like crystal. Καὶ ἐν μέσῳ τοῦ θρόνου καὶ κύκλῳ τοῦ θρόνου And in the middle of the throne and around the throne τέσσαρα ζῷα γέμοντα ὀφθαλμῶν ἔμπροσθεν καὶ ὄπισθεν. [were] four living creatures being filled with eyes before and behind.	6 and before the throne was like a glassy sea, like crystal. And in the middle of the throne and around the throne were four living creatures (angels of the highest order), filled with eyes before and behind.	6 and before the throne was like a glassy sea, like crystal. And in the middle of the throne and around the throne were four living creatures (angels of the highest order), filled with eyes before and behind.	6 and before the throne was like a glassy sea, like crystal. And in the middle of the throne and around the throne were four living creatures, filled with eyes before and behind.	6 and before the throne was like a glassy sea, like crystal. And in the middle of the throne and around the throne were four living creatures, filled with eyes before and behind.
4:7 καὶ τὸ ζῷον τὸ πρῶτον ὅμοιον λέοντι And the first living creature [is] like a lion καὶ τὸ δεύτερον ζῷον ὅμοιον μόσχῳ and the second living creature [is] like an ox καὶ τὸ τρίτον ζῷον ἔχον τὸ πρόσωπον ὡς ἀνθρώπου and the third living creature having the face like a man	7 And the first living creature is like a lion, and the second living creature is like an ox, and the third living creature has the face of a man, and the fourth living creature is like an eagle flying.	7 And the first living creature is like a lion, and the second living creature is like an ox, and the third living creature has the face of a man, and the fourth living creature is like an eagle flying.	7 And the first living creature is like a lion, and the second living creature is like an ox, and the third living creature has the face of a man, and the fourth living creature is like an eagle flying. These creatures represent the messages of the four Gospels. Thus the lion corresponds	7 And the first living creature is like a lion, and the second living creature is like an ox, and the third living creature has the face of a man, and the fourth living creature is like an eagle flying.

Greek / Literal	Version 2	Version 3	Version 4	Commentary
καὶ τὸ τέταρτον ζῷον ὅμοιον ἀετῷ πετομένῳ. and the fourth living creature [is] like an eagle flying.			to Matthew's portrayal of Jesus as the Davidic king, the Lion of the tribe of Judah; the ox corresponds to Mark with its message that Jesus is the Servant (ox, the beast of burden); the man corresponds to Luke's presentation of Christ as the perfect man; the eagle corresponds to John's message that Jesus is the Son of God, the most soaring (as an eagle soars) title for Jesus in the NT.	
4:8 καὶ τὰ τέσσαρα ζῷα, And the four living creatures,	8 And the four living creatures, one by one of them, each has six wings, around and within being full of eyes, and rest they do not have, day and night saying: "Holy, holy, holy, Lord God Almighty, who was and who is and who is coming."	8 And the four living creatures, one by one of them, each has six wings, around and within being full of eyes, and rest they do not have, day and night saying: "Holy, holy, holy, Lord God Almighty, who was and who is and who is coming."	8 And the four living creatures, one by one of them, each has six wings, around and within being full of eyes, and rest they do not have, day and night saying: "Holy, holy, holy, Lord God Almighty, who was and who is and who is coming." (Compare this phrase with the outline of Revelation 1:19: the past, present, and the future.)	8 And the four living creatures, one by one of them, each has six wings, around and within being full of eyes, and rest they do not have, day and night saying: "Holy, holy, holy, Lord God Almighty, who was and who is and who is coming." Thus the twenty-four elders represent saved humanity, while the four living creatures represent the animal creation. So, both the human and animal created orders, along with the angelic realm, worship God on the throne.
ἓν καθ᾽ ἓν αὐτῶν ἔχον ἀνὰ πτέρυγος ἕξ, one by one of them having six wings,				
κυκλόθεν καὶ ἔσωθεν γέμουσιν ὀφθαλμῶν, around and within being full of eyes,				
καὶ ἀνάπαυσιν οὐκ ἔχουσιν ἡμέρας καὶ νυκτὸς λέγοντες· and do not have rest day and night, saying,				
ἅγιος ἅγιος ἅγιος κύριος ὁ θεὸς ὁ παντοκράτωρ, "Holy, holy, holy, Lord God Almighty,				
ὁ ἦν καὶ ὁ ὢν καὶ ὁ ἐρχόμενος. the one who was and the one who is and the one who is coming."				
4:9 Καὶ ὅταν δώσουσιν τὰ ζῷα δόξαν καὶ τιμὴν And whenever the living creatures give glory and honor	9 And whenever the living creatures give glory and honor and thanks to the one sitting	9 And whenever the living creatures give glory and honor and thanks to the one sitting	9 And whenever the living creatures give glory and honor and thanks to the one sitting	9 And whenever the living creatures give glory and honor and thanks to the one sitting

Greek Text and English Translation	Preterist View	Historicist View	Futurist View	Idealist View
καὶ εὐχαριστίαν τῷ καθημένῳ ἐπὶ τῷ θρόνῳ and thanks to the one sitting upon the throne τῷ ζῶντι εἰς τοὺς αἰῶνας τῶν αἰῶνων, to the one who lives forever,	upon the throne, the one who lives forever,	upon the throne, the one who lives forever,	upon the throne, the one who lives forever,	upon the throne, the one who lives forever,
4:10 πεσοῦνται οἱ εἴκοσι τέσσαρες πρεσβύτεροι ἐνώπιον τοῦ καθημένου ἐπὶ τοῦ θρόνου the twenty-four elders will fall down before the one sitting upon the throne καὶ προσκυνήσουσιν τῷ ζῶντι εἰς τοὺς αἰῶνας τῶν αἰῶνων and will worship the one living forever καὶ βαλοῦσιν τοὺς στεφάνους αὐτῶν ἐνώπιον τοῦ θρόνου λέγοντες· and will cast their crowns before the throne, saying,	10 the twenty-four elders will fall down before the one sitting upon the throne and will worship the one living forever, and they will cast their crowns before the throne, saying,	10 the twenty-four elders will fall down before the one sitting upon the throne and will worship the one living forever, and they will cast their crowns before the throne, (which indicates that the Christian's works/rewards are based solely on God's grace, not the merits of the dead or the living) saying,	10 the twenty-four elders will fall down before the one sitting upon the throne and will worship the one living forever, and they will cast their crowns before the throne, saying,	10 the twenty-four elders will fall down before the one sitting upon the throne and will worship the one living forever, and they will cast their crowns before the throne, saying,
4:11 ἄξιος εἶ, ὁ κύριος καὶ ὁ θεὸς ἡμῶν, "You are worthy, our Lord and God, λαβεῖν τὴν δόξαν καὶ τὴν τιμὴν καὶ τὴν δύναμιν, to receive the glory and the honor and the power, ὅτι σὺ ἔκτισας τὰ πάντα καὶ διὰ τὸ θέλημά σου ἦσαν καὶ ἐκτίσθησαν. because you created all things and because of your will they were and were created."	11 "You are worthy, our Lord and God, to receive the glory and the honor and the power, because you created all things, and because of your will they existed and were created."	11 "You are worthy, our Lord and God, to receive the glory and the honor and the power, because you created all things, and because of your will they existed and were created."	11 "You are worthy, our Lord and God, to receive the glory and the honor and the power, because you created all things, and because of your will they existed and were created."	11 "You are worthy, our Lord and God, to receive the glory and the honor and the power, because you created all things, and because of your will they existed and were created."
5:1 Καὶ εἶδον ἐπὶ τὴν δεξιὰν τοῦ καθημένου And I saw in the right hand of the one sitting ἐπὶ τοῦ θρόνου βιβλίον γεγραμμένον ἔσωθεν upon the throne a scroll having been written within	1 And I saw in the right hand of the one sitting on the throne a scroll (God's divorce decree against Israel to be executed	1 And I saw in the right hand of the one sitting on the throne a scroll (God's government of the world), having been	1 And I saw in the right hand of the one sitting on the throne a scroll (the title deed to the universe, reminiscent of ancient	1 And I saw in the right hand of the one sitting on the throne a scroll (God's redemptive plan), having been written within

καὶ ὄπισθεν κατεσφραγισμένον σφραγῖσιν ἑπτά. and on the outside having been sealed with seven seals.	upon Jerusalem in A.D. 70, which symbolizes the replacement of the old covenant with the new covenant), having been written within and having been sealed with seven seals on the outside.	written within and having been sealed with seven seals on the outside.	Roman wills, sealed seven times), having been written within and having been sealed with seven seals on the outside, the mighty judgments of God by which he will reclaim his universe.	and having been sealed with seven seals on the outside, the recurring judgments of God upon the pagan world, which demonstrate he is the real Lord of the universe.
5:2 καὶ εἶδον ἄγγελον ἰσχυρὸν κηρύσσοντα ἐν φωνῇ μεγάλῃ· τίς ἄξιος ἀνοῖξαι τὸ βιβλίον καὶ λῦσαι τὰς σφραγῖδας αὐτοῦ; And I saw a strong angel proclaiming in a great voice, "Who is worthy to open the scroll and to loose its seals?"	2 And I saw a strong angel proclaiming in a great voice, "Who is worthy to open the scroll and loose its seals?"	2 And I saw a strong angel proclaiming in a great voice, "Who is worthy to open the scroll and loose its seals?"	2 And I saw a strong angel proclaiming in a great voice, "Who is worthy to open the scroll and loose its seals?"	2 And I saw a strong angel proclaiming in a great voice, "Who is worthy to open the scroll and loose its seals?"
5:3 καὶ οὐδεὶς ἐδύνατο ἐν τῷ οὐρανῷ οὐδὲ ἐπὶ τῆς γῆς οὐδὲ ὑποκάτω τῆς γῆς ἀνοῖξαι τὸ βιβλίον οὔτε βλέπειν αὐτό. And no one was able in heaven or upon the earth or under the earth to open the scroll or to look [into] it.	3 And no one was able in heaven or upon the earth or under the earth to open the scroll or to look into it.	3 And no one was able in heaven or upon the earth or under the earth to open the scroll or to look into it.	3 And no one was able in heaven or upon the earth or under the earth to open the scroll or to look into it.	3 And no one was able in heaven or upon the earth or under the earth to open the scroll or to look into it.
5:4 καὶ ἔκλαιον πολύ, ὅτι οὐδεὶς ἄξιος εὑρέθη ἀνοῖξαι τὸ βιβλίον οὔτε βλέπειν αὐτό. And I was weeping much, because no one worthy was found to open the scroll nor to look [into] it.	4 And I was weeping much, because no one worthy was found to open the scroll nor to look into it.	4 And I was weeping much, because no one worthy was found to open the scroll nor to look into it.	4 And I was weeping much, because no one worthy was found to open the scroll nor to look into it.	4 And I was weeping much, because no one worthy was found to open the scroll nor to look into it.
5:5 καὶ εἷς ἐκ τῶν πρεσβυτέρων λέγει μοι· μὴ κλαῖε, And one of the elders says to me, "Do not weep!	5 And one of the elders says to me, "Do not weep! Behold, the Lion has overcome—the one from the tribe of Judah, the Root of David—to open the scroll and its	5 And one of the elders says to me, "Do not weep! Behold, the Lion has overcome—the one from the tribe of Judah (Jesus' humanity) the Root of David (Jesus'	5 And one of the elders says to me, "Do not weep! Behold, the Lion has overcome—the one from the tribe of Judah, the Root of David—to open the scroll and its seven	5 And one of the elders says to me, Behold, the Lion has overcome—the one from the tribe of Judah, the Root of David—to open the scroll and its

Greek Text and English Translation	Preterist View	Historicist View	Futurist View	Idealist View
ἰδοὺ ἐνίκησεν ὁ λέων ὁ ἐκ τῆς φυλῆς Ἰούδα, ἡ ῥίζα Δαυίδ, Behold, the Lion has overcome—the one from the tribe of Judah, the Root of David— ἀνοῖξαι τὸ βιβλίον καὶ τὰς ἑπτὰ σφραγῖδας αὐτοῦ. to open the scroll and its seven seals."	seven seals." Jesus is the true Davidic heir who established the Davidic reign, the kingdom of God. As such, it replaced Jerusalem as the throne of God. Jesus will come to Jerusalem to destroy it by unleashing the judgments of Revelation, symbolized by the seven-sealed scroll.	deity)—to open the scroll and its seven seals." Jesus is the true Davidic heir who establishes the Davidic reign, the kingdom of God, that is, the Protestant Reformation and its return to the teachings of the early church and the church fathers. This is in contrast to Roman Catholicism.	seals." By these judgments Jesus will establish the Davidic kingdom in Jerusalem at his second coming, which was promised to Israel in the OT.	seven seals." Jesus is the true Davidic heir who is establishing the kingdom of God on earth now, despite the opposition of the enemies of Christ.
5:6 Καὶ εἶδον ἐν μέσῳ τοῦ θρόνου And I saw in the middle of the throne καὶ τῶν τεσσάρων ζῴων καὶ ἐν μέσῳ and of the four living creatures and in the middle τῶν πρεσβυτέρων ἀρνίον ἑστηκὸς of the elders a Lamb standing ὡς ἐσφαγμένον ἔχων κέρατα ἑπτὰ as though having been slain, having seven horns καὶ ὀφθαλμοὺς ἑπτὰ οἵ εἰσιν τὰ [ἑπτὰ] πνεύματα and seven eyes—these are the seven Spirits τοῦ θεοῦ ἀπεσταλμένοι εἰς πᾶσαν τὴν γῆν. of God having been sent into all the earth.	6 And I saw in the middle of the throne and the four living creatures and in the middle of the elders a Lamb standing, as though having been slain, having seven horns and seven eyes—these are the seven spirits of God (the Holy Spirit) having been sent into all the earth. The Lion of the tribe of Judah is the Messiah, who suffered death on the cross and who will retaliate against those Jews who crucified him.	6 And I saw in the middle of the throne and the four living creatures and in the middle of the elders a Lamb standing, as though having been slain, having seven horns and seven eyes—these are the seven spirits of God (the Holy Spirit) having been sent into all the earth. The Lion of the tribe of Judah is the Messiah, who suffered death on the cross.	6 And I saw in the middle of the throne and the four living creatures and in the middle of the elders a Lamb standing, as though having been slain, having seven horns and seven eyes—these are the seven spirits of God (the Holy Spirit) having been sent into all the earth. The Lion of the tribe of Judah is the Messiah, who suffered death on the cross.	6 And I saw in the middle of the throne and the four living creatures and in the middle of the elders a Lamb standing, as though having been slain, having seven horns and seven eyes—these are the seven spirits of God (the Holy Spirit) having been sent into all the earth. The Lion of the tribe of Judah is the Messiah, who suffered death on the cross. Jesus' path of suffering leading to the glory of the kingdom of God is the paradigm for the church: it too suffers persecution all the while representing

Greek (5:6)	Column 1	Column 2	Column 3	Column 4
5:7 καὶ ἦλθεν καὶ εἴληφεν ἐκ τῆς δεξιᾶς And he came and took [the scroll] out of the right [hand] τοῦ καθημένου ἐπὶ τοῦ θρόνου. of the one sitting on the throne.	7 And he came and took the scroll out of the right hand of the one sitting on the throne.	7 And he came and took the scroll out of the right hand of the one sitting on the throne.	7 And he came and took the scroll out of the right hand of the one sitting on the throne.	the kingdom of God on earth. 7 And he came and took the scroll out of the right hand of the one sitting on the throne.
5:8 Καὶ ὅτε ἔλαβεν τὸ βιβλίον, τὰ τέσσαρα ζῷα And when he took the scroll, the four living creatures καὶ οἱ εἴκοσι τέσσαρες πρεσβύτεροι ἔπεσαν and the twenty-four elders fell ἐνώπιον τοῦ ἀρνίου ἔχοντες ἕκαστος κιθάραν before the Lamb, each having a harp καὶ φιάλας χρυσᾶς γεμούσας θυμιαμάτων, and golden bowls being full of incense, αἵ εἰσιν αἱ προσευχαὶ τῶν ἁγίων, which are the prayers of the saints,	8 And when he took the scroll, the four living creatures and the twenty-four elders fell before the Lamb, each having a harp and golden bowls full of incense, which are the prayers of the saints (those persecuted by Jews and Caesar Nero),	8 And when he took the scroll, the four living creatures and the twenty-four elders fell before the Lamb, each having a harp and golden bowls full of incense, which are the prayers of the saints (those persecuted by the opponents of Christ throughout church history, especially at the hands of the papacy),	8 And when he took the scroll, the four living creatures and the twenty-four elders fell before the Lamb, each having a harp and golden bowls full of incense, which are the prayers of the saints (those persecuted by the opponents of Christ in the seven-year end-time Tribulation which is still yet to fall on the earth in the future, after the rapture of the church and before the second coming of Christ),	8 And when he took the scroll, the four living creatures and the twenty-four elders fell before the Lamb, each having a harp and golden bowls full of incense, which are the prayers of the saints (those persecuted by the opponents of Christ throughout church history),
5:9 καὶ ᾄδουσιν ᾠδὴν καινὴν λέγοντες· and they are singing a new song, saying, ἄξιος εἶ λαβεῖν τὸ βιβλίον καὶ ἀνοῖξαι τὰς σφραγῖδας αὐτοῦ, "Worthy are you to receive the scroll and to open its seals, ὅτι ἐσφάγης καὶ ἠγόρασας τῷ θεῷ because you were slain and you redeemed for God	9 and they are singing a new song, saying, "Worthy are you to receive the scroll and to open its seals, because you were slain and you have redeemed for God by your blood out of every tribe and people and tongue and nation (in other words, the true Israel)	9 and they are singing a new song, saying, "Worthy are you to receive the scroll and to open its seals, because you were slain and you have redeemed for God by your blood out of every tribe and people and tongue and nation (in other words, the true Israel)	9 and they are singing a new song, saying, "Worthy are you to receive the scroll and to open its seals, because you were slain and you have redeemed for God by your blood out of every tribe and tongue and people and nation (the 144,000 Christian Jewish evangelists will win many Gentiles to	9 and they are singing a new song, saying, "Worthy are you to receive the scroll and to open its seals, because you were slain and you have redeemed for God by your blood out of every tribe and tongue and people and nation (in other words, the true Israel).

Greek Text and English Translation	Preterist View	Historicist View	Futurist View	Idealist View
ἐν τῷ αἵματί σου ἐκ πάσης φυλῆς by your blood out of every tribe				
καὶ γλώσσης καὶ λαοῦ καὶ ἔθνους and tongue and and people and nation,				
			Christ during the end-time Tribulation)	
5:10 καὶ ἐποίησας αὐτοὺς τῷ θεῷ ἡμῶν βασιλείαν καὶ ἱερεῖς, and you have made them to our God a kingdom and priests,	10 and you have made them to our God a kingdom and priests, and that reign is fully here in the church."	10 and you have made them to our God a kingdom and priests, they will reign upon the earth" (and that reign has already begun).	10 and you have made them to our God a kingdom and priests, and they will reign upon the earth." After the end-time Tribulation, Christ will return to earth to establish his literal, thousand-year ("millennium") reign on earth, centered in Jerusalem. Christians raptured before the Tribulation will join those who became Christians during the Tribulation to rule with Christ over those unsaved people born in the Millennium.	10 and you have made them to our God a kingdom and priests, and they will reign upon the earth." And that reign has already begun despite enduring the end-time Tribulation (which is symbolic for the afflictions of the church).
καὶ βασιλεύσουσιν ἐπὶ τῆς γῆς. and they will rule upon the earth."				
5:11 Καὶ εἶδον, καὶ ἤκουσα φωνὴν ἀγγέλων πολλῶν κύκλῳ τοῦ θρόνου And I looked and I heard the voice of many angels around the throne	11 And I saw, and I heard the voice of many angels around the throne and of the living creatures and the elders, and their number was myriads of myriads and thousands of thousands,	11 And I saw, and I heard the voice of many angels around the throne and of the living creatures and the elders, and their number was myriads of myriads and thousands of thousands,	11 And I saw, and I heard the voice of many angels around the throne and of the living creatures and the elders, and their number was myriads of myriads and thousands of thousands,	11 And I saw, and I heard the voice of many angels around the throne and of the living creatures and the elders, and their number was myriads of myriads and thousands of thousands,
καὶ τῶν ζῴων καὶ τῶν πρεσβυτέρων, and of the living creatures and of the elders,				

12 saying in a great voice, "Worthy is the Lamb, the one having been slain, to receive power and riches and wisdom and strength and honor and glory and blessing."	12 saying in a great voice, "Worthy is the Lamb, the one having been slain, to receive power and riches and wisdom and strength and honor and glory and blessing."	12 saying in a great voice, "Worthy is the Lamb, the one having been slain, to receive power and riches and wisdom and strength and honor and glory and blessing."	12 saying in a great voice, "Worthy is the Lamb, the one having been slain, to receive power and riches and wisdom and strength and honor and glory and blessing."
13 And every creature which is in heaven and on earth and under the earth and on the sea and all things in them I heard saying, "To the one seated on the throne and to the Lamb be blessing and honor and glory and power forever."	13 And every creature which is in heaven and on earth and under the earth and on the sea and all things in them I heard saying, "To the one seated on the throne and to the Lamb be blessing and honor and glory and power forever."	13 And every creature which is in heaven and on earth and under the earth and on the sea and all things in them I heard saying, "To the one seated on the throne and to the Lamb be blessing and honor and glory and power forever."	13 And every creature which is in heaven and on earth and under the earth and on the sea and all things in them I heard saying, "To the one seated on the throne and to the Lamb be blessing and honor and glory and power forever."
14 And the four living creatures were saying, "Amen!" And the elders fell and worshipped.	14 And the four living creatures were saying, "Amen!" And the elders fell and worshipped.	14 And the four living creatures were saying, "Amen!" And the elders fell and worshipped.	14 And the four living creatures were saying, "Amen!" And the elders fell and worshipped.

καὶ ἦν ὁ ἀριθμὸς αὐτῶν μυριάδες μυριάδων καὶ χιλιάδες χιλιάδων
and their number was myriads of myriads and thousands of thousands,

5:12 λέγοντες φωνῇ μεγάλῃ· ἄξιόν ἐστιν τὸ ἀρνίον
saying in a great voice, "Worthy is the Lamb,

τὸ ἐσφαγμένον λαβεῖν τὴν δύναμιν
the one having been slain, to receive power

καὶ πλοῦτον καὶ σοφίαν καὶ ἰσχὺν καὶ τιμὴν καὶ δόξαν καὶ εὐλογίαν.
and riches and wisdom and strength and honor and glory and blessing."

5:13 καὶ πᾶν κτίσμα ὃ ἐν τῷ οὐρανῷ
And every creature which [is] in heaven

καὶ ἐπὶ τῆς γῆς καὶ ὑποκάτω τῆς γῆς
and on the earth and under the earth

καὶ ἐπὶ τῆς θαλάσσης καὶ τὰ ἐν αὐτοῖς πάντα
and on the sea and all the things in them

ἤκουσα λέγοντας· τῷ καθημένῳ ἐπὶ τῷ θρόνῳ καὶ τῷ ἀρνίῳ
I heard saying, "To the one seated on the throne and to the Lamb

ἡ εὐλογία καὶ ἡ τιμὴ καὶ ἡ δόξα καὶ τὸ κράτος εἰς τοὺς αἰῶνας τῶν αἰώνων.
[be] blessing and honor and glory and power forever."

5:14 καὶ τὰ τέσσαρα ζῷα ἔλεγον ἀμήν.
And the four living creatures were saying, "Amen!"

καὶ οἱ πρεσβύτεροι ἔπεσαν καὶ προσεκύνησαν.
And the elders fell and worshipped.

Greek Text and English Translation	Preterist View	Historicist View	Futurist View	Idealist View
6:1 Καὶ εἶδον ὅτε ἤνοιξεν τὸ ἀρνίον μίαν ἐκ τῶν ἑπτὰ σφραγίδων, And I saw when the Lamb opened one of the seven seals,	1 And I saw when the Lamb opened one of the seven seals (which correspond to the first half of the Jewish revolt against Rome, A.D. 66–68), and I heard one of the four living creatures saying with a thunderous voice, "Come!"	1 And I saw when the Lamb opened one of the seven seals (which summarize the unfolding of the fate of the Roman Empire, from Domitian's death in A.D. 96 to the fall of Rome in A.D. 476), and I heard one of the four living creatures saying with a thunderous voice, "Come!"	1 And I saw when the Lamb opened one of the seven seals (which forecast the judgments of the first three and a half years of the future Tribulation period [i.e., the first half of the Olivet Discourse, the beginning of the "birth pangs"]), and I heard one of the four living creatures saying with a thunderous voice, "Come!"	1 And I saw when the Lamb opened one of the seven seals (which are symbolic of both the progress of the gospel and the persecution of the church, and the divine judgment upon the unbelieving world throughout the history of Christianity; as such, the seal, trumpet, and bowl judgments are parallel, not three sequential sets of judgments), and I heard one of the four living creatures saying with a thunderous voice, "Come!"
καὶ ἤκουσα ἑνὸς ἐκ τῶν τεσσάρων ζῴων λέγοντος and I heard one of the four living creatures saying				
ὡς φωνὴ βροντῆς· ἔρχου. like a voice of thunder, "Come!"				
6:2 καὶ εἶδον, καὶ ἰδοὺ ἵππος λευκός, And I looked, and behold, a white horse,	2 And I saw, and behold, a white horse, and the one sitting upon it having a bow, and a crown was given to him, and he came conquering and in order to conquer. This rider represents the victorious Roman march toward Jerusalem to suppress the Jewish revolt (A.D. 67).	2 And I saw, and behold, a white horse, and the one sitting upon it having a bow, and a crown was given to him, and he came conquering and in order to conquer. This rider represents Rome's golden age, from the death of Domitian up to the peace made by Commodus with the Germans in A.D. 180. (This period of Roman history was known for its five good rulers:	2 And I saw, and behold, a white horse, and the one sitting upon it having a bow, and a crown was given to him, and he came conquering and in order to conquer. This rider will be the Antichrist, who, after the rapture of the church to heaven so that it will miss the Tribulation period, will head up the revived Roman Empire at the end of history (the European Union,	2 And I saw, and behold, a white horse, and the one sitting upon it having a bow, and a crown was given to him, and he came conquering and in order to conquer. This rider is a symbol of the progress of the gospel of the conquering Christ (cf. Rev. 5:5; 19:11–16).
καὶ ὁ καθήμενος ἐπ᾽ αὐτὸν ἔχων τόξον and the one sitting upon it having a bow				
καὶ ἐδόθη αὐτῷ στέφανος καὶ ἐξῆλθεν νικῶν καὶ ἵνα νικήσῃ. and a crown was given to him and he came conquering and in order to conquer.				

6:3 Καὶ ὅτε ἤνοιξεν τὴν σφραγῖδα τὴν δευτέραν, And when he opened the second seal,		Nerva [96–98], Trajan [98–117], Hadrian [117–138], Antonius Pius [138–161], and Marcus Aurelius [161–180].)	whose headquarters will be in rebuilt Babylon; cf. Dan. 9:26).	
ἤκουσα τοῦ δευτέρου ζῴου λέγοντος· ἔρχου. I heard the second living creature saying, "Come!"	3 And when he opened the second seal, I heard the second living creature saying, "Come!"	3 And when he opened the second seal, I heard the second living creature saying, "Come!"	3 And when he opened the second seal, I heard the second living creature saying, "Come!"	3 And when he opened the second seal, I heard the second living creature saying, "Come!"
6:4 καὶ ἐξῆλθεν ἄλλος ἵππος πυρρός, And there came another horse, bright red,	4 And there came another horse, bright red, and to the one sitting upon it was granted to him to take peace out of the earth and in order that men might slay one another, and there was given to him a great sword. This rider corresponds to the civil war among Jews, which dissipated their stand against Rome. (The Jewish revolt against Rome fractured into various factions in town after town, including Jerusalem eventually.)	4 And there came another horse, bright red, and to the one sitting upon it was granted to him to take peace out of the earth and in order that men might slay one another, and there was given to him a great sword. This second rider corresponds to the period from the rules of Commodus (180) to Diocletian (284), which was fraught with civil war. (Some thirty-two would-be emperors came and went during that time. This was the beginning of the end of the Roman Empire.)	4 And there came another horse, bright red, and to the one sitting upon it was granted to him to take peace out of the earth and in order that men might slay one another, and there was given to him a great sword. The Antichrist will unleash World War III, especially against those who become Christians after the Rapture. He will team up with his Arab allies in his bid to conquer the world (cf. Ezek. 38; Dan. 11). Before the Great Tribulation (the second half of the Tribulation period and the most intense part of it) is over, only Jerusalem will stand in his way to world supremacy.	4 And there came another horse, bright red, and to the one sitting upon it was granted to him to take peace out of the earth and in order that men might slay one another, and there was given to him a great sword. Seal judgments two through four represent the disintegration of both human civilization and creation resulting from their rejection of the Lamb of God. The rider on the red horse represents the slaughter and war that the kingdoms of men perpetrate against each other because they reject the King of Kings.
καὶ τῷ καθημένῳ ἐπ᾽ αὐτὸν ἐδόθη αὐτῷ and to the one sitting upon it was given to him				
λαβεῖν τὴν εἰρήνην ἐκ τῆς γῆς καὶ ἵνα ἀλλήλους σφάξουσιν to take peace out of the earth and in order that [men] might slay one another				
καὶ ἐδόθη αὐτῷ μάχαιρα μεγάλη. and there was given to him a great sword.				
6:5 Καὶ ὅτε ἤνοιξεν τὴν σφραγῖδα τὴν τρίτην, And when he opened the third seal,	5 And when he opened the third seal, I heard the third living creature	5 And when he opened the third seal, I heard the third living creature	5 And when he opened the third seal, I heard the third living creature	5 And when he opened the third seal, I heard the third living creature

Greek Text and English Translation	Preterist View	Historicist View	Futurist View	Idealist View
ἤκουσα τοῦ τρίτου ζῴου λέγοντος· ἔρχου. I heard the third living creature saying, "Come!"	saying, "Come!" And I saw, and behold, there was a black horse, and the one sitting upon it had a balance in his hand.	saying, "Come!" And I saw, and behold, there was a black horse, and the one sitting upon it had a balance in his hand.	saying, "Come!" And I saw, and behold, there was a black horse, and the one sitting upon it had a balance in his hand.	saying, "Come!" And I saw, and behold, there was a black horse, and the one sitting upon it had a balance in his hand.
καὶ εἶδον, καὶ ἰδοὺ ἵππος μέλας, And I looked, and behold, a black horse,				
καὶ ὁ καθήμενος ἐπ᾽ αὐτὸν ἔχον ζυγὸν ἐν τῇ χειρὶ αὐτοῦ. and the one sitting upon it having a balance in his hand.				
6:6 καὶ ἤκουσα ὡς φωνὴν ἐν μέσῳ τῶν τεσσάρων ζῴων λέγουσαν· And I heard [something] like a voice in the middle of the four living creatures saying,	6 And I heard something like a voice in the middle of the four living creatures saying, "A quart of wheat for a denarius and three quarts of barley for a denarius, and do not harm the oil and the wine!" This rider represents the famine that fell upon Jews as the Romans lay siege to their land. The famine was so bad that mothers ate their children to survive. Ironically, however, at the same time John Gischala (one of the leaders of the Jewish revolt) and his men consumed oil and wine—considered luxury items—from the Jerusalem temple.	6 And I heard something like a voice in the middle of the four living creatures saying, "A quart of wheat for a denarius and three quarts of barley for a denarius, and do not harm the oil and the wine!" The third seal alludes to the financial oppression on the Roman citizenry created by the heavy taxation imposed by the emperors in the third century. Taxes could be paid in grain, oil, and wine.	6 And I heard something like a voice in the middle of the four living creatures saying, "A quart of wheat for a denarius and three quarts of barley for a denarius, and do not harm the oil and the wine!" Inflation and famine heretofore unknown will plague the earth during World War III. Yet, while most will starve, the wealthy will enjoy the luxuries of oil and wine. This will constitute the third seal judgment.	6 And I heard something like a voice in the middle of the four living creatures saying, "A quart of wheat for a denarius and three quarts of barley for a denarius, and do not harm the oil and the wine!" This rider bespeaks the economic hardship and poverty that follow the unleashing of wars on humankind. Yet, in the midst of it all, the rich get richer.
χοῖνιξ σίτου δηναρίου καὶ τρεῖς χοίνικες κριθῶν δηναρίου, "A quart of wheat for a denarius and three quarts of barley for a denarius,				
καὶ τὸ ἔλαιον καὶ τὸν οἶνον μὴ ἀδικήσῃς. and do not harm the oil and the wine!"				

Greek	Col A	Col B	Col C	Col D
6:7 Καὶ ὅτε ἤνοιξεν τὴν σφραγῖδα τὴν τετάρτην, And when he opened the fourth seal, ἤκουσα φωνὴν τοῦ τετάρτου ζῴου λέγοντος· ἔρχου. I heard the voice of the fourth living creature saying, "Come!"	7 And when he opened the fourth seal, I heard the voice of the fourth living creature saying, "Come!"	7 And when he opened the fourth seal, I heard the voice of the fourth living creature saying, "Come!"	7 And when he opened the fourth seal, I heard the voice of the fourth living creature saying, "Come!"	7 And when he opened the fourth seal, I heard the voice of the fourth living creature saying, "Come!"
6:8 καὶ εἶδον, καὶ ἰδοὺ ἵππος χλωρός, And I looked, and behold, a pale horse, καὶ ὁ καθήμενος ἐπάνω αὐτοῦ ‘ ὄνομα αὐτῷ [ὁ] θάνατος, and the one sitting upon it, his name is Death, καὶ ὁ ᾅδης ἠκολούθει μετ᾿ αὐτοῦ and hades followed with him καὶ ἐδόθη αὐτοῖς ἐξουσία and there was given to them authority ἐπὶ τὸ τέταρτον τῆς γῆς ἀποκτεῖναι upon the fourth of the earth to kill ἐν ῥομφαίᾳ καὶ ἐν λιμῷ καὶ ἐν θανάτῳ by the sword and by famine and by death καὶ ὑπὸ τῶν θηρίων τῆς γῆς. and by wild beasts upon the earth.	8 And I looked, and behold, there was a pale horse, and the one sitting upon it, his name is Death, and hades followed with him, and there was given to them authority upon the fourth of the earth, to kill by the sword and by famine and by death and by wild beasts upon the earth. This rider speaks the widespread death of Jews in their fight against Rome (over a million of them).	8 And I looked, and behold, there was a pale horse, and the one sitting upon it, his name is Death, and hades followed with him, and there was given to them authority upon the fourth of the earth, to kill by the sword and by famine and by death and by wild beasts upon the earth. This rider signifies the twenty years of fighting, famine, and disease that plagued the reigns of Emperors Decius, Gallus, Aemilianus, Valerian, and Gallienus (248–268). These calamities came at the hands of military tyrants within the empire and barbarous invaders from outside the Empire. Dogs ("wild beasts") ate the skeletal remains of the dead, some five thousand daily in Rome alone. The fourth seal judgment will spell death for one-fourth of the earth's inhabitants (the equivalent today of the population of Europe and South America). The war begun by the Antichrist will not reach its finale until the bowl judgments (Rev. 15–18). (This indicates that the seal, trumpet, and bowl judgments will be sequential, not parallel. They will therefore increase in intensity with each succeeding set of judgments.)	8 And I looked, and behold, there was a pale horse, and the one sitting upon it, his name is Death, and hades followed with him, and there was given to them authority upon the fourth of the earth, to kill by the sword and by famine and by death and by wild beasts upon the earth. This rider symbolizes the death that results from war and famine when men turn against men.
6:9 Καὶ ὅτε ἤνοιξεν τὴν πέμπτην σφραγῖδα, εἶδον And when he opened the fifth seal, I saw	9 And when he opened the fifth seal, I saw under	9 And when he opened the fifth seal, I saw under	9 And when he opened the fifth seal, I saw under	9 And when he opened the fifth seal, I saw under

Greek Text and English Translation	Preterist View	Historicist View	Futurist View	Idealist View
ὑποκάτω τοῦ θυσιαστηρίου τὰς ψυχὰς τῶν ἐσφαγμένων under the altar the souls of those who had been slain διὰ τὸν λόγον τοῦ θεοῦ καὶ διὰ τὴν μαρτυρίαν ἣν εἶχον. for the word of God and for the testimony which they had.	the altar the souls of those who had been slain for the word of God and for the testimony which they had.	the altar the souls of those who had been slain for the word of God and for the testimony which they had.	the altar the souls of those who had been slain for the word of God and for the testimony which they had.	the altar the souls of those who had been slain for the word of God and for the testimony which they had.
6:10 καὶ ἔκραξαν φωνῇ μεγάλῃ λέγοντες· And they cried with a great voice, saying, ἕως πότε, ὁ δεσπότης ὁ ἅγιος καὶ ἀληθινός, "How long, O Sovereign, holy and true, οὐ κρίνεις καὶ ἐκδικεῖς τὸ αἷμα ἡμῶν ἐκ τῶν κατοικούντων ἐπὶ τῆς γῆς; will you not judge and avenge our blood on those who dwell on the earth?"	10 And they cried with a great voice, saying, "How long, O Sovereign, holy and true, will you not judge and avenge our blood on those who dwell on the earth?"	10 And they cried with a great voice, saying, "How long, O Sovereign, holy and true, will you not judge and avenge our blood on those who dwell on the earth?"	10 And they cried with a great voice, saying, "How long, O Sovereign, holy and true, will you not judge and avenge our blood on those who dwell on the earth?"	10 And they cried with a great voice, saying, "How long, O Sovereign, holy and true, will you not judge and avenge our blood on those who dwell on the earth?"
6:11 καὶ ἐδόθη αὐτοῖς ἑκάστῳ στολὴ λευκὴ And there was given to each one of them a white robe καὶ ἐρρέθη αὐτοῖς ἵνα ἀναπαύσωνται ἔτι χρόνον μικρόν, and was told to them that they might rest yet a little time, ἕως πληρωθῶσιν καὶ οἱ σύνδουλοι αὐτῶν καὶ οἱ ἀδελφοὶ αὐτῶν until also their fellow servants and their brothers should be fulfilled,	11 And there was given to each one a white robe and was told to them that they might rest yet a little time, until also their fellow servants and their brothers should be fulfilled, the ones who are about to be killed as also they were. The fifth seal—the cry for vindication by the martyrs—corresponds to the many Christians persecuted by Jews after Christ's death and leading up to the fall	11 And there was given to each one a white robe and was told to them that they might rest yet a little time, until also their fellow servants and their brothers should be fulfilled, the ones who are about to be killed as also they were. The fifth seal is the rule of martyred Christians who were persecuted by Emperor Diocletian (284–303). This was the tenth period of the persecution of	11 And there was given to each one a white robe and was told to them that they might rest yet a little time, until also their fellow servants and their brothers should be fulfilled, the ones who are about to be killed as also they were. The fifth seal judgment encompasses the Christians who will be martyred for their faith in Christ during the Tribulation period because they	11 And there was given to each one a white robe and was told to them that they might rest yet a little time, until also their fellow servants and their brothers should be fulfilled, the ones who are about to be killed as also they were. The fifth seal is a stark reminder that, even though Christ has inaugurated the kingdom of God through the preaching of the gospel by the true church, still

οἱ μέλλοντες ἀποκτέννεσθαι ὡς καὶ αὐτοί. / the ones who are about to be killed as also they [were].	of Jerusalem in A.D. 70. (The name "Jerusalem" had become synonymous with the persecution of the righteous. But God avenged the deaths of the righteous by handing the "holy city" over to the Romans. This, then, was in retaliation for the Jews having handed Jesus over to Pilate and the Romans. Divine turnabout is fair play!)	Christianity and the most severe, for it was world-wide. With Constantine's rise to power, however, Christianity became legalized (313) and the church was thereby vindicated.	will not bow before the Antichrist. Their deaths place them in the good company of the righteous throughout the ages.	God's people suffer the end-time Tribulation (which extends from the first coming of Christ to the second coming of Christ) at the hands of the enemies of God. So the end-time Tribulation stretches across world history, opposing the church. Thus, "already" the kingdom of God is in history, but "not yet" is it finally triumphant.
6:12 Καὶ εἶδον ὅτε ἤνοιξεν τὴν σφραγῖδα τὴν ἕκτην, / And I looked when he opened the sixth seal,	12 And I saw when he opened the sixth seal, and there was a great earthquake and the sun became black as sackcloth, and the full moon became like blood,	12 And I saw when he opened the sixth seal, and there was a great earthquake and the sun became black as sackcloth, and the full moon became like blood,	12 And I saw when he opened the sixth seal, and there was a great earthquake and the sun became black as sackcloth, and the full moon became like blood,	12 And I saw when he opened the sixth seal, and there was a great earthquake and the sun became black as sackcloth, and the full moon became like blood,
καὶ σεισμὸς μέγας ἐγένετο / and there was a great earthquake				
καὶ ὁ ἥλιος ἐγένετο μέλας ὡς σάκκος τρίχινος / and the sun became black as sackcloth,				
καὶ ἡ σελήνη ὅλη ἐγένετο ὡς αἷμα / and the full moon became like blood,				
6:13 καὶ οἱ ἀστέρες τοῦ οὐρανοῦ ἔπεσαν εἰς τὴν γῆν, / and the stars of heaven fell unto the earth,	13 and the stars of the heaven fell unto the earth, as a fig tree casts its winter fruit, being shaken by a great wind,	13 and the stars of the heaven fell unto the earth, as a fig tree casts its winter fruit, being shaken by a great wind,	13 and the stars of the heaven fell unto the earth, as a fig tree casts its winter fruit, being shaken by a great wind,	13 and the stars of the heaven fell unto the earth, as a fig tree casts its winter fruit, being shaken by a great wind,
ὡς συκῆ βάλλει τοὺς ὀλύνθους αὐτῆς / as a fig tree casts its winter fruit				
ὑπὸ ἀνέμου μεγάλου σειομένη, / being shaken by a great wind,				
6:14 καὶ ὁ οὐρανὸς ἀπεχωρίσθη ὡς βιβλίον ἑλισσόμενον / and heaven departed like a scroll being rolled up	14 and the heaven departed like a scroll being rolled up, and every	14 and the heaven departed like a scroll being rolled up, and	14 and the heaven departed like a scroll being rolled up, and every	14 and the heaven departed like a scroll being rolled up, and

Greek Text and English Translation	Preterist View	Historicist View	Futurist View	Idealist View
καὶ πᾶν ὄρος καὶ νῆσος ἐκ τῶν τόπων αὐτῶν ἐκινήθησαν. and every mountain and island was removed out of their places.	mountain and island was removed out of their places. (The sixth seal is symbolic language adapted from the OT and alludes to the environmental disturbances that fell upon Jerusalem before its fall in A.D. 70. Such figurative description is the language of judgment.)	every mountain and island was removed out of their places.	mountain and island was removed out of their places. The sixth seal will be the literal cosmic disturbances caused by nuclear war. The first nuclear explosion will trigger the worst earthquake ever. The smoke will darken the sun, make the moon appear red, and prompt massive meteor showers ("the stars . . . fell").	every mountain and island was removed out of their places.
6:15 Καὶ οἱ βασιλεῖς τῆς γῆς And the kings of the earth	15 And the kings of the earth and the great men and chiliarchs and the rich and the strong and every one, slave and free, hid themselves in the caves and among the rocks of the mountains	15 And the kings of the earth and the great men and chiliarchs and the rich and the strong and every one, slave and free, hid themselves in the caves and among the rocks of the mountains	15 And the kings of the earth and the great men and chiliarchs and the rich and the strong and every one, slave and free, hid themselves in the caves and among the rocks of the mountains	15 And the kings of the earth and the great men and chiliarchs and the rich and the strong and every one, slave and free, hid themselves in the caves and among the rocks of the mountains
καὶ οἱ μεγιστᾶνες καὶ οἱ χιλίαρχοι and the great men and chiliarchs				
καὶ οἱ πλούσιοι καὶ οἱ ἰσχυροὶ καὶ πᾶς and the rich and the strong and every one				
δοῦλος καὶ ἐλεύθερος ἔκρυψαν ἑαυτοὺς εἰς τὰ σπήλαια slave and free hid themselves in caves				
καὶ εἰς τὰς πέτρας τῶν ὀρέων and among the rocks of the mountains				
6:16 καὶ λέγουσιν τοῖς ὄρεσιν καὶ ταῖς πέτραις· and they say to the mountains and to the rocks,	16 and saying to the mountains and to the rocks, "Fall upon us and hide us from the face of the one sitting upon	16 and saying to the mountains and to the rocks, "Fall upon us and hide us from the face of the one sitting upon	16 and saying to the mountains and to the rocks, "Fall upon us and hide us from the face of the one sitting upon	16 and saying to the mountains and to the rocks, "Fall upon us and hide us from the face of the one sitting upon
πέσετε ἐφ᾿ ἡμᾶς καὶ κρύψατε ἡμᾶς "Fall upon us and hide us				

ἀπὸ προσώπου τοῦ καθημένου ἐπὶ τοῦ θρόνου from the face of the one sitting upon the throne καὶ ἀπὸ τῆς ὀργῆς τοῦ ἀρνίου, and from the wrath of the Lamb,	the throne and from the wrath of the Lamb,	the throne and from the wrath of the Lamb,	the throne and from the wrath of the Lamb,	the throne and from the wrath of the Lamb,
6:17 ὅτι ἦλθεν ἡ ἡμέρα ἡ μεγάλη τῆς ὀργῆς αὐτῶν, because the great day of their wrath has come, καὶ τίς δύναται σταθῆναι; and who is able to stand [before it?]	17 because the great day of their wrath has come, and who is able to stand before it?" (The reference to rocks falling may allude to the Roman legions removing obstacles in their path toward to Jerusalem. The mention of hiding in caves alludes to the many Jews who hid in caves and underground, but to no avail against mighty Rome. This was so because God's wrath was destined to fall on Israel for crucifying their Messiah.)	17 because the great day of their wrath has come, and who is able to stand before it?" The sixth seal corresponds to the political upheaval and collapse of the Roman Empire brought about by the invasions of the northern hordes of Goths and Vandals between 376 and 418.	17 because the great day of their wrath has come, and who is able to stand before it?" This sixth seal conveys the wrath of God upon the earth in the first half of the Tribulation period. Such wrath cannot harm the church, because it already will have been raptured before the beginning of the Tribulation (cf. 1 Thess. 5:9).	17 because the great day of their wrath has come, and who is able to stand before it?" The sixth seal represents the end of the world, when Christ returns. His second coming will bring cosmic upheaval on the enemies of God, the ones who persecute the church. These will stand before God at the Great White Throne Judgment and be condemned for all eternity (cf. Rev. 20:11–15). The righteous, however, will enjoy the presence of God forever, because they have been faithful to Christ.
7:1 Μετὰ τοῦτο εἶδον τέσσαρας ἀγγέλους After this I saw four angels ἑστῶτας ἐπὶ τὰς τέσσαρας γωνίας τῆς γῆς, standing upon the four corners of the earth, κρατοῦντας τοὺς τέσσαρας ἀνέμους τῆς γῆς holding back the four winds of the earth ἵνα μὴ πνέῃ ἄνεμος ἐπὶ τῆς γῆς in order that no wind may blow upon the earth μήτε ἐπὶ τῆς θαλάσσης μήτε ἐπὶ πᾶν δένδρον. nor upon the sea nor upon any tree.	1 After this I saw four angels standing upon the four corners of the earth, holding back the four winds of the earth in order that no wind may blow upon the earth or upon the sea neither upon any tree.	1 After this I saw four angels standing upon the four corners of the earth, holding back the four winds of the earth in order that no wind may blow upon the earth or upon the sea neither upon any tree.	1 After this I saw four angels standing upon the four corners of the earth, holding back the four winds of the earth in order that no wind may blow upon the earth or upon the sea neither upon any tree.	1 After this I saw four angels standing upon the four corners of the earth, holding back the four winds of the earth in order that no wind may blow upon the earth or upon the sea neither upon any tree.

Greek Text and English Translation	Preterist View	Historicist View	Futurist View	Idealist View
7:2 Καὶ εἶδον ἄλλον ἄγγελον ἀναβαίνοντα And I saw another angel coming up ἀπὸ ἀνατολῆς ἡλίου ἔχοντα σφραγῖδα θεοῦ ζῶντος, from the rising of the sun having the seal of the living God, καὶ ἔκραξεν φωνῇ μεγάλῃ τοῖς τέσσαρσιν ἀγγέλοις and he cried in a great voice to the four angels οἷς ἐδόθη αὐτοῖς to whom [power] had been given to them ἀδικῆσαι τὴν γῆν καὶ τὴν θάλασσαν to harm the earth and the sea,	2 And I saw another angel coming up from the rising of the sun, having the seal of the living God, and he cried in a great voice to whom power had been given to harm the earth and the sea,	2 And I saw another angel coming up from the rising of the sun, having the seal of the living God, and he cried in a great voice to whom power had been given to harm the earth and the sea,	2 And I saw another angel coming up from the rising of the sun, having the seal of the living God, and he cried in a great voice to the four angels to whom power had been given to harm the earth and the sea,	2 And I saw another angel coming up from the rising of the sun, having the seal of the living God, and he cried in a great voice to the four angels to whom power had been given to harm the earth and the sea,
7:3 λέγων· μὴ ἀδικήσητε τὴν γῆν saying, "Do not harm the earth μήτε τὴν θάλασσαν μήτε τὰ δένδρα, nor the sea nor the trees, ἄχρι σφραγίσωμεν τοὺς δούλους τοῦ θεοῦ ἡμῶν ἐπὶ τῶν μετώπων αὐτῶν. until we have sealed the servants of our God upon their foreheads."	3 saying, "Do not harm the earth, nor the sea, nor the trees, until we may have sealed the servants of our God upon their foreheads." (The first six seal judgments represent the early stage of the Jewish revolt, wherein the Roman general Vespasian fought his way through Galilee toward Jerusalem. But before he had advanced to Jerusalem itself, God providentially brought a brief halt to the war with the suicide of Caesar Nero back in	3 saying, "Do not harm the earth, nor the sea, nor the trees, until we may have sealed the servants of our God upon their foreheads." (The four angels will unleash the first trumpet judgments [Rev. 8], which are the barbaric invasions of the Roman Empire before its final fall; it succumbed to theological heresy from those within the church along the way. The sealing of the 144,000 was God's spiritual protection of his servants during	3 saying, "Do not harm the earth, nor the sea, neither the trees, until we may have sealed the servants of our God upon their foreheads." (The four angels who cover the four corners of the world will hold back the onslaught of the future end-time Tribulation just long enough to put God's protective mark upon the 144,000.)	3 saying, "Do not harm the earth, nor the sea, neither the trees, until we may have sealed the servants of our God upon their foreheads." (While the four winds of judgment fall upon the wicked throughout the history of the church, the sealed 144,000—the universal church—is safe.)

7:4 Καὶ ἤκουσα τὸν ἀριθμὸν τῶν ἐσφραγισμένον, And I heard the number of the ones having been sealed, ἑκατὸν τεσσεράκοντα τέσσαρες χιλιάδες, one hundred forty-four thousand	those military coups and theological upheavals.) Rome in A.D. 68. This event caused Vespasian to return to Rome, where eventually he was proclaimed the new caesar. His son, Titus, who had been serving with his father in the campaign against Israel, assumed command of the Roman advance upon Jerusalem. This break in the action allowed Jewish Christians to flee Jerusalem and Israel by crossing the Jordan River and hiding in the city of Pella. The fourth-century church historian Eusebius reported that a Christian prophet had warned Jewish Christians to do just that. The number—144,000—is a figurative allusion to those Jewish Christians who fled to Pella, for the church is the true Israel. The seal of God upon the 144,000 is a symbolic way of saying that God protected them from the Romans.)	4 And I heard the number of the ones having been sealed, one hundred and forty-four thousand, having been sealed out of every tribe of the sons of Israel:	4 And I heard the number of the ones having been sealed, one hundred and forty-four thousand, having been sealed out of every tribe of the sons of Israel:	4 And I heard the number of the ones having been sealed, one hundred and forty-four thousand, having been sealed out of every tribe of the sons of Israel:

Greek Text and English Translation	Preterist View	Historicist View	Futurist View	Idealist View
ἐσφραγισμένοι ἐκ πάσης φυλῆς υἱῶν Ἰσραήλ· having been sealed out of every tribe of the sons of Israel:				
7:5 ἐκ φυλῆς Ἰουδα δώδεκα χιλιάδες ἐσφραγισμένοι, out of the tribe of Judah twelve thousand having been sealed,	5 out of the tribe of Judah twelve thousand having been sealed, out of the tribe of Reuben twelve thousand, out of the tribe of Gad twelve thousand,	5 out of the tribe of Judah twelve thousand having been sealed, out of the tribe of Reuben twelve thousand, out of the tribe of Gad twelve thousand,	5 out of the tribe of Judah twelve thousand having been sealed, out of the tribe of Reuben twelve thousand, out of the tribe of Gad twelve thousand,	5 out of the tribe of Judah twelve thousand having been sealed, out of the tribe of Reuben twelve thousand, out of the tribe of Gad twelve thousand,
ἐκ φυλῆς Ῥουβὴν δώδεκα χιλιάδες, out of the tribe of Reuben twelve thousand,				
ἐκ φυλῆς Γὰδ δώδεκα χιλιάδες, out of the tribe of Gad twelve thousand,				
7:6 ἐκ φυλῆς Ἀσὴρ δώδεκα χιλιάδες, out of the tribe of Asher twelve thousand,	6 out of the tribe of Asher twelve thousand, out of the tribe of Naphtali twelve thousand, out of the tribe of Manasseh twelve thousand,	6 out of the tribe of Asher twelve thousand, out of the tribe of Naphtali twelve thousand, out of the tribe of Manasseh twelve thousand,	6 out of the tribe of Asher twelve thousand, out of the tribe of Naphtali twelve thousand, out of the tribe of Manasseh twelve thousand,	6 out of the tribe of Asher twelve thousand, out of the tribe of Naphtali twelve thousand, out of the tribe of Manasseh twelve thousand,
ἐκ φυλῆς Νεφθαλὶμ δώδεκα χιλιάδες, out of the tribe of Naphtali twelve thousand,				
ἐκ φυλῆς Μανασσῆ δώδεκα χιλιάδες, out of the tribe of Manasseh twelve thousand,				
7:7 ἐκ φυλῆς Συμεὼν δώδεκα χιλιάδες, out of the tribe of Simeon twelve thousand,	7 out of the tribe of Simeon twelve thousand, out of the tribe of Levi twelve thousand, out of the tribe of Issachar twelve thousand,	7 out of the tribe of Simeon twelve thousand, out of the tribe of Levi twelve thousand, out of the tribe of Issachar twelve thousand,	7 out of the tribe of Simeon twelve thousand, out of the tribe of Levi twelve thousand, out of the tribe of Issachar twelve thousand,	7 out of the tribe of Simeon twelve thousand, out of the tribe of Levi twelve thousand, out of the tribe of Issachar twelve thousand,
ἐκ φυλῆς Λευὶ δώδεκα χιλιάδες, out of the tribe of Levi twelve thousand,				
ἐκ φυλῆς Ἰσσαχὰρ δώδεκα χιλιάδες, out of the tribe of Issachar twelve thousand,				
7:8 ἐκ φυλῆς Ζαβουλὼν δώδεκα χιλιάδες, out of the tribe of Zebulun twelve thousand,	8 out of the tribe of Zebulun twelve thousand, out of the tribe	8 out of the tribe of Zebulun twelve thousand, out of the tribe of Joseph	8 out of the tribe of Zebulun twelve thousand, out of the tribe	8 out of the tribe of Zebulun twelve thousand, out of the tribe of Joseph

ἐκ φυλῆς Ἰωσὴφ δώδεκα χιλιάδες, out of the tribe of Joseph twelve thousand, ἐκ φυλῆς Βενιαμὶν δώδεκα χιλιάδες ἐσφραγισμένοι. out of the tribe of Benjamin twelve thousand having been sealed.	twelve thousand, out of the tribe of Benjamin twelve thousand having been sealed. (The 144,000 is the church, the true and spiritual Israel, which has replaced Jews as the people of God. These arose after Constantine's conversion and the subsequent legalizing of Christianity [A.D. 313] and were sealed for spiritual protection against the barbarian invasions of Rome and from theological compromise in the face of the heresies of Arius [fourth century, who denied Jesus' deity and that salvation is by faith in him alone]. Thus the sealing is spiritual in nature: it was God's earthly preservation of the true church's faith in Christ despite the threat of death at the hands of the papacy and abandonment of the true Christian faith at the hands of heretics.)	of Joseph twelve thousand, out of the tribe of Benjamin twelve thousand having been sealed. (The 144,000 are Jews who are converted to Christ right after the rapture of the church and are commissioned to be evangelists for Christ during the Tribulation period. There will be literally 12,000 Jewish Christians from each of the twelve tribes of Israel, not to be confused with the church, which will have already been raptured by this time. The mission of the 144,000 will be to bring Israel to faith in Christ during the end-time Tribulation as well as to convert Gentiles to Christianity. The 144,000 will be supernaturally protected and empowered by God to preach the gospel.)	twelve thousand, out of the tribe of Benjamin twelve thousand having been sealed. (The 144,000 is the true, spiritual Israel; the church. The irregular listing of the tribes indicates this: Judah is placed first as the tribe from which the Messiah was to originate; Dan [the tribe most associated with ancient Israel's idolatry] is omitted; Levi is included as a tribe, and Joseph replaces Ephraim. The number "144,000" is symbolic, derived by multiplying 1,000 [the basic military division in the camp of Israel; cf. Num. 31:4–5] by 144 [twelve squared], representing the faithful remnant of the OT and the NT, which results in the true, spiritual Israel, the true church of God. He protects his remnant, the church, in every age.)
7:9 Μετὰ ταῦτα εἶδον, καὶ ἰδοὺ ὄχλος πολύς, After these things I looked, and behold a great crowd, ὃν ἀριθμῆσαι αὐτὸν οὐδεὶς ἐδύνατο, which to number it no one was able,	9 After these things I looked, and behold, there was a great crowd, which no one is able to number, out of every nation, and out of all tribes and peoples and tongues, standing before	9 After these things I looked, and behold, there was a great crowd, which no one is able to number, out of every nation, and out of all tribes and peoples and tongues, standing before	9 After these things I looked, and behold, there was a great crowd, which no one is able to number, out of every nation, and out of all tribes and peoples and tongues, standing before

Greek Text and English Translation	Preterist View	Historicist View	Futurist View	Idealist View
ἐκ παντὸς ἔθνους καὶ φυλῶν καὶ λαῶν καὶ γλωσσῶν out of every nation and all tribes and peoples and tongues				
ἑστῶτες ἐνώπιον τοῦ θρόνου καὶ ἐνώπιον τοῦ ἀρνίου standing before the throne and before the Lamb,	the throne and before the Lamb, having been clothed in white robes and palm branches in their hands,	the throne and before the Lamb, having been clothed in white robes and palm branches in their hands,	the throne and before the Lamb, having been clothed in white robes and palm branches in their hands,	the throne and before the Lamb, having been clothed in white robes and palm branches in their hands,
περιβεβλημένους στολὰς λευκὰς having been clothed in white robes				
καὶ φοίνικες ἐν ταῖς χερσὶν αὐτῶν, and palm branches in their hands,				
7:10 καὶ κράζουσιν φωνῇ μεγάλῃ λέγοντες· and crying with a great voice, saying,	10 and crying with a great voice saying, "Salvation to our God, to the one seated upon the throne and to the Lamb!"	10 and crying with a great voice saying, "Salvation to our God, to the one seated upon the throne and to the Lamb!"	10 and crying with a great voice saying, "Salvation to our God, to the one seated upon the throne and to the Lamb!"	10 and crying with a great voice saying, "Salvation to our God, to the one seated upon the throne and to the Lamb!"
ἡ σωτηρία τῷ θεῷ ἡμῶν "Salvation to our God				
τῷ καθημένῳ ἐπὶ τῷ θρόνῳ καὶ τῷ ἀρνίῳ. to the one seated upon the throne and to the Lamb!"				
7:11 Καὶ πάντες οἱ ἄγγελοι εἱστήκεισαν And all the angels stood	11 And all the angels stood around the throne, and the elders and the four living creatures, and all fell before the throne upon their faces and worshipped God,	11 And all the angels stood around the throne, and the elders and the four living creatures, and all fell before the throne upon their faces and worshipped God,	11 And all the angels stood around the throne, and the elders and the four living creatures, and all fell before the throne upon their faces and worshipped God,	11 And all the angels stood around the throne, and the elders and the four living creatures, and all fell before the throne upon their faces and worshipped God,
κύκλῳ τοῦ θρόνου καὶ τῶν πρεσβυτέρων καὶ τῶν τεσσάρων ζῴων around the throne and the elders and the four living creatures				
καὶ ἔπεσαν ἐνώπιον τοῦ θρόνου ἐπὶ τὰ πρόσωπα αὐτῶν and all fell before the throne upon their faces				

καὶ προσεκύνησαν τῷ θεῷ
and worshipped God

7:12 λέγοντες· ἀμήν, ἡ εὐλογία καὶ ἡ δόξα
saying, "Amen! Blessing and glory

καὶ ἡ σοφία καὶ ἡ εὐχαριστία καὶ ἡ τιμὴ
and wisdom and thanksgiving and honor

καὶ ἡ δύναμις καὶ ἡ ἰσχὺς τῷ θεῷ ἡμῶν
and power and strength [be] to our God

εἰς τοὺς αἰῶνας τῶν αἰώνων· ἀμήν.
forever. Amen!"

7:13 Καὶ ἀπεκρίθη εἷς ἐκ τῶν πρεσβυτέρων λέγων μοι·
And one of the elders answered, saying to me,

οὗτοι οἱ περιβεβλημένοι τὰς στολὰς τὰς λευκὰς τίνες εἰσὶν
"Who are these having been clothed in white robes

καὶ πόθεν ἦλθον;
and from whence have they come?"

7:14 καὶ εἴρηκα αὐτῷ· κύριέ μου, σὺ οἶδας. καὶ εἶπέν μοι·
And I said to him, "My Lord, you know." And he said to me,

οὗτοί εἰσιν οἱ ἐρχόμενοι ἐκ τῆς θλίψεως τῆς μεγάλης
"These are the ones who are coming out of the Great Tribulation

καὶ ἔπλυναν τὰς στολὰς αὐτῶν
and they have washed their robes

καὶ ἐλεύκαναν αὐτὰς ἐν τῷ αἵματι τοῦ ἀρνίου.
and made them white in the blood of the Lamb.

---

12 saying, "Amen! Blessing and glory and wisdom and thanksgiving and honor and power and strength be to our God forever. Amen!"

13 And one of the elders answered, saying to me, "Who are these having been clothed in white robes, and from whence have they come?"

14 And I said to him, "My lord, you know." And he said to me, "These are the ones who are coming out of the Great Tribulation, and they have washed their robes and made them white in the blood of the Lamb.

---

12 saying, "Amen! Blessing and glory and wisdom and thanksgiving and honor and power and strength be to our God forever. Amen!"

13 And one of the elders answered, saying to me, "Who are these having been clothed in white robes, and from whence have they come?"

14 And I said to him, "My lord, you know." And he said to me, "These are the ones who are coming out of the Great Tribulation, and they have washed their robes and made them white in the blood of the Lamb.

---

12 saying, "Amen! Blessing and glory and wisdom and thanksgiving and honor and power and strength be to our God forever. Amen!"

13 And one of the elders answered, saying to me, "Who are these having been clothed in white robes, and from whence have they come?"

14 And I said to him, "My lord, you know." And he said to me, "These are the ones who are coming out of the Great Tribulation, and they have washed their robes and made them white in the blood of the Lamb.

---

12 saying, "Amen! Blessing and glory and wisdom and thanksgiving and honor and power and strength be to our God forever. Amen!"

13 And one of the elders answered, saying to me, "Who are these having been clothed in white robes, and from whence have they come?"

14 And I said to him, "My lord, you know." And he said to me, "These are the ones who are coming out of the Great Tribulation, and they have washed their robes and made them white in the blood of the Lamb.

Greek Text and English Translation	Preterist View	Historicist View	Futurist View	Idealist View
7:15 διὰ τοῦτό εἰσιν ἐνώπιον τοῦ θρόνου τοῦ θεοῦ Because of this they are before the throne of God καὶ λατρεύουσιν αὐτῷ ἡμέρας καὶ νυκτὸς ἐν τῷ ναῷ αὐτοῦ, and serve him day and night in his temple, καὶ ὁ καθήμενος ἐπὶ τοῦ θρόνου σκηνώσει ἐπ᾽ αὐτούς. and the one seated upon the throne will spread his tent upon them.	15 Because of this they are before the throne of God and night in his temple, and the one seated upon the throne will spread his tent upon them.	15 Because of this they are before the throne of God and serve him day and night in his temple, and the one seated upon the throne will spread his tent upon them.	15 Because of this they are before the throne of God and serve him day and night in his temple, and the one seated upon the throne will spread his tent upon them.	15 Because of this they are before the throne of God and serve him day and night in his temple, and the one seated upon the throne will spread his tent upon them.
7:16 οὐ πεινάσουσιν ἔτι οὐδὲ διψήσουσιν ἔτι They will not hunger again nor will they thirst again οὐδὲ μὴ πέση ἐπ᾽ αὐτοὺς ὁ ἥλιος οὐδὲ πᾶν καῦμα, nor will the sun fall upon them nor any heat,	16 They will not hunger again, nor will they thirst again, nor will the sun fall upon them, nor any heat,	16 They will not hunger again, nor will they thirst again, nor will the sun fall upon them, nor any heat,	16 They will not hunger again, nor will they thirst again, nor will the sun fall upon them, nor any heat,	16 They will not hunger again, nor will they thirst again, nor will the sun fall upon them, nor any heat,
7:17 ὅτι τὸ ἀρνίον τὸ ἀνὰ μέσον τοῦ θρόνου because the Lamb in the midst of the throne ποιμανεῖ αὐτοὺς καὶ ὁδηγήσει αὐτοὺς ἐπὶ ζωῆς πηγὰς ὑδάτων, will shepherd them and will lead them unto springs of living water, καὶ ἐξαλείψει ὁ θεὸς πᾶν δάκρυον ἐκ τῶν ὀφθαλμῶν αὐτῶν. and God will wipe away every tear from their eyes.”	17 because the Lamb in the midst of the throne will shepherd them and will lead them unto springs of living water, and God will wipe away every tear from their eyes.” (The "Great Tribulation" is a reference to the time in which many Gentile Christians were not protected from Nero in the city of Rome. These were the Gentile Christians in Rome who were persecuted by that madman, A.D. 64–68. Their suffering	17 because the Lamb in the midst of the throne will shepherd them and will lead them unto springs of living water, and God will wipe away every tear from their eyes.” (The innumerable multitude is the same group as the 144,000, but seen in a different light: their heavenly destiny. Though their bodies may suffer persecution and death at the hands of pagan attacks and heretics, their souls are	17 because the Lamb in the midst of the throne will shepherd them and will lead them unto springs of living water, and God will wipe away every tear from their eyes.” (The innumerable multitude will be the many Gentiles the 144,000 convert to Christ in the Tribulation period. That great multitude will not enjoy the divine protection that the 144,000 will have. Rather, they will be killed by the Antichrist for their	17 because the Lamb in the midst of the throne will shepherd them and will lead them unto springs of living water, and God will wipe away every tear from their eyes.” (The innumerable multitude is the 144,000, but seen from a different perspective: the 144,000 is the church sealed and protected spiritually by God on earth, while the countless host is the church finally glorified in heaven. The church as the 144,000 is

was a part of the end-time Tribulation that began with the first coming of Christ. Their deaths qualified them to become partakers of the kingdom of God. In dying for their faith, the great multitude followed in the footsteps of Jesus, the Lamb of God.)	secure in the heavenly kingdom of Christ.)	faith in Jesus. But their eternal destiny will be secure in the heavenly kingdom of God. When Christ returns, both the 144,000 and the innumerable multitude will rule with Christ and his church [which will return to the earth after the Tribulation with Christ at the second coming] in the Millennium.)	the true Israel, but the church as the innumerable multitude consists of Christians from all nations. Despite persecution and even death at the hands of the enemies of God, these will eventually triumph through the blood of the Lamb.)
1 And when the Lamb opened the seventh seal, there was silence in heaven for about a half hour. The silence is the preparation for the judgment about to fall upon Jerusalem in A.D. 70, which will be the divine response to the cry for vindication from those Christians martyred by Jerusalem (Stephen, James the brother of John, James the half-brother of Jesus, etc.).	1 And when the Lamb opened the seventh seal, there was silence in heaven for about a half hour. This represents the seventy years between Emperor Constantine's defeat of Licinius (A.D. 324) and Alaric's invasion of the Roman Empire (395).	1 And when the Lamb opened the seventh seal, there was silence in heaven for about a half hour. This is the hush of expectancy much as the courtroom waits quietly before the jury announces its verdict—in this case, the guilty verdict of the earth.	1 And when the Lamb opened the seventh seal, there was silence in heaven for about a half hour. This silence quiets heaven so that it can focus on what is about to be revealed. It is the lull before the storm.
2 And I saw the seven angels, the ones who have stood before God, and seven trumpets were given to them.	2 And I saw the seven angels, the ones who have stood before God, and seven trumpets were given to them.	2 And I saw the seven angels, the ones who have stood before God, and seven trumpets were given to them.	2 And I saw the seven angels, the ones who have stood before God, and seven trumpets were given to them.

8:1 Καὶ ὅταν ἤνοιξεν τὴν σφραγῖδα τὴν ἑβδόμην,
And when he opened the seventh seal,

ἐγένετο σιγὴ ἐν τῷ οὐρανῷ ὡς ἡμιώριον.
there was silence in heaven for about a half hour.

8:2 Καὶ εἶδον τοὺς ἑπτὰ ἀγγέλους οἳ ἐνώπιον τοῦ θεοῦ ἑστήκασιν,
And I saw the seven angels, the ones who stand before God,

καὶ ἐδόθησαν αὐτοῖς ἑπτὰ σάλπιγγες.
and seven trumpets were given to them.

Greek Text and English Translation	Preterist View	Historicist View	Futurist View	Idealist View
8:3 Καὶ ἄλλος ἄγγελος ἦλθεν καὶ ἐστάθη ἐπὶ τοῦ θυσιαστηρίου And another angel came and stood at the altar ἔχων λιβανωτὸν χρυσοῦν, καὶ ἐδόθη αὐτῷ θυμιάματα πολλά, having a golden censer, and much incense was given to him, ἵνα δώσει ταῖς προσευχαῖς τῶν ἁγίων πάντων in order that he might give [it] with the prayers of all the saints ἐπὶ τὸ θυσιαστήριον τὸ χρυσοῦν τὸ ἐνώπιον τοῦ θρόνου. upon the golden altar which is before the throne.	3 And another angel came and stood at the altar, having a golden censer, and much incense was given to him, in order that he might mingle it with the prayers of all the saints upon the golden altar which is before the throne.	3 And another angel came and stood at the altar, having a golden censer, and much incense was given to him, in order that he might mingle it with the prayers of all the saints upon the golden altar which is before the throne.	3 And another angel came and stood at the altar, having a golden censer, and much incense was given to him, in order that he might mingle it with the prayers of all the saints upon the golden altar which is before the throne.	3 And another angel came and stood at the altar, having a golden censer, and much incense was given to him, in order that he might mingle it with the prayers of all the saints upon the golden altar which is before the throne.
8:4 καὶ ἀνέβη ὁ καπνὸς τῶν θυμιαμάτων ταῖς προσευχαῖς τῶν ἁγίων And the smoke of the incense of the prayers of the saints rose ἐκ χειρὸς τοῦ ἀγγέλου ἐνώπιον τοῦ θεοῦ. from the hand of the angel before God.	4 And the smoke of the incense of the prayers of the saints rose from the hand of the angel before God.	4 And the smoke of the incense of the prayers of the saints rose from the hand of the angel before God.	4 And the smoke of the incense of the prayers of the saints rose from the hand of the angel before God.	4 And the smoke of the incense of the prayers of the saints rose from the hand of the angel before God.
8:5 καὶ εἴληφεν ὁ ἄγγελος τὸν λιβανωτὸν And the angel took the censer καὶ ἐγέμισεν αὐτὸν ἐκ τοῦ πυρὸς τοῦ θυσιαστηρίου and filled it with the fire of the altar καὶ ἔβαλεν εἰς τὴν γῆν, and cast it onto the earth,	5 And the angel took the censer and filled it with the fire of the altar and cast it onto the earth, and there came to be thunders and voices and lightnings and an earthquake. The irony of this scene is that it is apostate Jerusalem that is about to be destroyed as if it were	5 And the angel took the censer and filled it with the fire of the altar and cast it onto the earth, and there came to be thunders and voices and lightnings and an earthquake. The angel who offers the incense is Christ. The prayers are those of the Christians	5 And the angel took the censer and filled it with the fire of the altar and cast it onto the earth, and there came to be thunders and voices and lightnings and an earthquake. The prayers are those of the Christians who will be martyred by the Antichrist in the	5 And the angel took the censer and filled it with the fire of the altar and cast it onto the earth, and there came to be thunders and voices and lightnings and an earthquake. The ensuing judgments vindicate the Christian martyrs throughout the centuries,

	Column A	Column B	Column C	Column D
				whose prayers God hears and answers by judging their perpetrators.

8:5

καὶ ἐγένοντο βρονταὶ καὶ φωναὶ
and there came to be thunders and voices

καὶ ἀστραπαὶ καὶ σεισμός.
and lightnings and an earthquake.

Column A	Column B	Column C	Column D
a whole burnt offering. (This is how the OT declares an apostate city should be destroyed—the priest would burn the city's booty in the middle of the city square with fire from God's altar [Deut. 13:16; Judg. 20:40]. Thus Jerusalem is the apostate city about to be destroyed by God.)	martyred by pagan Rome during its earlier persecution of the church. The seven trumpets represent the judgments God pours out on the Roman Empire, a more intense description than that of the seal judgments.	Great Tribulation, the last three and a half years of the end-time tribulation. The angel offering the incense may be Christ, who in his heavenly intercessory ministry hears and answers the prayers of the persecuted righteous during the Tribulation period.	

8:6 Καὶ οἱ ἑπτὰ ἄγγελοι οἱ ἔχοντες τὰς ἑπτὰ σάλπιγγας
And the seven angels, the ones having the seven trumpets,

ἡτοίμασαν αὐτοὺς ἵνα σαλπίσωσιν.
prepared them in order to blow [them].

Column A	Column B	Column C	Column D
6 And the seven angels, the ones having the seven trumpets, prepared them in order to blow them. The seven archangels who attend the throne of God will blow the seven trumpets of judgment upon Jerusalem. (Those angels are Uriel, Raphael, Raguel, Michael, Saragel, Gabriel, and Remiel [cf. 1 Enoch 20:2–8; Tobit 12:15; etc.].)	6 And the seven angels, the ones having the seven trumpets, prepared them in order to blow them. The seven angels are the seven archangels who attend the throne of God.	6 And the seven angels, the ones having the seven trumpets, prepared them in order to blow them. The trumpet (Rev. 8–9) and bowl (Rev. 15–18) judgments will be unleashed on the wicked during the second half of the Tribulation period, called the "Great Tribulation." Thus the six seal judgments correspond to the first three and a half years of the Tribulation (cf. Matt. 24:3–14; Mark 13:3–23; Luke 21:8–24), while the trumpet and bowl judgments correspond to the second half of the Tribulation (cf. Matt. 24:15–31; Mark 13:24–31; Luke 21:25–33)—the Great Tribulation. The trumpet judgments go from bad (seal judgments destroy	6 And the seven angels, the ones having the seven trumpets, prepared them in order to blow them. So the seven archangels who attend the divine throne prepare to sound their trumpets. These judgments repeat the seal judgments and occur again and again in history, until the second coming of Christ. They, like the seal judgments, are not final (seal—one-fourth destruction; trumpets—one-third destruction).

Greek Text and English Translation	Preterist View	Historicist View	Futurist View	Idealist View
			one-fourth of the earth) to worse (the trumpet judgments destroy one-third of the earth).	
8:7 Καὶ ὁ πρῶτος ἐσάλπισεν· And the first blew [the trumpet], κ αὶ ἐγένετο χάλαζα καὶ πῦρ μεμιγμένα ἐν αἵματι καὶ ἐβλήθη εἰς τὴν γῆν, and there came hail and fire mixed with blood, and it was cast on the earth, καὶ τὸ τρίτον τῆς γῆς κατεκάη and one-third of the earth was burned, καὶ τὸ τρίτον τῶν δένδρων κατεκάη and one-third of the trees were burned, καὶ πᾶς χόρτος χλωρὸς κατεκάη. and all green grass was burned.	7 And the first angel blew the trumpet, and there came hail and fire mixed with blood, and it was cast on the earth, and one-third of the earth was burned, and one-third of the trees were burned, and all green grass was burned. The seven trumpets mark the progress of the Roman invasion of Israel, intensifying the campaign from A.D. 69 to 70. A violent storm beat upon Israel, like the Egyptian plague of hail (Exod. 9:13–34, the seventh plague). This first trumpet judgment was a portent of things to come, for the Romans burned up one-third of Israel's trees and grass.	7 And the first angel blew the trumpet, and there came hail and fire mixed with blood, and it was cast on the earth, and one-third of the earth was burned, and one-third of the trees were burned, and all green grass was burned. These first four trumpet judgments correspond to the four barbaric invasions of the Roman Empire that resulted in its demise in A.D. 476. Hail, fire (cf. the seventh Egyptian plague), blood, and the scorched earth recall the conflicts between the western Roman Empire (one-third of the Roman Empire) and the hordes of Goths and Vandals under Alaric. These barbarians attacked Gaul, Spain, and Italy from the north, burning or destroying everything in their path. In 410, they sacked Rome itself.	7 And the first angel blew the trumpet, and there came hail and fire mixed with blood, and it was cast on the earth, and one-third of the earth was burned, and one-third of the trees were burned, and all green grass was burned. Similar to the seventh Egyptian plague, ice, fire, and blood will rain on the earth during the Great Tribulation, burning up one-third of its trees and grass (cf. Joel 2:30). This will be an ecological disaster without parallel in human history thus far.	7 And the first angel blew the trumpet, and there came hail and fire mixed with blood, which was cast on the earth, and one-third of the earth was burned, and one-third of the trees were burned, and all green grass was burned. This trumpet judgment (cf. the seventh Egyptian plague)—with its hail and fire mingled with blood—symbolizes the repeated land disasters that are used by God to warn the wicked to repent of their sins.

8:8 Καὶ ὁ δεύτερος ἄγγελος ἐσάλπισεν· And the second angel blew [the trumpet] καὶ ὡς ὅρος μέγα πυρὶ καιόμενον ἐβλήθη εἰς τὴν θάλασσαν, and [something] like a great mountain burning with fire was cast into the sea, καὶ ἐγένετο τὸ τρίτον τῆς θαλάσσης αἷμα and one-third of the sea became blood. 8:9 καὶ ἀπέθανεν τὸ τρίτον τῶν κτισμάτων τῶν ἐν τῇ θαλάσσῃ τὰ ἔχοντα ψυχάς, And one-third of the creatures which are in the sea having souls died, καὶ τὸ τρίτον τῶν πλοίων διεφθάρησαν. and one-third part of the ships were destroyed. 8:10 Καὶ ὁ τρίτος ἄγγελος ἐσάλπισεν· And the third angel blew [the trumpet] καὶ ἔπεσεν ἐκ τοῦ οὐρανοῦ ἀστὴρ μέγας καιόμενος ὡς λαμπάς, and a great star fell out of heaven burning like a torch	8 And the second angel blew the trumpet, and something like a great mountain burning with fire was cast into the sea, and one-third of the sea became blood. 9 And one-third of the creatures in the sea having souls died, and one-third part of the ships were destroyed. The Romans destroyed the Jewish "fleet" near Syria, Phoenicia, and on the Sea of Galilee, and the dead Jewish bodies colored the waters with their blood, reminiscent of the first Egyptian plague (Exod. 7:14–21). 10 And the third angel blew the trumpet, and a great star fell out of heaven burning like a torch, and it fell upon one-third of the rivers and upon the fountains of the waters.	8 And the second angel blew the trumpet, and something like a great mountain burning with fire was cast into the sea, and one-third of the sea became blood. 9 And one-third of the creatures in the sea having souls died, and one-third of the ships were destroyed. This second trumpet judgment, reminiscent of the first Egyptian plague, features the Vandals led by Genseric (428–468) as a great mountain/kingdom that controlled the seas and polluted them with the blood of Romans. The Vandals left the Baltic Sea to defeat Carthage and then Rome. Defeating those armadas, the Vandals then controlled the seas. 10 And the third angel blew the trumpet, and a great star fell out of heaven burning like a torch, and it fell upon one-third of the rivers and upon the fountains of the waters.	8 And the second angel blew the trumpet, and something like a great mountain burning with fire was cast into the sea, and one-third of the sea became blood. 9 And one-third of the creatures in the sea having souls died, and one-third of the ships were destroyed. Enormous meteorites will be hurled into the seas, turning them into blood (cf. the first Egyptian plague). Consequently, one-third of the world's population will die. 10 And the third angel blew the trumpet, and a great star fell out of heaven burning like a torch, and it fell upon one-third of the rivers and upon the fountains of the waters.	8 And the second angel blew the trumpet, and something like a great mountain burning with fire was cast into the sea, and one-third of the sea became blood. 9 And one-third of the creatures in the sea having souls died, and one-third of the ships were destroyed. This judgment (cf. the first Egyptian plague) represents all sea disasters allowed by God to destroy his unrepentant enemies. 10 And the third angel blew the trumpet, and a great star fell out of heaven burning like a torch, and it fell upon one-third of the rivers and upon the fountains of the waters.

Greek Text and English Translation	Preterist View	Historicist View	Futurist View	Idealist View
καὶ ἔπεσεν ἐπὶ τὸ τρίτον τῶν ποταμῶν and it fell upon one-third of the rivers καὶ ἐπὶ τὰς πηγὰς τῶν ὑδάτων, and upon the fountains of the waters. 8:11 καὶ τὸ ὄνομα τοῦ ἀστέρος λέγεται ὁ ῎Αψινθος, And the name of the star is called Wormwood, καὶ ἐγένετο τὸ τρίτον τῶν ὑδάτων εἰς ἄψινθον and one-third of the waters became wormwood καὶ πολλοὶ τῶν ἀνθρώπων ἀπέθανον ἐκ τῶν ὑδάτων ὅτι ἐπικράνθησαν. and many of the men died of the waters because they were made bitter.	11 And the name of the star is called Wormwood, and one-third of the waters became wormwood, and many of the waters because they were made bitter. The dead bodies caused a stench, and disease contaminated Israel's drinking water from the Sea of Galilee, as well as putrified the air (cf. again the first Egyptian plague and also the miracle of the waters at Marah [Exod. 15:23–26], but as a parody).	11 And the name of the star is called Wormwood, and one-third of the waters became wormwood, and many of the men died of the waters because they were made bitter. The star, Wormwood, is Attica, the leader of the Huns in 440. If the Vandals were masters of the seas, the Huns were masters of the rivers. They took over the regions of the Rhine, the Upper Danube, and Po rivers. In the Italian Alps they shed so much blood that they polluted its springs. Overall, the Huns slaughtered 300,000 people in those rivers, polluting them and spreading disease and death.	11 And the name of the star is called Wormwood, and one-third of the waters became wormwood, and many of the men died of the waters because they were made bitter.	11 And the name of the star is called Wormwood, and one-third of the waters became wormwood, and many of the men died of the waters because they were made bitter. This divine judgment represents the disturbance of rivers, causing flooding, epidemic, chemical pollution, etc., and thereby widespread death.
8:12 Καὶ ὁ τέταρτος ἄγγελος ἐσάλπισεν· And the fourth angel blew [the trumpet],	12 And the fourth angel blew the trumpet, and one-third of the sun was struck and one-third	12 And the fourth angel blew the trumpet, and one-third of the sun was struck and one-third	12 And the fourth angel blew the trumpet, and one-third of the sun was struck and one-third	12 And the fourth angel blew the trumpet, and one- third of the sun was struck and one-third

καὶ ἐπλήγη τὸ τρίτον τοῦ ἡλίου and one-third of the sun was struck καὶ τὸ τρίτον τῆς σελήνης καὶ τὸ τρίτον τῶν ἀστέρων, and one-third of the moon and one-third of the stars, ἵνα σκοτισθῇ τὸ τρίτον αὐτῶν so that one-third of them was darkened καὶ ἡ ἡμέρα μὴ φάνῃ τὸ τρίτον αὐτῆς καὶ ἡ νὺξ ὁμοίως, and the day did not shine for one-third of it and the night also.	of the moon and one-third of the stars, so that one-third of them were darkened and the day did not shine for one-third of it and the night also. This is the OT symbolic language of end-time judgment now applied to apostate Israel itself (Isa. 13:9–11; Ezek. 32:7–8; Joel 2:10, 28–32). It recalls the ninth Egyptian plague (Exod. 10:21–23).	of the moon and one-third of the stars, so that one-third of them were darkened and the day did not shine for one-third of it and the night also. This trumpet heralding darkness (cf. the ninth Egyptian plague) symbolizes the light of civilization going out with the fall of the city of Rome in 476 to King Odoacer of the Heruli. He became known as the "King of Italy" from 476 to 490.	of the moon and one-third of the stars, so that one-third of them were darkened and the day did not shine for one-third of it and the night also. Like the ninth Egyptian plague, the fourth trumpet judgment will cast darkness over one-third of the heavens and earth (cf. Luke 21:25–26).	of the moon and one-third of the stars, so that one-third of them were darkened and the day did not shine for one-third of it and the night also. This judgment recalls the ninth Egyptian plague as well as the OT prophetic language of judgment (cf. Isa. 13:9–11; Ezek. 32:7–8; Joel 2:10, 28–32; etc.) pronounced upon the wicked. The darkness motif heralds the judgments of God upon unbelieving humankind during the age of the church.
8:13 Καὶ εἶδον, καὶ ἤκουσα ἑνὸς ἀετοῦ πετομένου And I looked, and I heard one eagle flying ἐν μεσουρανήματι λέγοντος φωνῇ μεγάλῃ· in the middle of the heavens saying in a great voice, οὐαὶ οὐαὶ οὐαὶ τοὺς κατοικοῦντας ἐπὶ τῆς γῆς "Woe, Woe, Woe to the ones dwelling upon the earth ἐκ τῶν λοιπῶν φωνῶν τῆς σάλπιγγος at the remaining blasts of the trumpets τῶν τριῶν ἀγγέλων τῶν μελλόντων σαλπίζειν. of the three angels who are about to blow [their trumpets]."	13 And I looked, and I heard one eagle flying in the middle of the heavens, saying in a great voice, "Woe, woe, woe to the inhabitants upon the earth at the remaining blasts of the trumpets of the three angels who are about to blow their trumpets" of judgments 5, 6, and 7. (The eagle was a feared symbol to the first century because it was stamped on the Roman standards/flags. Thus the next three judgments correspond to the advance of the Roman legions on Jerusalem.)	13 And I looked, and I heard one eagle flying in the middle of the heavens, saying in a great voice, "Woe, woe, woe to the inhabitants upon the earth at the remaining blasts of the trumpets of the three angels who are about to blow their trumpets." These three trumpets/woes—5, 6, and 7—allude to the overthrow of the eastern Roman Empire by Saracen, the Turks, and the French Revolution (see Rev. 9).	13 And I looked, and I heard one eagle flying in the middle of the heavens, saying in a great voice, "Woe, woe, woe to the inhabitants upon the earth at the remaining blasts of the trumpets of the three angels who are about to blow their trumpets." The three woes—trumpet judgments 5, 6, and 7; the last of which heralds the seven bowl judgments.	13 And I looked, and I heard one eagle flying in the middle of the heavens, saying in a great voice, "Woe, woe, woe to the inhabitants upon the earth at the remaining blasts of the trumpets of the three angels who are about to blow [their trumpets]." The three woes—trumpet judgments 5, 6, and 7—suggest that the calamities that occur throughout history will become more intense at the end of history, when the return of Christ approaches.

Greek Text and English Translation	Preterist View	Historicist View	Futurist View	Idealist View
9:1 Καὶ ὁ πέμπτος ἄγγελος ἐσάλπισεν· And the fifth angel blew [the trumpet], καὶ εἶδον ἀστέρα ἐκ τοῦ οὐρανοῦ πεπτωκότα εἰς τὴν γῆν, and I saw a star out of heaven having fallen unto the earth, καὶ ἐδόθη αὐτῷ ἡ κλεὶς τοῦ φρέατος τῆς ἀβύσσου and there was given to him the key to the shaft of the [bottomless] abyss,	1 And the fifth angel blew the trumpet, and I saw a star out of heaven, having fallen unto earth, and there was given to him the key to the shaft of the bottomless abyss,	1 And the fifth angel blew the trumpet, and I saw a star out of heaven, having fallen unto earth, and there was given to him the key to the shaft of the bottomless abyss,	1 And the fifth angel blew the trumpet, and I saw a star out of heaven, having fallen unto earth, and there was given to him the key to the shaft of the bottomless abyss,	1 And the fifth angel blew the trumpet, and I saw a star out of heaven, having fallen unto earth, and there was given to him the key to the shaft of the bottomless abyss,
9:2 καὶ ἤνοιξεν τὸ φρέαρ τῆς ἀβύσσου, καὶ ἀνέβη καπνὸς and he opened the shaft of the abyss, and smoke arose ἐκ τοῦ φρέατος ὡς καπνὸς καμίνου μεγάλης, from the shaft like the smoke of a great furnace, καὶ ἐσκοτώθη ὁ ἥλιος καὶ ὁ ἀήρ and the sun and the air were darkened ἐκ τοῦ καπνοῦ τοῦ φρέατος, with the smoke from the shaft.	2 and he opened the shaft of the abyss, and smoke arose from the shaft like the smoke of a great furnace, and the sun and the air were darkened with the smoke from the shaft.	2 and he opened the shaft of the abyss, and smoke arose from the shaft like the smoke of a great furnace, and the sun and the air were darkened with the smoke from the shaft.	2 and he opened the shaft of the abyss, and smoke arose from the shaft like the smoke of a great furnace, and the sun and the air were darkened with the smoke from the shaft.	2 and he opened the shaft of the abyss, and smoke arose from the shaft like the smoke of a great furnace, and the sun and the air were darkened with the smoke from the shaft.
9:3 καὶ ἐκ τοῦ καπνοῦ ἐξῆλθον ἀκρίδες εἰς τὴν γῆν, And out of the smoke came locusts unto the earth, καὶ ἐδόθη αὐταῖς ἐξουσία and there was given to them authority ὡς ἔχουσιν ἐξουσίαν οἱ σκορπίοι τῆς γῆς. as the scorpions of the earth have authority.	3 And out of the smoke came locusts unto the earth, and there was given to them authority as the scorpions of the earth have authority.	3 And out of the smoke came locusts unto the earth, and there was given to them authority as the scorpions of the earth have authority.	3 And out of the smoke came locusts unto the earth, and there was given to them authority as the scorpions of the earth have authority.	3 And out of the smoke came locusts unto the earth, and there was given to them authority as the scorpions of the earth have authority.

9:4 καὶ ἐρρέθη αὐταῖς ἵνα μὴ ἀδικήσουσιν And it was told to them that they should not harm τὸν χόρτον τῆς γῆς οὐδὲ πᾶν χλωρὸν οὐδὲ πᾶν δένδρον, the grass of the earth, nor any vegetation, nor any tree, εἰ μὴ τοὺς ἀνθρώπους οἴτινες οὐκ ἔχουσι τὴν σφραγῖδα except those men who do not have the seal τοῦ θεοῦ ἐπὶ τῶν μετώπων. of God upon the foreheads.	4 And it was told to them that they should not harm the grass of the earth, nor any vegetation, nor any tree, except those men who do not have the seal of God upon their foreheads. Satan (the falling star; see Isa. 14:12–15; Ezek. 28:11–19) was allowed by God to open the bottomless pit to release the demons (the fallen angels of 2 Peter 2:4; Jude 6) upon Jerusalem during the days of its siege by General Titus (A.D. 70). These were Jews who did not believe in Christ and therefore were not protected by the seal of God, in contrast to the 144,000 (Rev. 7:1–8). The generation of Palestinian Jews became increasingly demon-possessed, which reached its zenith during the Romans' siege of Jerusalem. The divisions among the inhabitants of the "holy city" (for example, those for the Zealots and those against them); the frenzied mobs; the false prophets; the desperate searching for food resulting in murder, even of children; and the suicides—all these attest to the demonic hordes' control of Israel at that time.	4 And it was told to them that they should not harm the grass of the earth, nor any vegetation, nor any tree, except those men who do not have the seal of God upon their foreheads. The fifth angel blew the trumpet, and a star—Mohammed—appeared on the scene. The star's fall alludes to the decline of Mohammed's family from princely rule but his rise to power in A.D. 612, when he began to command the Muslim army. The locusts are Mohammed's Arabian followers. Indeed, locust plagues literally come from Arabia. Moreover, the word "Arbeh" sounds like "Arab." Thus, the Saracens (Muslim Arabs), like a locust invasion (cf. the eighth Egyptian plague), plagued the eastern Roman Empire from A.D. 612 to 763. The Koran forbade Muslims to destroy trees, grass, and produce. Rather, the Muslims' intent was to harm corrupt and idolatrous Christianity—Catholicism, a false religion without the seal of God's approval and protection.	4 And it was told to them that they should not harm the grass of the earth, nor any vegetation, nor any tree, except those men who do not have the seal of God upon their foreheads. The star falling from heaven is Satan, the fallen angel (cf. Isa. 14:12–15; Ezek. 28:11–19), who will be allowed by God to open the bottomless pit to unleash the demons now incarcerated there (cf. 2 Peter 2:4; Jude 6). They will afflict those not sealed by God during the Great Tribulation.	4 And it was told to them that they should not harm the grass of the earth, nor any vegetation, nor any tree, except those men who do not have the seal of God upon their foreheads. Satan is allowed by God to let loose the demonic horde, heretofore reserved in the bottomless pit (cf. 2 Peter 2:4; Jude 6), to punish an unrepentant world. But God's chosen people will be unaffected by the demons because they have Christ's power over God's enemies (cf. Luke 10:19).

Greek Text and English Translation	Preterist View	Historicist View	Futurist View	Idealist View
9:5 καὶ ἐδόθη αὐτοῖς ἵνα μὴ ἀποκτείνωσιν αὐτούς, And it was granted to them that they should not kill them, ἀλλ᾽ ἵνα βασανισθήσονται μῆνας πέντε, but that they should be tormented for five months, καὶ ὁ βασανισμὸς αὐτῶν ὡς βασανισμὸς σκορπίου ὅταν παίσῃ ἄνθρωπον. and their torment [is] like the torment of a scorpion whenever it stings a man.	5 And there was given to them that they should not kill them, but that they should be allowed to torment them for five months, and their torment is like the torment of the scorpion whenever it stings a man.	5 And there was given to them that they should not kill them, but that they should be allowed to torment them for five months, and their torment is like the torment of the scorpion whenever it stings a man.	5 And there was given to them that they should not kill them, but that they should be allowed to torment them for five months, and their torment is like the torment of the scorpion whenever it stings a man.	5 And there was given to them that they should not kill them, but that they should be allowed to torment them for five months, and their torment is like the torment of the scorpion whenever it stings a man.
9:6 καὶ ἐν ταῖς ἡμέραις ἐκείναις ζητήσουσιν οἱ ἄνθρωποι τὸν θάνατον And in those days men will seek death καὶ οὐ μὴ εὑρήσουσιν αὐτόν, and never ever will find it, καὶ ἐπιθυμήσουσιν ἀποθανεῖν and they will desire to die, καὶ φεύγει ὁ θάνατος ἀπ᾽ αὐτῶν. and death will flee from them.	6 And in those days men will seek death and never ever will find it, and they will desire to die, and death will flee from them. The five months of torture inflicted upon Jerusalemites by the demons refers to the five months General Titus laid siege to that city (April to August A.D. 70), resulting in its fall. That period of time was the worst part of the Jewish revolt.	6 And in those days men will seek death and never ever will find it, and they will desire to die, and death will flee from them. The Saracens were not able to kill papal Rome as a political body, but only to torment it for a while. "Five months" are prophetic months of thirty days each, totaling 150 days. And since "day" stands for a year, the five months equals 150 years—A.D. 612 to 763, the time of the Saracens' "plague."	6 And in those days men will seek death and never ever will find it, and they will desire to die, and death will flee from them. The pain inflicted by the demonic horde will not actually kill the unrepentant but, like a scorpion's sting, will make them wish they could die. The pain will last five months (the life span of a locust). Nor do they harm the earth.	6 And in those days men will seek death and never ever will find it, and they will desire to die, and death will flee from them. The demons do not have the authority to take life; only God has that power. And the demons' influence is only temporary ("five months"), though tormenting.
9:7 Καὶ τὰ ὁμοιώματα τῶν ἀκρίδων ὅμοια ἵπποις And the likeness of the locusts [is] like horses ἡτοιμασμένοις εἰς πόλεμον, having been prepared for battle,	7 And the likeness of the locusts is like horses having been prepared for battle, and upon their heads are like crowns like	7 And the likeness of the locusts is like horses having been prepared for battle, and upon their heads are like crowns like	7 And the likeness of the locusts is like horses having been prepared for battle, and upon their heads are like crowns like	7 And the likeness of the locusts is like horses having been prepared for battle, and upon their heads are like crowns like

καὶ ἐπὶ τὰς κεφαλὰς αὐτῶν ὡς στέφανοι ὅμοιοι χρυσῷ, and upon their heads [are] like crowns like gold, καὶ τὰ πρόσωπα αὐτῶν ὡς πρόσωπα ἀνθρώπων, and their faces [are] like the faces of men,	gold, and their faces are like the faces of men,	gold, and their faces are like the faces of men,	gold, and their faces are like the faces of men,	gold, and their faces are like the faces of men,
9:8 καὶ εἶχον τρίχας ὡς τρίχας γυναικῶν, and they were having hair like hair of women, καὶ οἱ ὀδόντες αὐτῶν ὡς λεόντων ἦσαν, and their teeth were like lions' teeth,	8 and they were having hair of women, and their teeth were like lions' teeth,	8 and they were having hair like women's hair, and their teeth were like lions' teeth,	8 and they were having hair like women's hair, and their teeth were like lions' teeth,	8 and they were having hair like women's hair, and their teeth were like lions' teeth,
9:9 καὶ εἶχον θώρακας ὡς θώρακας σιδηροῦς, and they were having scales like scales of iron, καὶ ἡ φωνὴ τῶν πτερύγων αὐτῶν ὡς φωνὴ ἁρμάτων and the sound of their wings [is] like the sound of chariots ἵππων πολλῶν τρεχόντων εἰς πόλεμον, of many horses rushing into battle,	9 and they were having scales like scales of iron, and the noise of their wings is like the noise of chariots of many horses rushing into battle,	9 and they were having scales like scales of iron, and the noise of their wings is like the noise of chariots of many horses rushing into battle,	9 and they were having scales like scales of iron, and the noise of their wings is like the noise of chariots of many horses rushing into battle,	9 and they were having scales like scales of iron, and the noise of their wings is like the noise of chariots of many horses rushing into battle,
9:10 καὶ ἔχουσιν οὐρὰς ὁμοίας σκορπίοις καὶ κέντρα, and they have tails like scorpions and stings, καὶ ἐν ταῖς οὐραῖς αὐτῶν ἡ ἐξουσία αὐτῶν and in their tails [is] their power ἀδικῆσαι τοὺς ἀνθρώπους μῆνας πέντε, to harm men for five months,	10 and they have tails like scorpions and stings, and in their tails is their power to harm men for five months;	10 and they have tails like scorpions and stings, and in their tails is their power to harm men for five months;	10 and they have tails like scorpions and stings, and in their tails is their power to harm men for five months;	10 and they have tails like scorpions and stings, and in their tails is their power to harm men for five months;
9:11 ἔχουσιν ἐπ᾽ αὐτῶν βασιλέα they have over them a ruler, τὸν ἄγγελον τῆς ἀβύσσου, the angel of the [bottomless] abyss; ὄνομα αὐτῷ Ἑβραϊστὶ Ἀβαδδών, the name of him in Hebrew is Abaddon,	11 they have over them a ruler, the angel of the bottomless abyss; the name of him in Hebrew is Abaddon, and in Greek he has the name Apollyon.	11 they have over them a ruler, the angel of the bottomless abyss; the name of him in Hebrew is Abaddon, and in Greek he has the name Apollyon.	11 they have over them a ruler, the angel of the bottomless abyss; the name of him in Hebrew is Abaddon, and in Greek he has the name Apollyon.	11 they have over them a ruler, the angel of the bottomless abyss; the name of him in Hebrew is Abaddon, and in Greek he has the name Apollyon.

Greek Text and English Translation	Preterist View	Historicist View	Futurist View	Idealist View
καὶ ἐν τῇ Ἑλληνικῇ ὄνομα ἔχει Ἀπολλύων. and in the Greek he has the name Apollyon. 9:12 Ἡ οὐαὶ ἡ μία ἀπῆλθεν· ἰδοὺ ἔρχεται ἔτι δύο οὐαὶ μετὰ ταῦτα. The first woe has passed; behold there is still coming the second woe after these.	12 The first woe has passed; behold, there is still coming the second woe after these. In the fifth trumpet judgment, the demons appear as a combination of locusts and humans. The locust appearance recalls the eighth Egyptian plague (Exod. 10:3–19) as well as the prophet Joel's prophecy against Israel (Joel 1:6; 2:5). The crownlike head, scaled bodies, thunderous noise, and stinging tail like a scorpion's are various expressions of the locust appearance of the demons. The faces like men's, sharp teeth, and long hair of women are human expressions but exaggerated due to demonic possession. Their leader is Satan, "Abaddon" (which means "death"), or "Apollyon" (which means "destruction"). The red, blue, and yellow colors describe the demons' hellish,	12 The first woe has passed; behold, there is still coming the second woe after these. The Islamic hordes were known for their turbans ("crowns"), beards and long hair ("hair like hair of women"), iron coats of mail ("scales of iron"), fighting rearward and over the tails of their horses ("stings" in their tails). Their leader—Mohammed—unleashed on Western civilization destruction and death ("Apollyon" and "Abaddon"). They thundered roughshod over the Eastern Roman Empire. The Saracens' invasion constitutes the first woe, the fifth trumpet judgment. Darkness now covered Western civilization (cf. the ninth Egyptian plague).	12 The first woe has passed; behold, there is still coming the second woe after these. The grotesque appearance of the supernatural army accentuates its demonic character: long, disheveled hair; lionlike teeth; hellishlike color; terrifying creatures—locusts/horses, crowns of gold, scales of iron, thunderous advancement, scorpionlike tails. Their leader—Abaddon/Apollyon—is Satan, who is the author of destruction and death. This fifth trumpet judgment is the first woe.	12 The first woe has passed; behold, there is still coming the second woe after these. This fifth trumpet judgment portrays demons as locustlike. Like horses, the demons are an invading army. Their crowns symbolize their supernatural authority. Like the faces of men, the demons are intelligent. Like women with long hair, they can be seductive. Like the lion's teeth, they are ferocious. Like scorpions, they are malicious (even as Satan the serpent is malicious; cf. Rev. 12). Their breastplates of iron give the impression that thereby they are invincible; and their ruler is Satan, the destroyer. The locust-demon invasion is reminiscent of the eighth Egyptian plague. And the darkness they bring recalls the ninth Egyptian plague. This is the first woe.

9:13 Καὶ ὁ ἕκτος ἄγγελος ἐσάλπισεν· And the sixth angel blew [the trumpet],	*(supernatural aura. The darkness they cause recalls the ninth Egyptian plague. The fifth trumpet judgment is the first woe.)*			
καὶ ἤκουσα φωνὴν μίαν ἐκ τῶν [τεσσάρων] κεράτων and I heard a voice out of the four horns	13 And the sixth angel blew the trumpet, and I heard a voice out of the four horns of the golden altar that is before God,	13 And the sixth angel blew the trumpet, and I heard a voice out of the four horns of the golden altar that is before God,	13 And the sixth angel blew the trumpet, and I heard a voice out of the four horns of the golden altar that is before God,	13 And the sixth angel blew the trumpet, and I heard a voice out of the four horns of the golden altar that is before God,
τοῦ θυσιαστηρίου τοῦ χρυσοῦ τοῦ ἐνώπιον τοῦ θεοῦ, of the golden altar that is before God,				
9:14 λέγοντα τῷ ἕκτῳ ἀγγέλῳ, ὁ ἔχων τὴν σάλπιγγα· saying to the sixth angel, the one having the trumpet,	14 saying to the sixth angel, the one having the trumpet, "Loose the four angels who have been imprisoned at the great river, Euphrates!"	14 saying to the sixth angel, the one having the trumpet, "Loose the four angels who have been imprisoned at the great river, Euphrates!"	14 saying to the sixth angel, the one having the trumpet, "Loose the four angels who have been imprisoned at the great river, Euphrates!"	14 saying to the sixth angel, the one having the trumpet, "Loose the four angels who have been imprisoned at the great river, Euphrates!"
λῦσον τοὺς τέσσαρας ἀγγέλους "Loose the four angels				
τοὺς δεδεμένους ἐπὶ τῷ ποταμῷ τῷ μεγάλῳ Εὐφράτῃ. who have been imprisoned at the great river, Euphrates!"				
9:15 καὶ ἐλύθησαν οἱ τέσσαρες ἄγγελοι And the four angels were loosed,	15 And the four angels were loosed, the ones having been prepared for the hour and the day and the month and the year, that they might kill one-third of men. The Euphrates River was the boundary between ancient Israel and her captors. From across	15 And the four angels were loosed, the ones having been prepared for the hour and the day and the month and the year, that they might kill one-third of men. The sixth angel blew the sixth plague trumpet, which unleashed the Turkish invasion of the eastern	15 And the four angels were loosed, the ones having been prepared for the hour and the day and the month and the year, that they might kill one-third of men. The sixth trumpet judgment unleashes a massive human army onto the world scene during the	15 And the four angels were loosed, the ones having been prepared for the hour and the day and the month and the year, that they might kill one-third of men. The sixth trumpet judgment/ second woe envisions the demonic horde as empowering human
οἱ ἡτοιμασμένοι εἰς τὴν ὥραν the ones having been prepared for the hour				
καὶ ἡμέραν καὶ μῆνα καὶ ἐνιαυτόν, and the day and the month and the year,				
ἵνα ἀποκτείνωσιν τὸ τρίτον τῶν ἀνθρώπων. that they might kill one-third of men.				

REVELATION

Greek Text and English Translation	Preterist View	Historicist View	Futurist View	Idealist View
	the Euphrates came Assyria, Babylonia, and Medo-Persia, and now Rome. It was where the Euphrates River touches Syria that four Roman legions stayed. And four Roman legions assaulted Jerusalem in A.D. 70. The specifics of the time of the attack ("hour," "day," "month," "year") indicate that the fall of Jerusalem to the Romans was in fulfillment of inspired prophecy (Dan. 9:24, 26; Luke 21:6; etc.).	Roman Empire (A.D. 1062 to 1453). Their original leader was Togrul, whose successor, Malek Shah, crossed the Euphrates and made assaults upon the Byzantine Empire. The Turkish Empire was divided into four principalities under Shah's four sons. If the Saracens defeated the southern and eastern thirds of the Roman Empire, then the Turks conquered the remaining third in the east. By the fall of Constantinople in 1453 to the Turks, the latter were now known as the "Ottoman Empire." The "hour," "day," "month," and "year" is a prophetic figure based on the "year-for-a-day" method of reckoning time. Thus, adding together 1 day (= 1 year), 1 month (= 30 years), and 1 year (= 360 years) totals 391 years (the "hour" is only a fraction of time). Thus, the sixth trumpet judgment covers A.D. 1062 (the year the Turks crossed the Euphrates River) to 1453 (the fall of Constantinople); that is, 391 years!	Great Tribulation. It is unleashed by four evil angels stationed at the Euphrates River. This army will kill one-third of the human population.	armies to wage war with each other. The unleashing of the demonic/human force to judge the earth is in answer to the martyrs' prayers for vindication (it comes from the heavenly altar; cf. Rev. 8:3). Just as the Euphrates River served as a barrier for the West to marauding armies from the East, its crossing by the Satanic herd indicates that humans are no longer protected from Satan and his denizens.

Column 1

16 And the number of the troops of the cavalry is two hundred million; I heard their number.

17 And thus I saw the horses in the vision and the ones sitting upon them, having breastplates the color of fire and of sapphire, and sulfurous, and the heads of the horses were like heads of lions, and out of their mouths proceed fire and smoke and sulfur.

18 By these three plagues one-third of men were killed, by the fire and the smoke and the sulfur proceeding from their mouths.

19 For the power of the horses is in their mouths and in their tails, for their tails are like serpents,

Column 2

16 And the number of the troops of the cavalry is two hundred million; I heard their number.

17 And thus I saw the horses in the vision and the ones sitting upon them, having breastplates the color of fire and of sapphire, and sulfurous, and the heads of the horses were like heads of lions, and out of their mouths proceed fire and smoke and sulfur.

18 By these three plagues one-third of men were killed, by the fire and the smoke and the sulfur proceeding from their mouths.

19 For the power of the horses is in their mouths and in their tails, for their tails are

Column 3

16 And the number of the troops of the cavalry is two hundred million; I heard their number.

17 And thus I saw the horses in the vision and the ones sitting upon them, having breastplates the color of fire and of sapphire, and sulfurous, and the heads of the horses were like heads of lions, and out of their mouths proceed fire and smoke and sulfur.

18 By these three plagues one-third of men were killed, by the fire and the smoke and the sulfur proceeding from their mouths.

19 For the power of the horses is in their mouths and in their tails, for their tails are serpents,

Column 4

16 And the number of the troops of the cavalry is two hundred million; I heard their number.

17 And thus I saw the horses in the vision and the ones sitting upon them, having breastplates the color of fire and of sapphire, and sulfurous, and the heads of the horses were like heads of lions, and out of their mouths proceed fire and smoke and sulfur.

18 By these three plagues one-third of men were killed, by the fire and the smoke and the sulfur proceeding from their mouths.

19 For the power of the horses is in their mouths and in their tails, for their tails are like serpents,

Greek/Interlinear Column

9:16 καὶ ὁ ἀριθμὸς τῶν στρατευμάτων τοῦ ἱππικοῦ
And the number of the troops of the cavalry

δισμυριάδες μυριάδων, ἤκουσα τὸν ἀριθμὸν αὐτῶν.
[is] two myriads of myriads; I heard their number.

9:17 Καὶ οὕτως εἶδον τοὺς ἵππους ἐν τῇ ὁράσει
And thus I saw the horses in the vision

καὶ τοὺς καθημένους ἐπ᾽ αὐτῶν,
and the ones sitting upon them,

ἔχοντας θώρακας πυρίνους καὶ ὑακινθίνους καὶ θειώδεις,
having breastplates the color of fire and of sapphire, and sulfurous,

καὶ αἱ κεφαλαὶ τῶν ἵππων ὡς κεφαλαὶ λεόντων,
and the heads of the horses [were] like heads of lions,

καὶ ἐκ τῶν στομάτων αὐτῶν ἐκπορεύεται πῦρ καὶ καπνὸς καὶ θεῖον.
and out of their mouths proceed fire and smoke and sulfur.

9:18 ἀπὸ τῶν τριῶν πληγῶν τούτων ἀπεκτάνθησαν τὸ τρίτον τῶν ἀνθρώπων,
By these three plagues one-third of men were killed,

ἐκ τοῦ πυρὸς καὶ τοῦ καπνοῦ καὶ τοῦ θείου
by the fire and the smoke and the sulfur

τοῦ ἐκπορευομένου ἐκ τῶν στομάτων αὐτῶν.
proceeding out of their mouths.

9:19 ἡ γὰρ ἐξουσία τῶν ἵππων ἐν τῷ στόματι αὐτῶν ἐστιν
For the power of the horses is in their mouths

Greek Text and English Translation	Preterist View	Historicist View	Futurist View	Idealist View
καὶ ἐν ταῖς οὐραῖς αὐτῶν, and in their tails,	serpents, having heads, and by them they harm.	having heads, and by them they harm. The sixth trumpet heralds the advance of troops numbering into the "myriads," the very term Turks used to count their armies. Their troops were so numerous that they were indefinite in amount. The fiery red, hyacinth blue, and sulfur yellow refer to the Ottomans' warlike appearance of scarlet, blue, and yellow. The fire and smoke refer to the artillery of the Turks, who were the first to use great guns at the fall of Constantinople (67 cannons each with 1,200-pound cannon-balls). The power of the horse's tail alludes to the Turkish military custom of attaching two or three horses' tails to a pole as a standard.	like serpents, having heads, and by them they harm. The two-hundred-million-man army will be composed of Chinese soldiers, who will cross the Euphrates River (the divide between the Orient and the Occident) in order to attack Western civilization. Behind their plan is the orchestration of God. The Chinese army will use helicopters armed with nuclear missiles to conduct their invasion. Hence the locust appearance of the choppers, which shoot nuclear missiles, which account for the presence of smoke (clouds of radioactive fallout) and sulfur (melted material).	having heads, and by them they harm. The war horses represent war engines and war tools of every generation. "Two hundred million" is a symbol for all the warring armies throughout history. The tail like serpents represents the aftermath of the hellishness of war.
αἱ γὰρ οὐραὶ αὐτῶν ὅμοιαι ὄφεσιν, for their tails are like serpents,				
ἔχουσαι κεφαλάς καὶ ἐν αὐταῖς ἀδικοῦσιν. having heads and by them they harm.				
9:20 Καὶ οἱ λοιποὶ τῶν ἀνθρώπων, And the rest of the men,	20 And the rest of men, who had not been killed by these plagues, did not repent of the works of their hands, in order that they might not worship the demons and the	20 And the rest of men, who had not been killed by these plagues, did not repent of the works of their hands, in order that they might not worship the demons and	20 And the rest of men, who had not been killed by these plagues, did not repent of the works of their hands, in order that they might not worship the demons and	20 And the rest of men, who had not been killed by these plagues, did not repent of the works of their hands, in order that they might not worship the demons and
οἳ οὐκ ἀπεκτάνθησαν ἐν ταῖς πληγαῖς ταύταις, who had not been killed by these plagues,				

οὐδὲ μετενόησαν ἐκ τῶν ἔργων τῶν χειρῶν αὐτῶν, did not repent of the works of their hands, ἵνα μὴ προσκυνήσουσιν τὰ δαιμόνια in order that they might worship the demons καὶ τὰ εἴδωλα τὰ χρυσᾶ καὶ τὰ ἀργυρᾶ καὶ τὰ χαλκᾶ καὶ τὰ λίθινα and the idols of gold and silver and bronze and stone καὶ τὰ ξύλινα, ἃ οὔτε βλέπειν δύνανται and wood, which are able neither to see οὔτε ἀκούειν οὔτε περιπατεῖν, nor to hear nor to walk, 9:21 καὶ οὐ μετενόησαν ἐκ τῶν φόνον αὐτῶν and they did not repent of their murders οὔτε ἐκ τῶν φαρμάκων αὐτῶν οὔτε ἐκ τῆς πορνείας αὐτῶν or their sorceries or their immoralities οὔτε ἐκ τῶν κλεμμάτων αὐτῶν. or their thefts.	idols of gold and silver and bronze and stone and wood, which are able neither to see nor to hear nor to walk, 21 and they did not repent of their murders or their sorceries or their immoralities or their thefts. The sixth trumpet judgment unleashes an astronomical number of soldiers against a small Jewish army. The weaponry of the Roman legions is impressive: armored horsemen, iron-plated towers, battering rams, catapults producing fire and smoke. All of this was empowered by the demonic horde, which meted out massive destruction upon the Jews held hostage by the siege of Jerusalem. Yet, none of this persuaded the Jews to repent of their sins. They continued to be inspired by demons;	idols of gold and silver and bronze and stone and wood, which are able neither to see nor to hear nor to walk, 21 and they did not repent of their murders or their sorceries or their immoralities or their thefts. God used the Saracens and the Turks to judge the unrepentant Catholic church with its worship of icons; perpetration of murder after murder of Albigenses and Waldensians, and others; immorality of every kind by the popes; demonic sorcery-like sacramental sway over the people through the Mass; and thefts through the sale of indulgences.	idols of gold and silver and bronze and stone and wood, which are able neither to see nor to hear nor to walk, 21 and they did not repent of their murders or their im-moralities or their thefts. Despite the terrifying fifth trumpet (first woe) and the sixth trumpet (second woe) judgments, non-Christians in the Great Tribulation will not repent of their sin and convert to Christ. Instead, they will worship all the more the Antichrist, whose mark of the beast will seduce people to bow before him. And yet, that image is nothing more than an idol. And men will follow the practices of the Antichrist—greed, murder, and im-morality—and all will be energized by the realm of the occult.	idols of gold and silver and bronze and stone and wood, which are able neither to see nor to walk, 21 and they did not re-pent of their murders or their sorceries or their immoralities or their thefts. Behind God's judgments on earth is his mercy, which waits for men to repent; but the Lord waits to no avail. Humans prefer to wor-ship the idols their hands have created: egocentri-cism, hostility, immo-rality, and witchcraft.

9:21					10:1
Greek Text and English Translation	Preterist View	Historicist View	Futurist View		Idealist View
	committed idolatry by worshipping their temple with its gold coverings, silver trumpets, bronze laver, and stone edifices; stole food from each other during Titus's campaign; believed in the sorcery of false prophets like John Girschala the Zealot; and even committed acts of transvestitism. Little wonder the curses of the covenant fell on Jerusalem in A.D. 70, even as they did in 586 B.C. (cf. Deut. 28).				
10:1 Καὶ εἶδον ἄλλον ἄγγελον ἰσχυρὸν And I saw another strong ange	1 And I saw another strong angel (Christ) descending out of heaven, clothed in a cloud; a rainbow was upon his head, and his face were like the sun and his feet and legs were like pillars of fire.	1 And I saw another strong angel (Christ) descending out of heaven, clothed in a cloud; and a rainbow was upon his head, and his face were like the sun and his feet and legs were like pillars of fire.	1 And I saw another strong angel descending out of heaven, clothed in a cloud, and a rainbow was upon his head; and his face was like the sun and his feet and legs were like pillars of fire.		1 And I saw another strong angel descending out of heaven, clothed in a cloud; and a rainbow was upon his head, and his face was like the sun and his feet and legs were like pillars of fire. Being clothed in a cloud and having legs and feet like pillars of fire is a symbol for the church, which is the true Israel, not the one in the wilderness. God's presence is with his new people, the church.
καταβαίνοντα ἐκ τοῦ οὐρανοῦ descending out of heaven					
περιβεβλημένον νεφέλην, καὶ ἡ ἶρις clothed in a cloud, and a rainbow					
ἐπὶ τῆς κεφαλῆς αὐτοῦ καὶ τὸ πρόσωπον αὐτοῦ upon his head and his face					
ὡς ὁ ἥλιος καὶ οἱ πόδες αὐτοῦ ὡς στῦλοι πυρός, like the sun and his feet [and legs] like pillars of fire.					

10:2 καὶ ἔχων ἐν τῇ χειρὶ αὐτοῦ βιβλαρίδιον ἠνεῳγμένον. And having in his hand a little scroll having been opened καὶ ἔθηκεν τὸν πόδα αὐτοῦ τὸν δεξιὸν ἐπὶ τῆς θαλάσσης, and he placed his right foot upon the sea, τὸν δὲ εὐώνυμον ἐπὶ τῆς γῆς, and his left [foot] upon the earth.	2 And he had in his hand a little scroll (God's divorce bill against Israel) having been opened, and he placed his right foot upon the sea and his left foot upon the earth.	2 And he had in his hand a little scroll (the Bible) having been opened (which, with the Protestant Reformation in 1517, was translated into the language of the people and thus was "opened" to all to read), and he placed his right foot upon the sea and his left foot upon the earth.	2 And he had in his hand a little scroll (the title deed of the universe) having been opened, and he placed his right foot upon the sea and his left foot upon the earth.	2 And he had in his hand a little scroll (God's sovereignty over the world) having been opened, and he placed his right foot stood upon the sea and his left foot upon the earth.
10:3 καὶ ἔκραξεν φωνῇ μεγάλῃ ὥσπερ λέων μυκᾶται. And he cried in a loud voice like a lion roars. καὶ ὅτε ἔκραξεν, ἐλάλησαν αἱ ἑπτὰ βρονταὶ τὰς ἑαυτῶν φωνάς, And when he cried, the seven thunders sounded their own voices.	3 And he cried in a loud voice like a lion roars. And when he cried, the seven thunders sounded their own voices.	3 And he cried in a loud voice like a lion roars, which was Christ's challenge to the doctrines of Roman Catholicism through the Reformers—Luther, Calvin, Zwingli, and their predecessors, Wycliffe and Hus. And when he cried, the seven thunders sounded their own voices, which were the papal anathemas denouncing Martin Luther and promoting the seven sacraments: baptism, confirmation, eucharist, penance, extreme unction, holy orders, and matrimony.	3 And he cried in a loud voice like a lion roars. And when he cried, the seven thunders (seven unthinkable judgments to be unleashed on the earth) sounded their own voices.	3 And he cried in a loud voice like a lion roars. And when he cried, the seven thunders (God's judgments on the unbelieving world throughout history) sounded their own voices.
10:4 καὶ ὅτε ἐλάλησαν αἱ ἑπτὰ βρονταί, ἤμελλον γράφειν, And when the seven thunders spoke, I was about to write, καὶ ἤκουσα φωνὴν ἐκ τοῦ οὐρανοῦ λέγουσαν, and I heard a voice out of heaven saying,	4 And when the seven thunders spoke, I was about to write, and I heard a voice out of heaven saying, "Seal what the seven thunders spoke, and do not write these	4 And when the seven thunders spoke, I was about to write, and I heard a voice out of heaven saying, "Seal what the seven thunders spoke, and do not write	4 And when the seven thunders spoke, I was about to write, and I heard a voice out of heaven saying, "Seal what the seven thunders spoke, and do not	4 And when the seven thunders spoke, I was about to write, and I heard a voice out of heaven saying, "Seal what the seven thunders spoke, and do not write

REVELATION

Greek Text and English Translation	Preterist View	Historicist View	Futurist View	Idealist View
σφράγισον ἃ ἐλάλησαν αἱ ἑπτὰ βρονταί, "Seal what the seven thunders spoke, καὶ μὴ αὐτὰ γράψῃς. and do not write these things!"	things!" (yet, for these seven thunders will be unveiled in the last set of judgments, namely, the bowl judgments—Revelation 15–18—these will be God's final punishment on Jerusalem).	these things!" (because they are invalid and unworthy of record).	write these things!" (so terrible are they).	these things!" God's ways are mysterious and therefore beyond human comprehension.
10:5 Καὶ ὁ ἄγγελος, ὃν εἶδον ἑστῶτα And the angel, which I saw standing ἐπὶ τῆς θαλάσσης καὶ ἐπὶ τῆς γῆς, upon the sea and upon the earth, ἦρεν τὴν χεῖρα αὐτοῦ τὴν δεξιὰν εἰς τὸν οὐρανὸν raised his right hand unto heaven	5 And the angel which I saw standing upon the sea and upon the earth raised his right hand unto heaven	5 And the angel which I saw standing upon the sea and upon the earth raised his right hand unto heaven	5 And the angel which I saw standing upon the sea and upon the earth raised his right hand unto heaven	5 And the angel which I saw standing upon the sea and upon the earth raised his right hand unto heaven
10:6 καὶ ὤμοσεν ἐν τῷ ζῶντι εἰς τοὺς αἰῶνας τῶν αἰώνων, and swore by the one who lives forever, ὃς ἔκτισεν τὸν οὐρανὸν καὶ τὰ who created heaven and the things in it ἐν αὐτῷ καὶ τὴν γῆν καὶ τὰ ἐν αὐτῇ and the earth and the things in it καὶ τὴν θάλασσαν καὶ τὰ ἐν αὐτῇ, and the sea and the things in it, ὅτι χρόνος οὐκέτι ἔσται, that time no longer will be,	6 and swore by the one who lives forever, who created the heaven and the things in it and the earth and the things in it and the sea and the things in it, that time no longer will be (before judgment falls upon Jerusalem).	6 and swore by the one who lives forever, who created the heaven and the things in it and the earth and the things in it and the sea and the things in it, that time no longer will be, until God judges the Antichrist—the pope and his followers.	6 and swore by the one who lives forever, who created the heaven and the things in it and the earth and the things in it and the sea and the things in it, that time no longer will be, now that the second half of the Tribulation is here.	6 and swore by the one who lives forever, who created the heaven and the things in it and the earth and the things in it and the sea and the things in it, that time no longer will be, for history is moving toward God's predestined purposes.

10:7				
10:7 ἀλλ᾽ ἐν ταῖς ἡμέραις τῆς φωνῆς τοῦ ἑβδόμου ἀγγέλου, but in the days of the voice of the seventh angel,	7 But in the days of the seventh angel, when he is about to blow the trumpet, and the mystery of God has been completed, as he an- nounced to his servants the prophets. The mystery of God is that believing Gentiles are now the people of God, because the church has perma- nently replaced Israel as God's chosen people.	7 But in those days of the voice of the seventh angel, when he is about to blow the trumpet, and the mystery of God has been completed, as he an- nounced to his servants the prophets.	7 But in those days of the voice of the seventh angel, when he is about to blow the trumpet, and the mystery of God has been completed, as he an- nounced to his servants the prophets about the coming of the kingdom of God to earth at the second coming of Christ.	7 But in those days of the voice of the seventh angel, when he is about to blow the trumpet, and the mystery of God has been completed, as he an- nounced to his servants the prophets. That mys- tery is that the kingdom of God is currently being manifested through the church until the second coming of Christ.
ὅταν μέλλῃ σαλπίζειν, when he is about to blow [the trumpet],				
καὶ ἐτελέσθη τὸ μυστήριον τοῦ θεοῦ, and the mystery of God has been completed,				
ὡς εὐηγγέλισεν τοὺς ἑαυτοῦ δούλους τοὺς προφήτας, as he announced to his servants the prophets.				
10:8 Καὶ ἡ φωνὴ ἣν ἤκουσα ἐκ τοῦ οὐρανοῦ πάλιν And the voice which I heard out of heaven again	8 And the voice which I heard out of heaven again speaking with me and saying, "Go, take the little scroll, the one having been opened in the hand of the angel standing upon the sea and upon the earth!"	8 And the voice which I heard out of heaven again speaking with me and saying, "Go, take the little scroll, the one having been opened in the hand of the angel standing upon the sea and upon the earth!"	8 And the voice which I heard out of heaven again speaking with me and saying, "Go, take the little scroll, the one having been opened in the hand of the angel standing upon the sea and upon the earth!"	8 And the voice which I heard out of heaven again speaking with me and saying, "Go, take the little scroll, the one having been opened in the hand of the angel standing upon the sea and upon the earth!"
λαλοῦσαν μετ᾽ ἐμοῦ καὶ λέγουσαν· speaking with me and saying,				
ὕπαγε λάβε τὸ βιβλίον τὸ ἠνεῳγμένον "Go, take the [little] scroll, the one having been opened				
ἐν τῇ χειρὶ τοῦ ἀγγέλου τοῦ ἑστῶτος in the hand of the angel standing				
ἐπὶ τῆς θαλάσσης καὶ ἐπὶ τῆς γῆς. upon the sea and upon the earth!"				
10:9 καὶ ἀπῆλθα πρὸς τὸν ἄγγελον λέγων αὐτῷ And I went to the angel, saying to him,	9 And I went to the angel, saying to him, "Give me the little scroll!" and he said to me, "Take and eat it, and it will make your stomach bitter, but it will be sweet as honey in your mouth."	9 And I went to the angel, saying to him, "Give me the little scroll!" and he said to me, "Take and eat it, and it will make your stomach bitter, but it will be sweet as honey in your mouth."	9 And I went to the angel, saying to him, "Give me the little scroll!" and he said to me, "Take and eat it, and it will make your stomach bitter, but it will be sweet as honey in your mouth."	9 And I went to the angel, saying to him, "Give me the little scroll!" and he said to me, "Take and eat it, and it will make your stomach bitter, but it will be sweet as honey in your mouth."
δοῦναί μοι τὸ βιβλαρίδιον. καὶ λέγει μοι· "Give me the little scroll!" and he said to me,				
λάβε καὶ κατάφαγε αὐτό, καὶ πικρανεῖ σου τὴν κοιλίαν, "Take and eat it, and it will make your stomach bitter,				

	Greek Text and English Translation	Preterist View	Historicist View	Futurist View	Idealist View
10:9	ἀλλ᾽ ἐν τῷστόματί σου ἔσται γλυκὺ ὡς μέλι. but it will be sweet as honey in your mouth.				
	10:10 Καὶ ἔλαβον τὸ βιβλαρίδιον τοῦ And I took the little scroll	10 Then, like Ezekiel the prophet, who found God's word at first sweet but then bitter because it announced the imminent fall of Jerusalem to Babylonia in 586 B.C., I took the little scroll out of the hand of the angel and ate it, and it was like sweet honey in my mouth, and when I ate it, my stomach was made bitter, because it announced the imminent fall of Jerusalem to Rome.	10 Then, like Ezekiel the prophet, who found God's word at first sweet but then bitter. The Bible was translated and enthusiastically received by the true church as though it were honey, even through the persecution it elicited from Catholicism was bitter.	10 And I took the little scroll out of the hand of the angel and ate it, and it was like sweet honey in my mouth, and when I ate it, my stomach was made bitter. The prophecies of John contained both the message of salvation to those who accept Christ in the Great Tribulation and the message of judgment to those who remain followers of the Antichrist.	10 And I took the little scroll out of the hand of the angel and ate it, and it was like sweet honey in my mouth, and when I ate it, my stomach was made bitter. The advancement of the kingdom of God is bittersweet: sweet, because the church triumphs over evil through the kingdom of God; and bitter, because the world persecutes the church because of its message.
	ἐκ τῆς χειρὸς ἀγγέλου καὶ κατέφαγον αὐτό, out of the hand of the angel and ate it,				
	καὶ ἦν ἐν τῷ στόματί μου ὡς μέλι γλυκὺ and it was like sweet honey in my mouth,				
	καὶ ὅτε ἔφαγον αὐτό, ἐπικράνθη ἡ κοιλία μου. and when I ate it, my stomach was made bitter.				
	10:11 καὶ λέγουσίν μοι· δεῖ σε πάλιν And they said to me, "It is again necessary for you	11 And they said to me, "It is again necessary for you to prophesy about many peoples and nations and tongues and kings."	11 And they said to me, "It is again necessary for you to prophesy about many peoples and nations and tongues and kings." Like John, the ministry of the Reformation will go forth to prophesy God's word to the nations.	11 And they said to me, "It is again necessary for you to prophesy about many peoples and nations and tongues and kings." John will now resume his prophecies about the end times of the world.	11 And they said to me, "It is again necessary for you to prophesy about many peoples and nations and tongues and kings." The command to prophesy returns the reader to the vision of the seal and trumpet judgments, which, like the bowl judgments to come, are parallel, not sequential in order.
	προφητεῦσαι ἐπὶ λαοῖς καὶ ἔθνεσιν καὶ γλώσσαις καὶ βασιλεῦσιν πολλοῖς. to prophesy about many peoples and nations and tongues and and kings."				

11:1 Καὶ ἐδόθη μοι κάλαμος ὅμοιος ῥάβδῳ, λέγων· And there was given to me a measuring reed like a staff, saying, ἔγειρε καὶ μέτρησον τὸν ναὸν τοῦ θεοῦ "Rise and measure the temple of God καὶ τὸ θυσιαστήριον καὶ τοὺς προσκυνοῦντας ἐν αὐτῷ. and the altar and those who are worshipping in it,	1 And there was given to me a measuring reed like a staff, saying, "Rise and measure the temple of God and the altar and those who are worshipping in it." These are the 144,000, the Jewish Christians, members of the true temple of God, who fled Jerusalem before it fell to the Romans in A.D. 70; they were thereby spared.	1 And there was given to me a measuring reed like a staff, saying, "Rise and measure the temple of God and the altar and those who are worshipping in it." These three items allude to the true church ("the temple of God"), which is based on the one-time sacrifice of Christ, not the repetition of the death of Christ in the papal mass ("altar") and is entered into by faith alone in Jesus' substitutionary death, not by the works of "righteousness" of the Catholic Church ("who—true Christians—are worshipping in it"); these items were highlighted by the Protestant Reformers.	1 And there was given to me a measuring reed like a staff, saying, "Rise and measure the temple of God and the altar and those who are worshipping in it." This is symbolic for the 144,000, the Jewish Christian evangelists in the end-time Tribulation, who are a part of the true temple.	1 And there was given to me a measuring reed like a staff, saying, "Rise and measure the temple of God and the altar and those who are worshipping in it." This is the true church.
11:2 καὶ τὴν αὐλὴν τὴν ἔξωθεν τοῦ ναοῦ ἔκβαλε ἔξωθεν and cast out outside the court that is outside of the temple καὶ αὐτὴν μὴ μετρήσῃς, ὅτι ἐδόθη τοῖς ἔθνεσιν, and do not measure it, because it has been given to the Gentiles, καὶ τὴν πόλιν τὴν ἁγίαν πατήσουσιν μῆνας τεσσεράκοντα [καὶ] δύο. and they will trample the Holy City forty-two months!"	2 "And cast out outside the court that is outside of the temple and do not measure it, because it has been given to the Gentiles," This happened when the Romans (the Gentiles) destroyed Jerusalem, the culmination of the three and a half years of the Jewish revolt against Rome, 66–70.	2 "And cast out outside the court that is outside of the temple and do not measure it, because it has been given to the Gentiles," This is the false, apostate church of Roman Catholicism, which persecuted the Holy City (the true church) for 1,266 years (1 day = 1 year; cf. Ezek. 4:6); that is, from A.D. 303 and the decree of Diocletian against Christianity, which was	2 "And cast out outside the court that is outside of the temple and do not measure it, because it has been given to the Gentiles, and they will trample the Holy City forty-two months!" This will be the rebuilt temple in Jerusalem prophesied about in Dan. 9:27; 11:31; Matt. 24:15; and 2 Thess. 2:3–4. This temple will be built over the current Dome of the Rock and will reinstate the	2 "And cast out outside the court that is outside of the temple and do not measure it, because it has been given to the Gentiles, and they will trample the Holy City forty-two months!" Here we learn that the false church is Christendom invaded by worldliness. And the fight between the true church and the apostate church will not go on forever but will last only during the church age.

REVELATION

Greek Text and English Translation	Preterist View	Historicist View	Futurist View	Idealist View
		carried on by the papacy—the revived Roman Empire—against the true church, until the publication of the Bishops' Bible in 1568, the culmination point of the triumph of the Reformation in that it, along with its predecessor translations in the English language, freed the masses to read the Bible in English and thus supplanted the Latin Vulgate. The Catholic persecution of Wycliffe, Huss, and Tyndale did not stop the progress of the Word of God. "And they will trample the Holy City forty-two months."	OT sacrificial system. According to Dan. 9:27, the end-time Tribulation period will begin when the Antichrist signs a seven-year covenant of peace with Israel. After three and a half years, the future Antichrist will betray the Jews by seating himself in the Holy of Holies as God. This will spark the Great Tribulation, the second and most intense half of the Tribulation period—the last three and a half years. As a Gentile, the Antichrist will control the temple during that time. This will be the "abomination of desolation" predicted in Daniel and in the Olivet Discourse.	
11:3 Καὶ δώσω τοῖς δυσὶν μάρτυσίν μου And I will grant to my two witnesses καὶ προφητεύσουσιν ἡμέρας χιλίας διακοσίας ἑξήκοντα and they will prophesy 1,260 days περιβεβλημένοι σάκκους, having been clothed with sackcloth.	3 "And I will grant to my two witnesses and they will prophesy 1,260 days, having been clothed with sackcloth."	3 "And I will grant to my two witnesses and they will prophesy 1,260 days, having been clothed with sackcloth."	3 "And I will grant to my two witnesses and they will prophesy 1,260 days, having been clothed with sackcloth."	3 "And I will grant to my two witnesses and they will prophesy 1,260 days, having been clothed with sackcloth."

11:4 οὗτοί εἰσιν αἱ δύο ἐλαῖαι καὶ αἱ δύο λυχνίαι These are the two olive trees and the two lampstands who are standing αἱ ἐνώπιον τοῦ κυρίου τῆς γῆς ἑστῶσες. before the Lord of the earth.	4 These are the two olive trees and the two lampstands who are standing before the Lord of the earth.	4 These are the two olive trees and the two lampstands who are standing before the Lord of the earth. These represent the true church, which has been persecuted from the time of Diocletian's edict to the Reformation.	4 These are the two olive trees and the two lampstands who are standing before the Lord of the earth.	4 These are the two olive trees and the two lampstands who are standing before the Lord of the earth.
11:5 καὶ εἴ τις αὐτοὺς θέλει ἀδικῆσαι And if anyone wishes to harm them πῦρ ἐκπορεύεται ἐκ τοῦ στόματος αὐτῶν fire proceeds out of their mouths καὶ κατεσθίει τοὺς ἐχθροὺς αὐτῶν· and devours their enemies; καὶ εἴ τις θελήσῃ αὐτοὺς ἀδικῆσαι, and if anyone wishes to harm them οὕτως δεῖ αὐτὸν ἀποκτανθῆναι. in this way it is necessary for him to be killed.	5 And if anyone wishes to harm them, fire proceeds out of their mouths and devours their enemies; and if anyone wishes to harm them, in this way it is necessary for him to be killed.	5 And if anyone wishes to harm them, fire proceeds out of their mouths and devours their enemies; and if anyone wishes to harm them, in this way it is necessary for him to be killed. Such is the fiery Word of God that proceeds from the mouth of the true church.	5 And if anyone wishes to harm them, fire proceeds out of their mouths and devours their enemies; and if anyone wishes to harm them, in this way it is necessary for him to be killed.	5 And if anyone wishes to harm them, fire proceeds out of their mouths and devours their enemies; and if anyone wishes to harm them, in this way it is necessary for him to be killed.
11:6 οὗτοι ἔχουσιν τὴν ἐξουσίαν κλεῖσαι τὸν οὐρανόν, These have the authority to shut the heavens, ἵνα μὴ ὑετὸς βρέχῃ τὰς ἡμέρας τῆς προφητείας αὐτῶν, in order that rain may not fall in the days of their prophecy, καὶ ἐξουσίαν ἔχουσιν ἐπὶ τῶν ὑδάτων and they will have authority upon the waters στρέφειν αὐτὰ εἰς αἷμα καὶ πατάξαι τὴν γῆν to turn them into blood and to strike the earth	6 These have the authority to shut the heavens, in order that rain may not fall in the days of their prophecy, and they will have authority to turn them into blood and to strike the earth with every plague as often as they wish. The two olive trees and two lampstands remind one of Joshua the high priest and Zerubbabel the governor of the Jews	6 These have the authority to shut the heavens, in order that rain may not fall in the days of their prophecy, and they will have authority to turn them into blood and to strike the earth with every plague as often as they wish. Thus Catholicism's rejection of the prophetic word of the church caused God to withhold his blessings from the Catholic	6 These have the authority to shut the heavens, in order that rain may not fall in the days of their prophecy, and they will have authority to turn them into blood and to strike the earth with every plague as often as they wish. But during that time, God will raise up his two witnesses, Moses and Elijah, who will call down God's wrath (fire, drought,	6 These have the authority to shut the heavens, in order that rain may not fall in the days of their prophecy, and they will have authority to turn them into blood and to strike the earth with every plague as often as they wish. The church's witness is thereby one of repentance ("clothed with sackcloth"); proclaimed by the people of God, the royal and priestly agents

Greek Text and English Translation	Preterist View	Historicist View	Futurist View	Idealist View
ἐν πάσῃ πληγῇ ὁσάκις ἐὰν θελήσωσιν. with every plague as often as they wish.	who returned to Israel in 516 B.C. (cf. Zech. 3–4; 6:19–14). Furthermore, the two witnesses' miracles remind one of Moses and Elijah (Exod. 7–11; 1 Kings 17–18; 2 Kings 2). But for John, the two witnesses are the church, which testifies to Christ as the fulfillment of the Law (Moses) and the Prophets (Elijah). More specifically, the two witnesses are Peter and Paul, who represent the persecuted church during Nero's reign of terror, which corresponded to the Jewish revolt, from 66 to 70.	Church, and this often took the form of military disasters that befell the papacy in return for its persecution of the Waldensians, the Albigenses, the Bohemian Brethren, Wycliffe, Huss, and all nonconformists.	plagues on water and on land) upon the Antichrist and his followers.	(Zerubbabel, the Davidic ruler, and Joshua, the high priest); as the fulfillment of the Law (Moses) and the Prophets (Elijah).
11:7 Καὶ ὅταν τελέσωσιν τὴν μαρτυρίαν αὐτῶν, And when they finish their witness, τὸ θηρίον τὸ ἀναβαῖνον ἐκ τῆς ἀβύσσου ποιήσει μετ᾽ αὐτῶν πόλεμον the beast who rises up from the abyss will make war with them καὶ νικήσει αὐτοὺς καὶ ἀποκτενεῖ αὐτούς, and will overcome them and will kill them.	7 And when they finish their witness, the beast who rises up from the abyss will make war with them and will overcome them and will kill them.	7 And when they finish their witness, the beast (the papacy, the Antichrist) who rises up from the abyss will make war with them and will overcome them and will kill them. Thus the papacy especially persecuted the true church: Pope "Innocent" III (12th century), the Third Lateran Council	7 And when they (Moses and Elijah) finish their witness, the beast (Satan, through the Antichrist) who rises up from the abyss will make war with them and will overcome them and will kill them.	7 And when they (the true church) finish their witness, the beast (the anti-Christian powers that seek to silence the church's witness) who rises up from the abyss will make war with them and will overcome them and will kill them.

(Greek / English)				
11:8 καὶ τὸ πτῶμα αὐτῶν ἐπὶ τῆς πλατείας τῆς πόλεως τῆς μεγάλης, And their corpses [will lie] upon the street of the great city,	8 And their corpses will lie upon the street of the great city, which is spiritually called "Sodom and Egypt," where also their Lord was crucified,	in 1179, the inquisitions beginning in 1231, etc. 8 And their corpses will lie upon the street of the great city, which is spiritually called "Sodom and Egypt," where also their Lord was crucified,	8 And their corpses will lie upon the street of the great city, which is spiritually called "Sodom and Egypt" (Jerusalem under the control of the Antichrist), where also their Lord was crucified,	8 And their corpses will lie upon the street of the great city, which is spiritually called "Sodom and Egypt" (the world in rebellion against God), where also their Lord was crucified,
ἥτις καλεῖται πνευματικῶς Σόδομα καὶ Αἴγυπτος, which is spiritually called "Sodom and Egypt,"				
ὅπου καὶ ὁ κύριος αὐτῶν ἐσταυρώθη. where also their Lord was crucified,				
11:9 καὶ βλέπουσιν ἐκ τῶν λαῶν καὶ φυλῶν and they see—of the people and tribes	9 and they—of the people and tongues and nations—see their corpses for three and a half days, and they do not allow their corpses to be placed in a tomb.	9 and they—of the people and tribes and tongues and nations—see their corpses for three and a half days, and they do not allow their corpses to be placed in a tomb. Thus Rome denied proper burial of nonconformists, at both the Third and Fourth Lateran Councils (1179 and 1215, respectively) and in the papal decrees in 1227 and in 1422. This applied to Wycliffe, Huss, and Savanarola, leaders of the Reformed movement.	9 and they—of the people and tribes and tongues and nations—see (through TV, cell phone, satellites, etc.) their corpses for three and a half days, and they do not allow their corpses to be placed in a tomb.	9 and they—of the people and tribes and tongues and nations—see their corpses for three and a half days, and they do not allow their corpses to be placed in a tomb.
καὶ γλωσσῶν καὶ ἐθνῶν τὸ πτῶμα αὐτῶν ἡμέρας τρεῖς καὶ ἥμισυ and tongues and nations—their corpses for three days and a half,				
καὶ τὰ πτώματα αὐτῶν οὐκ ἀφίουσιν τεθῆναι εἰς μνῆμα. and their corpses they do not allow to be placed in a tomb.				
11:10 καὶ οἱ κατοικοῦντες ἐπὶ τῆς γῆς χαίρουσιν ἐπ᾽ αὐτοῖς And those dwelling upon the earth rejoice over them	10 And those dwelling upon the earth rejoice over them and will send gifts to one another, because these two prophets tormented those dwelling upon the earth. So the	10 And those dwelling upon the earth rejoice over them and will send gifts to one another, because these two prophets tormented those dwelling upon the earth. So complete was	10 And those dwelling upon the earth rejoice over them and are glad and will send gifts to one another, because these two prophets tormented those dwelling upon the earth. Thus	10 And those dwelling upon the earth rejoice over them and are glad and will send gifts to one another, because these two prophets tormented those dwelling upon the earth. Thus
καὶ εὐφραίνονται καὶ δῶρα πέμψουσιν ἀλλήλοις, and are glad and will send gifts to one another,				

11:10				
Greek Text and English Translation	**Preterist View**	**Historicist View**	**Futurist View**	**Idealist View**
ὅτι οὗτοι οἱ δύο προφῆται ἐβασάνισαν τοὺς κατοικοῦντας ἐπὶ τῆς γῆς. because these two prophets tormented those dwelling upon the earth.	beast—Caesar Nero—had Peter and Paul and many Christians in Rome killed as the scapegoats for his guilt in burning Rome. The persecution of the Christians in Rome by Nero is reminiscent of the Jewish authorities' crucifixion of Jesus and the killing of his followers in Jerusalem. And both cities—Rome and Jerusalem—are spiritual Sodom and Egypt and will be destroyed by God: Jerusalem in A.D. 70 and Rome very soon. So even though the followers of the Antichrist gloated over the deaths of Peter, Paul, and the early Christians, their own judgment is imminent.	Rome's victory over the nonconformists that, on May 5, 1514 at the Ninth Session of the Fifth Lateran Council, Pope Leo X threw a great celebration for the attendees.		the pagan world rejoices at the apparent defeat of the church.
11:11 Καὶ μετὰ τὰς τρεῖς ἡμέρας καὶ ἥμισυ πνεῦμα ζωῆς And after three days and a half, the spirit of life	11 And after three and a half days, the spirit of life from God entered in them, and they stood upon their feet, and great fear fell upon those beholding them.	11 And after three and a half days, the spirit of life from God entered in them, and they stood upon their feet, and great fear fell upon those beholding them.	11 And after three and a half days, the spirit of life from God entered in them, and they stood upon their feet, and great fear fell upon those beholding them (via modern technologies).	11 And after three and a half days, the spirit of life from God entered in them, and they stood upon their feet, and great fear fell upon those beholding them.
ἐκ τοῦ θεοῦ εἰσῆλθεν ἐν αὐτοῖς, from God entered in them,				
καὶ ἔστησαν ἐπὶ τοὺς πόδας αὐτῶν, and they stood upon their feet,				

καὶ φόβος μέγας ἐπέπεσεν ἐπὶ τοὺς θεωροῦντας αὐτούς. and great fear fell upon those beholding them. 11:12 καὶ ἤκουσαν φωνῆς μεγάλης And I heard a great voice ἐκ τοῦ οὐρανοῦ λεγούσης αὐτοῖς· ἀνάβατε ὧδε. out of heaven saying to them, " Come up here!" καὶ ἀνέβησαν εἰς τὸν οὐρανὸν ἐν τῇ νεφέλῃ, And they arose into heaven in the cloud, καὶ ἐθεώρησαν αὐτοὺς οἱ ἐχθροὶ αὐτῶν. and their enemies saw them. 11:13 Καὶ ἐν ἐκείνῃ τῇ ὥρᾳ ἐγένετο σεισμὸς μέγας And in that hour a great earthquake came to be, καὶ τὸ δέκατον τῆς πόλεως ἔπεσεν and the tenth of the city fell, καὶ ἀπεκτάνθησαν ἐν τῷ σεισμῷ ὀνόματα ἀνθρώπων χιλιάδες ἑπτά and 7,000 of the names of men were killed in the earthquake, καὶ οἱ λοιποὶ ἔμφοβοι ἐγένοντο and the rest became afraid	12 And I heard a great voice out of heaven saying to them, "Come up here!" And they arose into heaven in the cloud, and their enemies saw them. 13 And in that hour a great earthquake came to be, and the tenth of the city fell, and 7,000 of the names of men were killed in the earthquake, and the rest became afraid and gave glory to the God of heaven.	12 And I heard a great voice out of heaven saying to them, "Come up here!" And they arose into heaven in the cloud, and their enemies saw them. So it was that, three and a half years from the papal declaration that the nonconformist movement was dead (May 5, 1514), on October 31, 1517, Martin Luther nailed his ninety-five theses to the door of Wittenburg Church! As even Pope Hadrian later admitted in 1523, "The heretics Huss and Jerome of Prague seem now to be alive again in the person of Luther." 13 And in that hour a great earthquake came to be, and the tenth of the city fell, and 7,000 of the names of men were killed in the earthquake, and the rest became afraid and gave glory to the God of heaven. The earthquake came in the form of the political convulsions that shook Europe after the Reformation. The "tenth of the city"	12 And I heard a great voice out of heaven saying to them, "Come up here!" And they arose into heaven in the cloud, and their enemies saw them. 13 And in that hour a great earthquake came to be, and the tenth of the city fell, and 7,000 of the names of men were killed in the earthquake, and the rest became afraid and gave glory to the God of heaven. The resurrection of the two witnesses and the earthquake will cause the majority of the Jews in Jerusalem (all but 7,000 of them)	12 And I heard a great voice out of heaven saying to them, "Come up here!" And they arose into heaven in the cloud, and their enemies saw them. Thus God always raises his church up from the ashes of persecution and defeat to triumph over her enemies through the preaching of the gospel. 13 And in that hour a great earthquake came to be, and the tenth of the city fell, and 7,000 of the names of men were killed in the earthquake, and the rest became afraid and gave glory to the God of heaven. God's judgments on the world throughout history vindicate his church, all the while affording men

Greek Text and English Translation	Preterist View	Historicist View	Futurist View	Idealist View
καὶ ἔδωκαν δόξαν τῷ θεῷ τοῦ οὐρανοῦ. and gave glory to the God of heaven.		that fell was the Church of England breaking away from Rome in 1529, making England the first nation to become independent of the papacy. The 7,000 that were lost to Catholicism were the seven chiliads (provinces) that broke away from Rome: Holland, Zealand, Utrecht, Frieseland, Groningen, Overyssel, and Guiderland, the countries of the Union of Utrecht.	to repent and believe in Jesus as Messiah (cf. Rom. 11:25–27).	time to repent; and some do, but most do not.
11:14 Ἡ οὐαὶ ἡ δευτέρα ἀπῆλθεν· The second woe has come; ἰδοὺ ἡ οὐαὶ ἡ τρίτη ἔρχεται ταχύ. behold, the third woe is coming quickly.	14 The second woe has come; behold, the third woe is coming quickly. Thus the deaths of the Christian martyrs released their souls to the presence of God and (based on Jesus' resurrection from the dead after three days) prompted God to destroy Jerusalem in A.D. 70, which by the end of the second woe had engulfed a tenth of that city. The rest of Jerusalem will fall by the end of the third woe, the seven bowl judgments. The beginning of	14 The second woe has come (that is, the 1,260 years of papal persecution of the true church and the rise of the Reformation and the advances of Islam, both of which defeated Rome in their own ways); behold, the third woe is coming quickly, in the form of the bowl judgments.	14 The second woe has come; behold, the third woe is coming quickly. The second woe corresponds to the trumpet judgments (Rev. 8–9); the third woe corresponds to the bowl judgments (Rev. 15–18).	14 The second woe has come; behold, the third woe is coming quickly. God's judgments on the idolatrous world recur throughout history.

11:15 Καὶ ὁ ἕβδομος ἄγγελος ἐσάλπισεν· And the seventh angel blew [the trumpet]; καὶ ἐγένοντο φωναὶ μεγάλαι ἐν τῷ οὐρανῷ λέγοντες· and there were great voices in heaven saying, ἐγένετο ἡ βασιλεία τοῦ κόσμου τοῦ κυρίου ἡμῶν "The kingdom of the world has become [the kingdom] of our Lord καὶ τοῦ χριστοῦ αὐτοῦ, καὶ βασιλεύσει εἰς τοὺς αἰῶνας τῶν αἰώνων. and of his Christ, and he will rule forever." 11:16 Καὶ οἱ εἴκοσι τέσσαρες πρεσβύτεροι And the twenty-four elders, [οἱ] ἐνώπιον τοῦ θεοῦ καθήμενοι ἐπὶ τοὺς θρόνους αὐτῶν the ones who are seated before God upon their thrones, ἔπεσαν ἐπὶ τὰ πρόσωπα αὐτῶν καὶ προσεκύνησαν τῷ θεῷ λέγοντες· fell upon their faces and worshipped God, saying,	the fall of Jerusalem will shock many Jews into converting to Christ. These will join the ranks of the true remnant. 15 And the seventh angel blew the trumpet; and there were great voices in the heaven saying, "The kingdom of the world has become the kingdom of our Lord and his Christ, and he will rule forever." 16 And the twenty-four elders, the ones who are seated before God upon their thrones, fell upon their faces and worshipped God, saying,	15 And the seventh angel blew the trumpet (which will unfold in the French Revolution to the end of history as we know it); and there were great voices in the heaven saying, "The kingdom of the world has become the kingdom of our Lord and his Christ, and he will rule forever." By the end of the seventh trumpet/seven bowl judgments (Rev. 15–18), Roman Catholicism, the apostate church, will be replaced by the Reformation church, the true temple of God and the new covenant. 16 And the twenty-four elders, the ones who are seated before God upon their thrones, fell upon their faces and worshipped God, saying,	15 And the seventh angel blew the trumpet; and there were great voices in the heaven saying, "The kingdom of the world has become the kingdom of our Lord and his Christ, and he will rule forever." Thus when Christ returns in glory, his kingdom will be established on earth to begin the Millennium. 16 And the twenty-four elders (the church, which will be raptured to heaven before the start of the Tribulation period), the ones who are seated before God upon their thrones, fell upon their faces and worshipped God saying,	15 And the seventh angel blew the trumpet; and there were great voices in the heaven saying, "The kingdom of the world has become the kingdom of our Lord and his Christ, and he will rule forever." 16 And the twenty-four elders, the ones who are seated before God upon their thrones, fell upon their faces and worshipped God, saying,

Greek Text and English Translation	Preterist View	Historicist View	Futurist View	Idealist View
11:17 εὐχαριστοῦμέν σοι, κύριε ὁ θεὸς ὁ παντοκράτωρ, ὁ ὢν καὶ ὁ ἦν, "Blessed [are] you, Lord God Almighty, the one who is and who was,	17 "Blessed are you, Lord God Almighty, the one who is and who was, because you have taken your great power and you have reigned.	17 "Blessed are you, Lord God Almighty, the one who is and who was, because you have taken your great power and you have reigned.	17 "Blessed are you, Lord God Almighty, the one who is and who was, because you have taken your great power and you have reigned.	17 "Blessed are you, Lord God Almighty, the one who is and who was, because you have taken your great power and you have reigned.
ὅτι εἴληφας τὴν δύναμίν σου τὴν μεγάλην καὶ ἐβασίλευσας. because you have taken your great power and you have reigned.				
11:18 καὶ τὰ ἔθνη ὠργίσθησαν, καὶ ἦλθεν ἡ ὀργή σου And the nations were filled with wrath, and your wrath came	18 And the nations were filled with wrath, and your wrath came and the time of the dead to be judged and the time to give the reward to your servants, the prophets and the saints and the ones who fear your name, the small and the great, and to destroy the ones who are destroying the earth."	18 And the nations were filled with wrath, and your wrath came and the time of the dead to be judged and the time to give the reward to your servants, the prophets and the saints and the ones who fear your name, the small and the great, and to destroy the ones who are destroying the earth."	18 And the nations were filled with wrath, and your wrath came and the time of the dead to be judged and the time to give the reward to your servants, the prophets and the saints and the ones who fear your name, the small and the great"—those martyred for their faith in Christ during the Tribulation period and who therefore will have places of honor in the millennial kingdom—"and to destroy the ones who are destroying the earth." Thus there will be three resurrections: one of the church at the Rapture prior to the Tribulation; a second, of the Tribulation martyred saints at the second coming of Christ (Rev.	18 And the nations were filled with wrath, and your wrath came and the time of the dead to be judged and the time to give the reward to your servants, the prophets and the saints and the ones who fear your name, the small and the great, and to destroy the ones who are destroying the earth."
καὶ ὁ καιρὸς τῶν νεκρῶν κριθῆναι and the time of the dead to be judged				
καὶ δοῦναι τὸν μισθὸν τοῖς δούλοις σου and to give the reward to your servants,				
τοῖς προφήταις καὶ τοῖς ἁγίοις the prophets and the saints				
καὶ τοῖς φοβουμένοις τὸ ὄνομά σου, τοὺς μικροὺς καὶ τοὺς μεγάλους, and the ones who fear your name, the small and the great,				
καὶ διαφθεῖραι τοὺς διαφθείροντας τὴν γῆν. and to destroy the ones who are destroying the earth."				

11:19 Καὶ ἠνοίγη ὁ ναὸς τοῦ θεοῦ ὁ ἐν τῷοὐρανῷ And the temple of God was opened in heaven,	19 And the temple of God was opened in the heaven, and the ark of his covenant appeared in his temple, and there were lightnings and voices and thunders and an earthquake and great hail. So the contrast is stark: Jerusalem will be destroyed and replaced by the church, the true temple and the new covenant. All of this unfolds in the seven trumpet judgments.	19 And the temple of God was opened in the heaven, and the ark of his covenant appeared in his temple, and there were lightnings and voices and thunders and an earthquake and great hail.	11:18); and a third one, of the wicked dead at the end of the Millennium at the Great White Throne judgment (Rev. 20:5–6).	
καὶ ὤφθη ἡ κιβωτὸς τῆς διαθήκης αὐτοῦ ἐν τῷ ναῷ αὐτοῦ, and the ark of his covenant appeared in his temple,			19 And the temple of God was opened in the heaven, and the ark of his covenant appeared in his temple, and there were lightnings and voices and thunders and an earthquake and great hail. This heavenly temple, contrasted to the temple polluted by the Antichrist (Rev. 11:2), will descend to earth at the beginning of the Millennium, when Christ returns to earth to establish his literal thousand-year reign.	19 And the temple of God was opened in the heaven, and the ark of his covenant appeared in his temple, and there were lightnings and voices and thunders and an earthquake and great hail. Thus the heavenly kingdom of God currently rules through the true church on earth, though it must at the same time encounter the wrath of a godless world. This is the already/not yet eschatological tension of the kingdom of God.
καὶ ἐγένοντο ἀστραπαὶ καὶ φωναὶ and there were lightnings and voices				
καὶ βρονταὶ καὶ σεισμὸς καὶ χάλαζα μεγάλη. and thunders and an earthquake and great hail.				
12:1 Καὶ σημεῖον μέγα ὤφθη ἐν τῷ οὐρανῷ, And a great sign appeared in heaven,	1 And a great sign appeared in heaven, a woman having been clothed with the sun, and the moon under her feet, and upon her head a crown of twelve stars. This is righteous Israel (cf. Gen. 37:1–9; Isa. 54:1; 66:7–10; etc.), the faithful remnant of the OT now joined with the church.	1 And a great sign appeared in heaven, a woman having been clothed with the sun, and the moon under her feet, and upon her head a crown of twelve stars.	1 And a great sign appeared in heaven, a woman having been clothed with the sun, and the moon under her feet, and upon her head a crown of twelve stars. This is the nation of Israel.	1 And a great sign appeared in heaven, a woman (the church) having been clothed with the sun, and the moon under her feet, and upon her head a crown of twelve stars. Thus the church is glorious from heaven's perspective.
γυνὴ περιβεβλημένη τὸν ἥλιον, a woman having been clothed with the sun,				
καὶ ἡ σελήνη ὑποκάτω τῶν ποδῶν αὐτῆς and the moon under her feet,				
καὶ ἐπὶ τῆς κεφαλῆς αὐτῆς στέφανος ἀστέρων δώδεκα, and upon her head a crown of twelve stars.				
12:2 καὶ ἐν γαστρὶ ἔχουσα, And having in the womb [a child],	2 And she has in her womb a child, and she cries, having labor pangs	2 And she has in her womb a child, and she cries, having labor pangs	2 And she has in her womb a child (Jesus Christ, who as a Jew, was	2 And she has in womb a child, and she cries, having labor pangs and

Greek Text and English Translation	Preterist View	Historicist View	Futurist View	Idealist View
καὶ κράζει ὠδίνουσα καὶ βασανιζομένη τεκεῖν. and she cries, having labor pangs and being distressed to bear a child.	and being distressed to bear a child. Thus righteous Israel, represented by Mary, suffered the birth pangs of the Messiah in giving birth to Jesus Christ.	and being distressed to bear a child. This scene symbolizes Christianity's great promise of success and growth in A.D. 313, the year Emperor Constantine legalized Christianity.	born of the Jewish race; the woman of v. 1), and she cries, having labor pangs and being distressed to bear a child.	being distressed to bear a child. This signifies that Christ's birth began the messianic woes.
12:3 καὶ ὤφθη ἄλλο σημεῖον ἐν τῷ οὐρανῷ, And another sign appeared in heaven,	3 And another sign appeared in heaven, and behold, a great red dragon, who empowers the Roman emperor, having seven heads (the seven hills of Rome) and ten horns (the ten Caesars of the first century) and upon his heads seven diadems,	3 And another sign appeared in heaven, and behold, a great red dragon, having seven heads and ten horns and upon his heads seven diadems,	3 And another sign appeared in heaven, and behold, a great red dragon, having seven heads and ten horns and upon his heads seven diadems (this is Satan, who will revive the geographical Roman Empire in the end-time Tribulation period),	3 And another sign appeared in heaven, and behold, a great red dragon, Satan, having seven heads (universal authority) and ten horns (military authority) and upon his heads seven diadems (political authority),
καὶ ἰδοὺ δράκων μέγας πυρρός, and behold, a great red dragon,				
ἔχων κεφαλὰς ἑπτὰ καὶ κέρατα δέκα having seven heads and ten horns				
καὶ ἐπὶ τὰς κεφαλὰς αὐτοῦ ἑπτὰ διαδήματα, and upon his heads seven diadems,				
12:4 καὶ ἡ οὐρὰ αὐτοῦ σύρει τὸ τρίτον τῶν ἀστέρων τοῦ οὐρανοῦ and his tail draws one-third of the stars of heaven	4 and his tail draws one-third of the stars of heaven and cast them unto the earth (which symbolizes the fall of Satan and a third of the angels; cf. Gen. 3; Isa. 14:12–15; Ezek. 28:17; Jude 6; 2 Peter 2:4–5). And the dragon stood before the woman who is about to give birth, in order that when she gives birth to her child, he might eat it. This	4 and his tail draws one-third of the stars of heaven and cast them unto the earth. This was the Roman ruler Maximim, who governed the Asiatic third of the Roman Empire in A.D. 313. The remaining two thirds of the Roman Empire were under Constantine's reign. And the dragon stood before the woman who is about to give birth, in order that	4 and his tail draws one-third of the stars of heaven and cast them unto the earth, which recalls the fall of Satan and his angels (Gen. 3; Isa. 14:12–15; Ezek. 28:17; Jude 6; 2 Peter 2:4–5). Thus, Satan from the past will empower the Antichrist in the future (cf. Rev. 13). And the dragon stood before the woman who is about to give birth, in order that	4 and his tail draws one-third of the stars of heaven and cast them unto the earth. This was the fall of Satan at the beginning of time, along with one third of the angels (cf. Gen. 3; Isa. 14:12–15; Ezek. 28:17; Jude 6; 2 Peter 2:4–5). And the dragon stood before the woman who is about to give birth, in order that whenever
καὶ ἔβαλεν αὐτοὺς εἰς τὴν γῆν. and cast them unto the earth.				
Καὶ ὁ δράκων ἕστηκεν ἐνώπιον τῆς γυναικὸς τῆς μελλούσης τεκεῖν, And the dragon stood before the woman who is about to give birth,				
ἵνα ὅταν τέκῃ τὸ τέκνον αὐτῆς καταφάγῃ. in order that when she gives birth to her child, he might eat [it].				

Greek Text	Interpretation 1	Interpretation 2	Interpretation 3	Interpretation 4
12:5 καὶ ἔτεκεν υἱὸν ἄρσεν, ὃς μέλλει ποιμαίνειν And she bore a son, a male, who is about to shepherd πάντα τὰ ἔθνη ἐν ῥάβδῳ σιδηρᾷ. all the nations with a rod of iron. καὶ ἡρπάσθη τὸ τέκνον αὐτῆς πρὸς τὸν θεὸν καὶ πρὸς τὸν θρόνον αὐτοῦ. And her child was caught up to God and to his throne. 12:6 καὶ ἡ γυνὴ ἔφυγεν εἰς τὴν ἔρημον, And the woman fled into the desert, ὅπου ἔχει ἐκεῖ τόπον ἡτοιμασμένον where she has a place prepared there ἀπὸ τοῦ θεοῦ, ἵνα ἐκεῖ τρέφωσιν αὐτὴν by God, in order that they might nourish her there ἡμέρας χιλίας διακοσίας ἑξήκοντα. for 1,260 days.	was Satan inspiring Herod, the Roman client-king of Israel who attempted to kill baby Jesus (Matt. 2:1–18). 5 And she bore a son, a male, the Davidic Messiah (Ps. 2:9; Rev. 2:27; 19:15), who is about to shepherd all the nations with a rod of iron. And her child was caught up to God and to his throne, which fast-forwards in time from Jesus' birth to his resurrection. 6 And the woman fled into the desert, where she has a place prepared there by God, in order that they might nourish her there for 1,260 days. The woman is now an allusion to the 144,000 Jewish Christians who fled Jerusalem in A.D. 68 during the Jewish revolt. These were a part of the remnant. They fled to Pella in the Transjordan, where they remained safe for the rest of the war (cf. Rev. 7; 11:1). Even though Satan was cast out of heaven before or	when she gives birth to her child, he might eat it. 5 And she bore a son, a male, who is about to shepherd all the nations with a rod of iron. And her child was caught up to God and to his throne. So Constantine legalized Christianity in A.D. 313, allowing the church to prosper in security. In A.D. 324, Constantine was enthroned over the entire Roman Empire, thus promising a bright future for Christianity. 6 And the woman fled into the desert, where she has a place prepared there by God, in order that they might nourish her there for 1,260 days.	when she gives birth to her child, he might eat it. 5 And she bore a son, a male (Jesus the Davidic Messiah), who is about to shepherd all the nations with a rod of iron at his second coming to earth to establish his millennial kingdom. And her child was caught up to God and to his throne (at Jesus' resurrection). 6 And the woman (national Israel in the Tribulation period) fled into the desert (Petra in the Jordanian wilderness, south of the Dead Sea), where she has a place prepared there by God, in order that they might nourish her there for 1,260 days—the last three and a half years of the Tribulation, the Great Tribulation; cf. Dan. 9:24–27; 12:1–4. (The over two-thousand-year gap presupposed between v. 5 and v. 6 is typical of biblical prophecy.)	she gives birth to her child to eat [it]. 5 And she bore a son, a male, who is about to shepherd all the nations with a rod of iron. This is Jesus the Davidic Messiah, who will return to earth to make his triumphant kingdom visible to all (Ps. 2:9; Rev. 2:27; 19:15). And her child was caught up to God and to his throne (at Jesus' resurrection). 6 And the woman fled into the desert, where she has a place prepared there by God, in order that they might nourish her there for 1,260 days. Satan persecutes the church for 1,260 days, a symbolic number representing the time between the first and second comings of Christ.

Greek Text and English Translation	Preterist View	Historicist View	Futurist View	Idealist View
	at creation, he continued to have access to God's throne as the accuser of the brethren (Job 1:6, 7, 9, 12; Zech. 3:1; Eph. 6:10–17). But upon Jesus' death on the cross "there was war in heaven," and Satan was permanently cast out of heaven (John 12:31–33; Luke 10:18–19).			
12:7 Καὶ ἐγένετο πόλεμος ἐν τῷ οὐρανῷ, And there was war in heaven, ὁ Μιχαὴλ καὶ οἱ ἄγγελοι αὐτοῦ τοῦ πολεμῆσαι μετὰ τοῦ δράκοντος. so that Michael and his angels might make war with the dragon. καὶ ὁ δράκων ἐπολέμησεν καὶ οἱ ἄγγελοι αὐτοῦ, Both the dragon and his angels warred.	7 And there was war in heaven, so that Michael and his angels might make war with the dragon. Both the dragon and his angels warred.	7 And there was war in heaven, so that Michael and his angels might make war with the dragon. Both the dragon and his angels warred.	7 And there was war in heaven, so that Michael and his angels might make war with the dragon. Both the dragon and his angels warred.	7 And there was war in heaven, so that Michael and his angels might make war with the dragon. Both the dragon and his angels warred.
12:8 καὶ οὐκ ἴσχυσεν οὐδὲ τόπος εὑρέθη αὐτῶν ἔτι ἐν τῷ οὐρανῷ. And he was not strong, nor was a place found any longer for them in heaven.	8 And he was not strong, nor was a place found any longer for them in heaven.	8 And he was not strong, nor was a place found any longer for them in heaven.	8 And he was not strong, nor was a place found any longer for them in heaven.	8 And he was not strong, nor was a place found any longer for them in heaven.
12:9 καὶ ἐβλήθη ὁ δράκων ὁ μέγας, And he was cast out, the great dragon, ὁ ὄφις ὁ ἀρχαῖος, ὁ καλούμενος Διάβολος the serpent from old, the one called the Devil	9 And he was cast out, the great dragon, the serpent from old, the one called the Devil and the Satan, the one deceiving the whole earth; he was cast out onto the	9 And he was cast out, the great dragon, the serpent from old, the one called the Devil and the Satan, the one deceiving the whole earth; he was cast out onto the earth,	9 And he was cast out, the great dragon, the serpent from old, the one called the Devil and the Satan, the one deceiving the whole earth; he was cast out onto the earth,	9 And he was cast out, the great dragon, the serpent from old, the one called the Devil and the Satan, the one deceiving the whole earth; he was cast out onto the

καὶ ὁ Σατανᾶς, ὁ πλανῶν τὴν οἰκουμένην ὅλην, and the Satan, the one deceiving the whole earth; ἐβλήθη εἰς τὴν γῆν, he was cast out unto the earth, καὶ οἱ ἄγγελοι αὐτοῦ μετ᾽ αὐτοῦ ἐβλήθησαν. and his angels were cast out with him. 12:10 καὶ ἤκουσα φωνὴν μεγάλην ἐν τῷ οὐρανῷ λέγουσαν And I heard a great voice in heaven saying, ἄρτι ἐγένετο ἡ σωτηρία καὶ ἡ δύναμις "Now has come the salvation and power καὶ ἡ βασιλεία τοῦ θεοῦ ἡμῶν καὶ ἡ ἐξουσία τοῦ χριστοῦ αὐτοῦ, and the kingdom of our God and the authority of his Christ, ὅτι ἐβλήθη ὁ κατήγωρ τῶν ἀδελφῶν ἡμῶν, because the accuser of our brethren was cast out, ὁ κατηγορῶν αὐτοὺς ἐνώπιον τοῦ θεοῦ ἡμῶν ἡμέρας καὶ νυκτός. the one who accuses them before our God day and night.	earth, and his angels were cast out with him. 10 And I heard a great voice in heaven saying, "Now has come the salvation and the power and the kingdom of our God and the authority of his Christ, because the accuser of our brethren was cast out, the one who accuses them before our God day and night."	and his angels were cast out with him. This is a dramatic portrayal of the Roman emperor Julian the Apostate's attempt to reestablish paganism in the empire from A.D. 361 to 363. But his death in battle ended that spiritual conflict in favor of Christianity. Julian's last words were, "O Galilean [Jesus], you have conquered!" 10 So certain is the future establishment of the kingdom of God on earth at the return of Christ that it is as good as done. And I heard a great voice in heaven saying, "Now has come the salvation and the power and the kingdom of our God and the authority of his Christ (Rome under Christian rulers), because the accuser of our brethren was cast out, the one who accuses them before our God day and night.	earth, and his angels were cast out with him. 10 And I heard a great voice in heaven saying, "Now has come the salvation and the power and the kingdom of our God and the authority of his Christ, because the accuser of our brethren was cast out, the one who accuses them before our God day and night."	and his angels were cast out with him. This heavenly war will take place in the middle of the Tribulation period. At that time, Michael will protect the nation of Israel on earth from the Antichrist (cf. Dan. 12:1). 10 So certain is the future establishment of the kingdom of God on earth at the return of Christ that it is as good as done. And I heard a great voice in heaven saying, "Now has come the salvation and the power and the kingdom of our God and the authority of his Christ, because the accuser of our brethren was cast out, the one who accuses them before our God day and night." So at the cross and resurrection of Jesus Christ, Satan was defeated and cast out of heaven to earth for good (John 12:31–33; Luke 10:18–19). This constituted the triumph of the kingdom of God in heaven and its advance on earth through the church. Thus the church is already triumphant, but its victory is not yet complete, for the saints will be persecuted and even

Greek Text and English Translation	Preterist View	Historicist View	Futurist View	Idealist View
				die at the hands of Satan and his idolatrous world. But Christians' death for Christ will paradoxically secure their ultimate victory over Satan.
12:11 καὶ αὐτοὶ ἐνίκησαν αὐτὸν διὰ τὸ αἷμα τοῦ ἀρνίου And they themselves overcame him through the blood of the Lamb καὶ διὰ τὸν λόγον τῆς μαρτυρίας αὐτῶν and through the word of their witness, καὶ οὐκ ἠγάπησαν τὴν ψυχὴν αὐτῶν ἄχρι θανάτου. and they did not love their lives until death.	11 And they themselves (the martyred Christians during the Neronian persecution; cf. v. 17) overcame him through the blood of the Lamb and through the word of their witness, and they did not love their lives until death.	11 And they themselves (the martyred Christians at the time of Julian the Apostate) overcame him through the blood of the Lamb and through the word of their witness, and they did not love their lives until death.	11 And they themselves (the martyred Christians during the Tribulation period) overcame him through the blood of the Lamb and through the word of their witness, and they did not love their lives until death.	11 And they themselves overcame him through the blood of the Lamb and through the word of their witness, and they did not love their lives until death.
12:12 διὰ τοῦτο εὐφραίνεσθε, [οἱ] οὐρανοὶ Because of this, rejoice you heavens καὶ οἱ ἐν αὐτοῖς σκηνοῦντες. οὐαὶ τὴν γῆν καὶ τὴν θάλασσαν, and the ones who dwell in them! Woe to the earth and the sea ὅτι κατέβη ὁ διάβολος πρὸς ὑμᾶς ἔχων θυμὸν μέγαν, because the devil has descended to you having great wrath, εἰδὼς ὅτι ὀλίγον καιρὸν ἔχει. knowing that he has little time."	12 Because of this, rejoice you heavens and the ones who dwell in them! Woe to the earth and the sea, because the devil has descended to you, having great wrath, knowing that he has little time."	12 Because of this, rejoice you heavens and the ones who dwell in them! Woe to the earth and the sea, because the devil has descended to you, having great wrath, knowing that he has little time."	12 Because of this, rejoice you heavens and the ones who dwell in them! Woe to the earth and the sea, because the devil has descended to you, having great wrath, knowing that he has little time," because Satan will unleash his fury on Christians through the machinations of the Antichrist during the last three and a half years of the Tribulation period.	12 Because of this, rejoice you heavens and the ones who dwell in them! Woe to the earth and the sea, because the devil has descended to you, having great wrath, knowing that he has little time," that is, the 1,260 days—the church age on earth—which, in the light of eternity, is very brief.

12:13 Καὶ ὅτε εἶδεν ὁ δράκων ὅτι ἐβλήθη εἰς τὴν γῆν, And when the dragon saw that he was cast unto the earth, ἐδίωξεν τὴν γυναῖκα ἥτις ἔτεκεν τὸν ἄρσενα. he pursued the woman who bore the male child.	13 And when the dragon saw that he was cast unto the earth, he pursued the woman who bore the male child.	13 And when the dragon saw that he was cast unto the earth, he pursued the woman who bore the male child. The scene in church history now changes. The dragon/Satan failed to stamp out the church through Julian the Apostate, so then Satan changed his tactics by raising up the Vatican, the revived Roman Empire, to persecute the true people of God.	13 And when the dragon saw that he was cast unto the earth, he pursued the woman who bore the male child.	13 And when the dragon saw that he was cast unto the earth, he pursued the woman (the church) who bore the male child.
12:14 καὶ ἐδόθησαν τῇ γυναικὶ αἱ δύο πτέρυγες τοῦ ἀετοῦ τοῦ μεγάλου, And there were given to the woman the two wings of a great eagle, ἵνα πέτηται εἰς τὴν ἔρημον εἰς τὸν τόπον αὐτῆς, in order that she might fly to the desert unto her place, ὅπου τρέφεται ἐκεῖ καιρὸν καὶ καιροὺς καὶ ἥμισυ καιροῦ where she might be nourished there for a time and times and a half of time ἀπὸ προσώπου τοῦ ὄφεως. from the face of the serpent.	14 And there were given to the woman the two wings of a great eagle, in order that she might fly to the desert unto her place, where she might be nourished there for a time and times and half a time (and protected) from the face of the serpent.	14 And there were given to the woman (the pure church, not the Roman Catholic Church) the two wings of a great eagle, in order that she might fly to the desert unto her place, where she might be nourished there for a time and times and half a time (and protected; from A.D. 254, the time of the beginning of the official Roman persecution of the church, to A.D. 1514, the end of the pre-Reformation persecution of the church by the papacy, the revived Roman Empire; cf. v. 6 and the 1,260 days/years) from the face of the serpent.	14 And there were given to the woman the two wings of a great eagle (the emblem of America, which will airlift Israel to safety in Petra), in order that she might fly to the desert unto her place, where she might be nourished there for a time and times and half a time (and protected) from the face of the serpent.	14 And there were given to the woman the two wings of a great eagle, in order that she might fly to the desert unto her place, where she might be nourished there for a time and times and half a time (and protected) from the face of the serpent.
12:15 καὶ ἔβαλεν ὁ ὄφις ἐκ τοῦ στόματος αὐτοῦ And the serpent threw out of his mouth	15 And the serpent threw water like a river out of	15 And the serpent threw water like a river out of	15 And the serpent threw water like a river out of	15 And the serpent threw water like a river out of

Greek Text and English Translation	Preterist View	Historicist View	Futurist View	Idealist View
ὀπίσω τῆς γυναικὸς ὕδωρ ὡς ποταμόν, behind the woman water like a river,	his mouth behind the woman, in order that he might make her to be carried off by the water.	his mouth behind the woman, in order that he might make her to be carried off by the water.	his mouth behind the woman, in order that he might make her to be carried off by the water.	his mouth behind the woman, in order that he might make her to be carried off by the water.
ἵνα αὐτὴν ποταμοφόρητον ποιήσῃ. in order that he might make her [to be] carried off by the water.				
12:16 καὶ ἐβοήθησεν ἡ γῆ τῇ γυναικί And the earth helped the woman	16 And the earth helped the woman, and the earth opened its mouth and swallowed the river which the dragon threw out of his mouth. Just as God delivered ancient Israel at the exodus by parting the Red Sea and delivering her from Pharaoh (Exod. 15; 19:4) and sustained Israel in the wilderness (Exod. 16:32; etc.), so God spared the 144,000 from the destruction of Jerusalem and from the pursuit of the Roman army by taking the 144,000 safely across the Jordan River to Pella. And in Pella in the desert, God kept watch over the Jewish Christian remnant.	16 And the earth helped the woman, and the earth opened its mouth and swallowed the river which the dragon threw out of his mouth.	16 And the earth helped the woman, and the earth opened its mouth through a giant earthquake and swallowed the river which the dragon threw out of his mouth.	16 And the earth helped the woman, and the earth opened its mouth and swallowed the river which the dragon threw out of his mouth. Just as God brought ancient Israel safely through the exodus and provided for her in the wilderness, so God will deliver and sustain his church during the messianic woes.
καὶ ἤνοιξεν ἡ γῆ τὸ στόμα αὐτῆς καὶ κατέπιεν τὸν ποταμόν and the earth opened its mouth and swallowed the river				
ὃν ἔβαλεν ὁ δράκων ἐκ τοῦ στόματος αὐτοῦ. which the dragon threw out of his mouth.				
12:17 καὶ ὠργίσθη ὁ δράκων And the dragon was filled with wrath	17 And the dragon was filled with wrath toward the woman and departed to make war with the	17 And the dragon was filled with wrath toward the woman and departed to make war with the	17 And the dragon was filled with wrath toward the woman and departed to make war with the rest	17 And the dragon was filled with wrath toward the woman (the church) and departed to make

ἐπὶ τῇ γυναικὶ καὶ ἀπῆλθεν ποιῆσαι πόλεμον — toward the woman and departed to make war μετὰ τῶν λοιπῶν τοῦ σπέρματος αὐτῆς — with the rest of her seed τῶν τηρούντων τὰς ἐντολὰς τοῦ θεοῦ — of the ones who keep the commandments of God καὶ ἐχόντων τὴν μαρτυρίαν Ἰησοῦ. — and who are having the witness of Jesus.	rest of her seed, the ones who keep the command-ments of God and who are having the witness of Jesus. These are the Gentile Christians who were faithful unto death during the Neronian persecution of the Roman church (A.D. 64–68).	rest of her seed, the ones who keep the command-ments of God and who are having the witness of Jesus. So the Lord protected the true church, the spiritual minority, even though she was relentlessly persecuted by Roman Catholicism. But the faithful few to Christ defeated the papacy by being true to the Word of God, the gospel of Christ alone, and not to church tradition.	of her seed—the 144,000 Jewish Christian evange-lists—the ones who keep the commandments of God and who are having the witness of Jesus.	war with the rest of her seed, the ones who keep the commandments of God and who are having the witness of Jesus. This is the apocalyptic drama of Genesis 3:15: the seed of the woman (Christ and his church) crushes the head of the serpent (Satan and his pagan followers).
12:18 Καὶ ἐστάθη ἐπὶ τὴν ἄμμον τῆς θαλάσσης. — And he stood upon the sand of the sea.	18 And he stood upon the sand of the sea.	18 And he stood upon the sand of the sea.	18 And he stood upon the sand of the sea.	18 And he stood upon the sand of the sea.
13:1 Καὶ εἶδον ἐκ τῆς θαλάσσης θηρίον ἀναβαῖνον, — And I saw a beast rising out of the sea, ἔχον κέρατα δέκα καὶ κεφαλὰς ἑπτὰ — having ten horns and seven heads καὶ ἐπὶ τῶν κεράτων αὐτοῦ δέκα διαδήματα — and upon his horns [were] ten diadems καὶ ἐπὶ τὰς κεφαλὰς αὐτοῦ ὄνομα [τα] βλασφημίας· — and upon his heads [were] the names of blasphemy.	1 And I saw a beast rising out of the sea (the Roman proconsuls of the Asian province who enforced Caesar/Antichrist wor-ship of Nero and then later Domitian), having ten horns (the ten prov-inces that comprised the first-century Roman Empire) and seven heads (the seven hills of Rome/seven Roman emperors by the time of John; see Rev. 17:9–10), and upon his horns were ten diadems and upon his heads were the names of blasphemy.	1 And I saw a beast (the papacy in its political power) rising out of the sea (the flood of Gothic invasions), having ten horns (the ten subordi-nate kingdoms of Rome arising out of the papal head: the Anglo-Saxons, Franks, Alleman-Franks, Burgundic-Franks, Visigoths, Suevi, Vandals, Ostrogoths, Bavarians, and Lombards) and seven heads/hills (the seven forms of govern-ment under which Rome had historically existed: kings, consuls, dictators, decemvirs, military tri-bunes, and the imperial	1 And I saw a beast (the Antichrist) rising out of the sea (signifying that he is a Gentile), having ten horns (the European Union: Belgium, Germany, France, Italy, Luxembourg, the Netherlands, Denmark, Ireland, the United Kingdom, and Greece—Daniel's fourth empire = the revived Rome Empire [see Dan. 2, 7, 8, 11]) and seven heads (seven world empires: five before John's day = Egypt, Assyria, Babylon, Persia, Greece; the sixth in John's day = Rome; and the seventh = the	1 And I saw a beast rising out of the sea, having ten horns and seven heads, and upon his horns were ten diadems and upon his heads were the names of blasphemy.

Greek Text and English Translation	Preterist View	Historicist View	Futurist View	Idealist View
		form in John's day; the seventh was Diocletian), and upon his horns were ten diadems and upon his heads were the names of blasphemy, in that the papacy/Antichrist accepted the praise and worship of men.	revived Roman Empire in the distant future beyond John), and upon his horns were ten diadems and upon his heads were the names of blasphemy.	
13:2 καὶ τὸ θηρίον ὃ εἶδον ἦν ὅμοιον παρδάλει And the beast which I saw was like a leopard καὶ οἱ πόδες αὐτοῦ ὡς ἄρκου and his feet like a bear's καὶ τὸ στόμα αὐτοῦ ὡς στόμα λέοντος. and his mouth like the mouth of a lion. καὶ ἔδωκεν αὐτῷ ὁ δράκων τὴν δύναμιν αὐτοῦ And the dragon gave to him his power καὶ τὸν θρόνον αὐτοῦ καὶ ἐξουσίαν μεγάλην. and his throne and great authority.	2 And the beast which I saw was like a leopard and his feet like a bear's and his mouth like the mouth of a lion. The beast combines in one figure the four beasts of Daniel 2, 7, 8, and 11: leopard, bear, lion, and hideous beast. And the dragon/Satan gave to him his power and his throne and great authority.	2 And the beast which I saw was like a leopard and his feet like a bear's and his mouth like the mouth of a lion (cf. Daniel 2, 7, 8, 11 and its four kingdoms/beast now combined into one). And the dragon/Satan gave to him (the Pope/beast/Antichrist) his power and his throne and great authority.	2 And the beast which I saw was like a leopard and his feet like a bear's and his mouth like the mouth of a lion. The beast/Antichrist combines into one the four kingdoms/beasts of Daniel 2, 7, 8, 11 (leopard, bear, lion, hideous beast). He is the little horn of Daniel 7:8, 11, 25–26; 9:24–27; 11:36–45. And the dragon gave to him his power and his throne and great authority.	2 And the beast which I saw was like a leopard and his feet like a bear's and his mouth like the mouth of a lion. And the dragon gave to him his power and his throne and great authority. The beast is a monster of horror rising from the sea, an emblem of the influence of the world insofar as it is opposed to God. The beast, a composite of animals that symbolize four kingdoms in Daniel 2, 7, 8, and 11, represents the spirit of the world that opposes God and persecutes the church. The ten horns symbolize the universal influence of evil, and the seven heads represent its "perfection" of depravity.

13:3 καὶ μίαν ἐκ τῶν κεφαλῶν αὐτοῦ ὡς ἐσφαγμένην εἰς θάνατον, And [I saw] one of his heads as having been slain unto death, καὶ ἡ πληγὴ τοῦ θανάτου αὐτοῦ ἐθεραπεύθη. and the stroke of his death was healed. Καὶ ἐθαυμάσθη ὅλη ἡ γῆ ὀπίσω τοῦ θηρίου And the whole earth was amazed after the beast,	3 And I saw one of his heads as having been slain unto death, and the stroke of his death was healed. This is the Nero Redivivus legend; that is, the belief arose that Nero (who reigned from A.D. 54 until he committed suicide in 68) was expected to rise from the dead and lead the Parthian army from the east to fight Rome. Emperor Domitian (A.D. 81–96) was thought to be Nero revived, demanding like Nero to be worshipped. And the whole earth was amazed after the beast,	3 And I saw one of his heads as having been slain unto death (the deadly wound when Julian the Apostate, the last heathen Roman emperor, died on the battle-field; after him came the decree of Theodosius, which brought an end to the tolerance of pagan ritual religion in the Roman Empire), and the stroke of his death was healed (the revival of pagan practices in the church through the influence of the papacy during the days of King Charlemagne). And the whole earth was amazed after the beast,	3 And I saw one of his heads as having been literally slain unto death, and the stroke of his death was healed when Satan will raise the Antichrist from the dead; this will be in parody of Christ's death and resurrection. And the whole earth was amazed after the beast,	3 And I saw one of his heads as having been slain unto death, and the stroke of his death was healed, symbolic of the resiliency of evil to keep bouncing back from apparent defeat to oppose the kingdom of God. And the whole earth was amazed after the beast,
13:4 καὶ προσεκύνησαν τῷ δράκοντι, and they worshipped the dragon, ὅτι ἔδωκεν τὴν ἐξουσίαν τῷ θηρίῳ, because he gave authority to the beast, καὶ προσεκύνησαν τῷ θηρίῳ λέγοντες· and they worshipped the beast saying, τίς ὅμοιος τῷ θηρίῳ καὶ τίς δύναται πολεμῆσαι μετ᾽ αὐτοῦ; "Who is like the beast, and who has power to make war with him?"	4 and they worshipped the dragon/Satan, because he gave authority to the beast, and they worshipped the beast (Domitian, Nero revived), saying, "Who is like the beast, and who has power to make war with him?"	4 and they worshipped the dragon, because he gave authority to the beast, and they worshipped the beast, saying, "Who is like the beast, and who has power to make war with him?"	4 and they gave worship to the dragon, because he gave authority to the beast, and they worshipped the beast, saying, "Who is like the beast, and who has power to make war with him?"	4 and they gave worship to the dragon (Satan), because he gave authority to the beast, and they worshipped the beast, saying, "Who is like the beast, and who has power to make war with him?"
13:5 Καὶ ἐδόθη αὐτῷ στόμα λαλοῦν μεγάλα καὶ βλασφημίας And there was given to him a mouth speaking great blasphemies,	5 And there was given to him a mouth speaking great blasphemies, and there was given to	5 And there was given to him a mouth speaking great blasphemies, claiming to be the vicar	5 And there was given to him a mouth speaking great blasphemies, and there was given to him	5 And there was given to him a mouth speaking great blasphemies, and there was given to him

REVELATION

Greek Text and English Translation	Preterist View	Historicist View	Futurist View	Idealist View
καὶ ἐδόθη αὐτῷ ἐξουσία and there was given to him authority ποιῆσαι μῆνας τεσσεράκοντα [καὶ] δύο. to make [war] forty-two months.	him authority to make war forty-two months, the time Nero persecuted the Christians in Rome (A.D. 64–68).	of Christ, God on earth, and there was given to him authority to make war forty-two months. (The 1,260 years from the beginning of the papacy [A.D. 533, the year when the Eastern emperor Justinian elevated the bishop of Rome to be head of the church, which emerged as full-blown Roman Catholicism under Pope Boniface III] to the French Revolution [1793], at which time the bowl judgments [Rev. 15–18] fell on the papacy [Rev. 16]. During these years, Rome killed untold numbers of true Christians, the nonconformists, the Vaudois, Lollards, Hussites, German Protestants, Anglican Protestants, and Huguenots.)	authority to make war forty-two months. The Antichrist will break his peace treaty with Israel midway through the Tribulation period (see Dan. 9:24–27) and will unleash three and a half years of Great Tribulation on the saints of God.	authority to make war forty-two months. This is the same time as the Holy City is trampled (cf. Rev. 11:2), that the two witnesses preach (cf. Rev. 11:3), and that the woman is sustained by God in the wilderness (cf. Rev. 12:6, 14), which is symbolic of the period between the first and second comings of Christ.
13:6 καὶ ἤνοιξεν τὸ στόμα αὐτοῦ εἰς βλασφημίας πρὸς τὸν θεὸν And his mouth opened unto blasphemies against God βλασφημῆσαι τὸ ὄνομα αὐτοῦ καὶ τὴν σκηνὴν αὐτοῦ, to blaspheme his name and his dwelling,	6 And his mouth opened unto blasphemies against God to blaspheme his name and his dwelling, those who are dwelling in the heavens.	6 And his mouth opened unto blasphemies against God to blaspheme his name and his dwelling, those who are dwelling in the heavens.	6 And his mouth opened unto blasphemies against God to blaspheme his name and his dwelling—the rebuilt temple in Jerusalem (this will be the act of abomination predicted in Dan. 9; Matt. 24;	6 And his mouth opened unto blasphemies against God to blaspheme his name and his dwelling, those who are dwelling in the heavens.

τοὺς ἐν τῷ οὐρανῷ σκηνοῦντας. *those who are dwelling in the heavens.*			Mark 13) — those who are dwelling in the heavens.	
13:7 καὶ ἐδόθη αὐτῷ ποιῆσαι πόλεμον *And there was given to him [authority] to make war* μετὰ τῶν ἁγίων καὶ νικῆσαι αὐτούς, *with the saints and to overcome them,* καὶ ἐδόθη αὐτῷ ἐξουσία ἐπὶ πᾶσαν φυλὴν *and there was given to him authority over every tribe* καὶ λαὸν καὶ γλῶσσαν καὶ ἔθνος. *and people and tongue and nation.*	7 And there was given to him authority to make war with the saints and to overcome them, there was given to him authority over every tribe and people and nation.	7 And there was given to him authority to make war with the saints and to overcome them, and there was given to him authority over every tribe and people and nation.	7 And there was given to him authority to make war with the saints and to overcome them, and there was given to him authority over every tribe and people and nation.	7 And there was given to him authority to make war with the saints and to overcome them, and there was given to him authority over every tribe and people and nation.
13:8 καὶ προσκυνήσουσιν αὐτὸν *And they worshipped him* πάντες οἱ κατοικοῦντες ἐπὶ τῆς γῆς, *all the inhabitants upon the earth,* οὗ οὐ γέγραπται τὸ ὄνομα αὐτοῦ *whose names have not been written* ἐν τῷ βιβλίῳ τῆς ζωῆς τοῦ ἀρνίου *in the book of life of the Lamb* τοῦ ἐσφαγμένου ἀπὸ καταβολῆς κόσμου. *having been slain from the foundation of the world.*	8 And they worshipped him, all the inhabitants upon the earth whose names have not been written in the book of life of the Lamb having been slain from the foundation of the world.	8 And they worshipped him, all the inhabitants upon the earth whose names have not been written in the book of life of the Lamb having been slain from the foundation of the world.	8 And they worshipped him, all the inhabitants upon the earth whose names have not been written in the book of life of the Lamb having been slain from the foundation of the world.	8 And they worshipped him, all the inhabitants upon the earth whose names have not been written in the book of life of the Lamb having been slain from the foundation of the world.
13:9 Εἴ τις ἔχει οὖς ἀκουσάτω. *If anyone has ears let him hear!*	9 If anyone has ears, let him hear!	9 If anyone has ears, let him hear!	9 If anyone has ears, let him hear!	9 If anyone has ears, let him hear!
13:10 εἴ τις εἰς αἰχμαλωσίαν, εἰς αἰχμαλωσίαν ὑπάγει· *If anyone [is to go] unto captivity, unto captivity let him go!* εἴ τις ἐν μαχαίρῃ ἀποκτανθῆναι αὐτὸν *If anyone is to die by the sword,*	10 If anyone is to go out unto captivity, unto captivity let him go! If anyone is to die by the sword, by the sword let him be killed! Here is	10 If anyone is to go unto captivity, unto captivity let him go! If anyone is to die by the sword, by the sword let him be killed! Thus a number of popes were in turn captured	10 If anyone is to go unto captivity, unto captivity let him go! If anyone is to die by the sword, by the sword let him be killed! Here is the perseverance and the faith of the saints.	10 If anyone is unto captivity, unto captivity let him go! If anyone is to die by the sword, by the sword let him be killed; that is, let them endure the attacks of evil

Greek Text and English Translation	Preterist View	Historicist View	Futurist View	Idealist View
ἐν μαχαίρῃ ἀποκτανθῆναι. by the sword let him be killed! ˚Ὧδέ ἐστιν ἡ ὑπομονὴ καὶ ἡ πίστις τῶν ἁγίων. Here is the perseverance and the faith of the saints.	the perseverance and the faith of the saints.	and killed. Thus, for example, Napoleon deposed the pope in 1798. Here is the perseverance and the faith of the saints.		against their souls! Here is the perseverance and the faith of the saints.
13:11 Καὶ εἶδον ἄλλο θηρίον ἀναβαῖνον ἐκ τῆς γῆς, And I saw another beast arising out of the earth, καὶ εἶχεν κέρατα δύο ὅμοια ἀρνίῳ and he was having two horns like a lamb καὶ ἐλάλει ὡς δράκων. and he was speaking like a dragon.	11 And I saw another beast arising out of the earth, and he was having like a lamb, and he was speaking like a dragon. This is the imperial priesthood in Asia Minor, which enforced the worship of Caesar, thus reinforcing the work of the Roman proconsul. The imperial priest is the false prophet who garners worship for Caesar, the Antichrist. The two horns show that the Antichrist and the false prophet are in union. The symbol of the lamb is a parody of Christ, the Lion-Lamb that was slain and resurrected (recall Rev. 5).	11 And I saw another beast arising out of the earth (the papacy in its ecclesiastical power through its priesthood), and he was having two horns like a lamb (bishops since Pope Gregory [590] wore a pallium of lamb's wool, and abbots wore a miter with two points and were known as the Goruti ["the horned ones"]; all of this in an evil parody of Christ the slain Lamb of Rev. 5), and he was speaking like a dragon (Satan).	11 And I saw another beast arising out of the earth (the Jewish false prophet of the Antichrist's apostate religion), and he was having two horns like a lamb (in imitation of Christ, the Lamb that was slain; cf. Rev. 5), and he was speaking like a dragon. So the false prophet will be the Antichrist's minister of propaganda.	11 And I saw another beast arising out of the earth (the symbol of false religion and false philosophy perpetrated by the false prophet), and he was having two horns like a lamb, and he was speaking like a dragon (the second beast resembles the Lamb but is really an agent of the dragon).
13:12 καὶ τὴν ἐξουσίαν τοῦ πρώτου θηρίου πᾶσαν And all the authority of the first beast, ποιεῖ ἐνώπιον αὐτοῦ, καὶ ποιεῖ τὴν γῆν he does before it, and he makes the earth	12 And he does all the authority of the first beast before it, and he makes the earth and those dwelling in it that they worship the first	12 And he does all the authority of the first beast before it, and he makes the earth and those dwelling in it that they worship the first	12 And he does all the authority of the first beast before it, and he makes the earth and those dwelling in it that they worship the first	12 And he does all the authority of the first beast before it, and he makes the earth and those dwelling in it that they worship the first beast, whose stroke of death

καὶ τοὺς ἐν αὐτῇ κατοικοῦντας and all those dwelling in it ἵνα προσκυνήσουσιν τὸ θηρίον τὸ πρῶτον, that they worship the first beast, οὗ ἐθεραπεύθη ἡ πληγὴ τοῦ θανάτου αὐτοῦ. of which his stroke of death was healed.	beast, whose stroke of death was healed.	beast, whose stroke of death was healed.	beast, whose stroke of death was healed.	was healed. The beast of the sea and the beast of the earth work hand in hand. This is the spirit of the world as found in anti-Christian government conspiring with anti-Christian religion and attacking Christ and his church. The work of these cohorts was obvious in the crucifixion of Jesus Christ, where the Sanhedrin partnered with Pilate to murder the Messiah. Their attacks continue throughout this dispensation.
13:13 καὶ ποιεῖ σημεῖα μεγάλα, And he does great signs, ἵνα καὶ πῦρ ποιῇ ἐκ τοῦ οὐρανοῦ in order also to make fire out of heaven καταβαίνειν εἰς τὴν γῆν ἐνώπιον τῶν ἀνθρώπων, to fall unto the earth before men,	13 And he does great signs, in order also to make fire out of heaven fall unto the earth before men,	13 And he does great signs, in order also to make fire out of heaven fall unto the earth before men,	13 And he does great signs, in order also to make fire out of heaven fall unto the earth before men,	13 And he does great signs, in order also to make fire out of heaven fall unto the earth before men,
13:14 καὶ πλανᾷ τοὺς κατοικοῦντας ἐπὶ τῆς γῆς and he deceives those dwelling upon the earth διὰ τὰ σημεῖα ἃ ἐδόθη αὐτῷ ποιῆσαι ἐνώπιον τοῦ θηρίου, through the signs which were given to him to do before the beast, λέγων τοῖς κατοικοῦσιν ἐπὶ τῆς γῆς saying to the inhabitants upon the earth ποιῆσαι εἰκόνα τῷ θηρίῳ, to make the image of the beast,	14 and he deceives those dwelling upon the earth through the signs which were given to him to do before the beast, saying to the inhabitants upon the earth to make the image of the beast, which has the stroke of the sword and lived.	14 and he is deceiving those dwelling upon the earth through the signs which were given to him to do before the beast, saying to the inhabitants upon the earth to make the image of the beast, which has the stroke of the sword and lived.	14 and he is deceiving those dwelling upon the earth through the signs which were given to him to do before the beast, saying to the inhabitants upon the earth to make the image of the beast (which will be a large statue of the Antichrist, like Nebuchadnezzar made of himself in Dan.	14 and he is deceiving those dwelling upon the earth through the signs which were given to him to do before the beast, saying to the inhabitants upon the earth to make the image of the beast, which has the stroke of the sword and lived.

Greek Text and English Translation	Preterist View	Historicist View	Futurist View	Idealist View
ὃς ἔχει τὴν πληγὴν τῆς μαχαίρης καὶ ἔζησεν. which has the stroke of the sword and he lived.			2), which has the stroke of the sword and lived.	
13:15 Καὶ ἐδόθη αὐτῷ δοῦναι πνεῦμα τῇ εἰκόνι τοῦ θηρίου, And it was granted to him to give the spirit of the image of the beast,	15 And it was granted to him to give the spirit of the image of the beast, in order that the image of the beast also might speak and might make as many as do not worship the image of the beast to be killed. Thus by manipulating miracles and overt force, the false prophet garners worship for the beast.	15 And it was granted to him to give the spirit of the image of the beast, in order that the image of the beast also might speak and might make as many as do not worship the image of the beast to be killed. Thus the Catholic Church, by manipulative miracles (images coming down and lighting candles; idols [supposedly] sweating, turning their eyes, moving their hands, opening their mouths, healing sicknesses, raising the dead; crucifixes speaking; stigmata of Christ appearing on hands and feet of people; Mary appearing to many; all of these), plus overt force, was inspired by the power of Satan to make the world worship the beast/pope.	15 And there was given to him to give the spirit of the image of the beast, in order that the image of the beast also might speak and might make as many as do not worship the image of the beast to be killed.	15 And there was given to him to give the spirit of the image of the beast, in order that the image of the beast also might speak and might make as many as do not worship the image of the beast to be killed. The beast's power can be either by tricks (ventriloquism) performed by chicanery or by occult power. An image reflects the reality behind it, thus mixing the two for the beholder. The image is the loss of the separation of church and state—the one becoming the glove, the other the hand. And together, state (hand) and religion (glove) deal a knock-out punch to righteousness.
ἵνα καὶ λαλήσῃ ἡ εἰκὼν τοῦ θηρίου in order that the image of the beast also might speak				
καὶ ποιήσῃ [ἵνα] ὅσοι ἐὰν μὴ προσκυνήσωσιν and might make as many as do not worship				
τῇ εἰκόνι τοῦ θηρίου ἀποκτανθῶσιν. the image of the beast to be killed.				
13:16 καὶ ποιεῖ πάντας, τοὺς μικροὺς καὶ τοὺς μεγάλους, And he makes all, the little and the great,	16 And he makes all, the little and the great, and the rich and the poor, and the free and	16 And he makes all, the little and the great, and the rich and the poor, and the free and the slaves, to	16 And he makes all, the little and the great, and the rich and the poor, and the free and the slaves, to	16 And he makes all, the little and the great, and the rich and the poor, and the free and the slaves, to

καὶ τοὺς πλουσίους καὶ τοὺς πτωχούς, καὶ τοὺς ἐλευθέρους καὶ τοὺς δούλους, and the rich and the poor, and the free and the slaves, ἵνα δῶσιν αὐτοῖς χάραγμα to be given to them a mark ἐπὶ τῆς χειρὸς αὐτῶν τῆς δεξιᾶς ἢ ἐπὶ τὸ μέτωπον αὐτῶν upon their right hand or upon their forehead.	the slaves, to be given to them a mark upon their right hand or upon their forehead. This is the imperial seal showing that a person had worshipped Caesar/Antichrist by offering wine and incense to his statue.	be given to them a mark upon their right hand or upon their forehead. This is the Latinizing of the world by Roman Catholicism: the Mass, prayers, hymns, litanies, canons, decretals, bulls, councils, even Scripture (the Latin Vulgate).	be given to them a mark upon their right hand or upon their forehead. This will be some type of literal mark, like a computer chip, credit card, or laser tattoo, without which people in the Tribulation period cannot buy or sell anything in a cashless society.	be given to them a mark upon their right hand or upon their forehead.
13:17 καὶ ἵνα μή τις δύνηται ἀγοράσαι ἢ πωλῆσαι And in order that no one might have the power to buy or to sell εἰ μὴ ὁ ἔχων τὸ χάραγμα τὸ ὄνομα τοῦ θηρίου unless he is one having the mark of the name of the beast ἢ τὸν ἀριθμὸν τοῦ ὀνόματος αὐτοῦ. or the number of his name.	17 And in order that no one might have the power to buy or to sell unless he is one having the mark of the name of the beast or the number of his name.	17 And in order that no one might have the power to buy or to sell unless he is one having the mark of the name of the beast or the number of his name. Thus popes have often forbidden commercial transactions with "heretics" or Protestants (e.g., Pope Alexander III at the Third Lateran Council in 1178).	17 And in order that no one might have the power to buy or to sell unless he is one having the mark of the name of the beast or the number of his name.	17 And in order that no one might have the power to buy or to sell unless he is one having the mark of the beast or the number of his name.
13:18 Ὧδε ἡ σοφία ἐστίν. ὁ ἔχων νοῦν ψηφισάτω Here is wisdom: the one having reason let him count τὸν ἀριθμὸν τοῦ θηρίου, ἀριθμὸς γὰρ ἀνθρώπου ἐστίν, the number of the beast, for the number [is] of man, καὶ ὁ ἀριθμὸς αὐτοῦ ἑξακόσιοι ἑξήκοντα ἕξ. and his number [is] 666!	18 Here is wisdom: the one having reason let him count the number of the beast, for the number is of man, and his number is 666! This is gematria; a mathematical cryptogram that assigns a numerical value to the letters of a name, in this case for the Hebrew consonants forming the name Neron Kaiser, NRWN QSR: N = 50, R = 200, W = 6,	18 Here is wisdom: the one having reason, let him count the number of the beast, for the number of man, and his number is 666! This is the pope's official Latin title: Vicarius filii Dei ("Vicar of the Son of God"), the value of which in terms of the Roman numerals it contains is V = 5, I = 1, C = 100, L = 60, D = 500.	18 Here is wisdom: the one having reason, let him count the number of the beast, for the number is of man, and his number is 666! This is perpetually the number of man (never able to approach the number of God = 7). Thus no matter how hard he tries, the Antichrist will never ever be able to supplant the true God. The Antichrist will relocate	18 Here is wisdom: the one having reason, let him count the number of the beast, for the number is of man, and his number is 666! The mark is the epitome of human endeavor to usurp the throne of God ("666" is contrasted to "7," the number for God in Revelation and thus the symbol of perfection). A mark on the forehead symbolizes

Greek Text and English Translation	Preterist View	Historicist View	Futurist View	Idealist View
	N = 50, Q = 100, S = 60, R = 200, totaling 666!		the headquarters of the European Union in literal, rebuilt Babylon and will attempt to rule the world from there (see Rev. 17–18).	the individual's mind, thought, and philosophy of life. A mark on the right hand indicates action, deeds, and enterprise. Those who receive the mark of the beast, then, belong to the army of those who persecute the church with mind and action.
14:1 Καὶ εἶδον, καὶ ἰδοὺ τὸ ἀρνίον ἑστὸς ἐπὶ τὸ ὄρος Σιὼν And I looked, and behold the Lamb standing upon Mount Zion καὶ μετ᾽ αὐτοῦ ἑκατὸν τεσσεράκοντα τέσσαρες χιλιάδες and with him the 144,000 ἔχουσαι τὸ ὄνομα αὐτοῦ καὶ τὸ ὄνομα τοῦ πατρὸς αὐτοῦ having his name and the name of his Father γεγραμμένον ἐπὶ τῶν μετώπων αὐτῶν. having been written upon their foreheads.	1 And I looked, and behold, the Lamb was standing upon Mount Zion and with him the 144,000 having his name and the name of his Father having been written upon their foreheads. These are the 144,000 Jewish Christians who were preserved from the fall of Jerusalem to the Romans, but now they are ready to descend on Christ's enemies.	1 And I looked, and behold, the Lamb was standing upon Mount Zion (the true church on earth; cf. Heb. 12:22) and with him the 144,000 (the faithful church during the age of the beast) having his name and the name of his Father having been written upon their foreheads, which signifies God's preservation of the people of God from false doctrine.	1 This vision is proleptic: it anticipates the bowl judgments (Rev. 15–16), the fall of Babylon (Rev. 17–18), and the return of Christ, at the end of history (Rev. 19). And I looked, and behold, the Lamb was standing upon Mount Zion (Jerusalem, the site of Jesus' return to earth at the end of the Great Tribulation to establish his kingdom in Israel) and with him the 144,000 having his name and the name of his Father having been written upon their foreheads. These are the 144,000 Jewish Christian evangelists who will be protected by God during the Tribulation period	1 This vision is that of the second coming of Christ, at the end of history. And I looked, and behold, the Lamb was standing upon Mount Zion (heaven, from whence Christ will return to earth to establish the eternal state) and with him the 144,000 (the true church throughout the church age) having his name and the name of his Father having been written upon their foreheads. These are protected spiritually even though they are killed for the sake of the gospel.

14:2 καὶ ἤκουσα φωνὴν ἐκ τοῦ οὐρανοῦ And I heard a voice out of heaven ὡς φωνὴν ὑδάτων πολλῶν καὶ ὡς φωνὴν βροντῆς μεγάλης, as a sound of many waters and as a sound of great thunder, καὶ ἡ φωνὴ ἣν ἤκουσα ὡς κιθαρῳδῶν and the voice which I heard [was] as of harpers κιθαριζόντων ἐν ταῖς κιθάραις αὐτῶν. harping upon their harps.	2 And I heard a voice out of heaven as a sound of many waters and as a sound of great thunder, and the voice which I heard was as of harpers harping upon their harps.	*(cf. Rev. 7:1–8) and then will meet Christ at his second coming to form his holy warriors against the Antichrist.* 2 And I heard a voice out of heaven as a sound of many waters and as a sound of great thunder, and the voice which I heard was as of harpers harping upon their harps.	2 And I heard a voice out of heaven as a sound of many waters and as a sound of great thunder, and the voice which I heard was as of harpers harping upon their harps.
14:3 καὶ ᾄδουσιν [ὡς] ᾠδὴν καινὴν And they sang like a new song ἐνώπιον τοῦ θρόνου καὶ ἐνώπιον τῶν τεσσάρων ζῴων before the throne and before the four living creatures καὶ τῶν πρεσβυτέρων, καὶ οὐδεὶς ἐδύνατο μαθεῖν τὴν ᾠδὴν and before the [twenty-four] elders, and no one was able to learn the song εἰ μὴ αἱ ἑκατὸν τεσσεράκοντα τέσσαρες χιλιάδες, except the 144,000, οἱ ἠγορασμένοι ἀπὸ τῆς γῆς. the ones having been redeemed from the earth.	3 And they sang like a new song before the throne and before the four living creatures and before the twenty-four elders, and no one was able to learn the song except the 144,000, the ones having been redeemed from the earth.	3 And they sang like a new song (the blessed truth of the Reformation message that justification is by faith apart from works) before the throne and before the four living creatures and before the twenty-four elders, and no one was able to learn the song except the 144,000, the ones having been redeemed from the earth.	3 And they sang like a new song (the song of the new exodus of deliverance [cf. Exod. 15]) before the throne and before the four living creatures and before the twenty-four elders, and no one was able to learn the song except the 144,000, the ones having been redeemed from the earth.

Greek Text and English Translation	Preterist View	Historicist View	Futurist View	Idealist View
14:4 οὗτοί εἰσιν οἱ μετὰ γυναικῶν οὐκ ἐμολύνθησαν, These are they who were not defiled with women, παρθένοι γάρ εἰσιν, οὗτοι οἱ ἀκολουθοῦντες for they are virgins, these are the ones following τῷ ἀρνίῳ ὅπου ἂν ὑπάγῃ. the Lamb wherever he may go. οὗτοι ἠγοράσθησαν ἀπὸ τῶν ἀνθρώπων These were redeemed from men, ἀπαρχὴ τῷ θεῷ καὶ τῷ ἀρνίῳ, firstfruits to God and to the Lamb,	4 These are they who were not defiled with women, for they are virgins (because they are holy warriors set apart for battle and who have not been polluted by Caesar worship); these are the ones following the Lamb wherever he may go. These were redeemed from men, firstfruits (Gentile Christians constituted the main harvest) to God and to the Lamb,	4 These are they who were not defiled with women, for they are virgins (in terms of spiritual purity, not in the sense of the so-called "sacrament of celibacy" practiced by Roman Catholicism); these are the ones following the Lamb wherever he may go. These were redeemed from men, firstfruits to God and to the Lamb (thus the 144,000 is representative of the whole of the redeemed),	4 These are they who were not defiled with women, for they are virgins (figurative for the spiritual purity of the 144,000 in the face of the onslaught of the evil trinity—Satan, beast/Antichrist, false prophet); these are the ones following the Lamb wherever he may go (the multitude of Gentiles who the 144,000 will win to Christ during the Tribulation; cf. Rev. 7:9–17). These were redeemed from men, firstfruits to God and to the Lamb,	4 These are they who were not defiled with women, for they are virgins; these are the ones following the Lamb wherever he may go. This is the true, pure church (cf. Rev. 21–22). These were redeemed from men, firstfruits to God and to the Lamb,
14:5 καὶ ἐν τῷ στόματι αὐτῶν οὐχ εὑρέθη ψεῦδος, ἄμωμοί εἰσιν. and in their mouths there was not found a lie; they are blameless.	5 and in their mouths there was not found a lie; they are blameless.	5 and in their mouths there was not found a lie; they are blameless.	5 and in their mouths there was not found a lie; they are blameless.	5 and in their mouths there was not found a lie; they are blameless.
14:6 Καὶ εἶδον ἄλλον ἄγγελον πετόμενον ἐν μεσουρανήματι, And I saw another angel flying in the midheaven, ἔχοντα εὐαγγέλιον αἰώνιον εὐαγγελίσαι having the eternal gospel to announce ἐπὶ τοὺς καθημένους ἐπὶ τῆς γῆς upon the ones residing upon the earth	6 And I saw another angel flying in the midheaven, having the eternal gospel to announce upon the ones residing upon the earth and upon every nation and tribe and tongue and people,	6 And I saw another angel flying in the midheaven, having the eternal gospel to announce upon the ones residing upon the earth and upon every nation and tribe and tongue and people (this occurred during the missionary era and the Great Awakening in the time of	6 And I saw another angel flying in the midheaven, having the eternal gospel to announce upon the ones residing upon the earth and upon every nation and tribe and tongue and people,	6 And I saw another angel flying in the midheaven, having the eternal gospel (the gospel of Christ to be preached by the church until the return of Christ; cf. Matt. 24:14; Mark 13:10) to announce upon the ones residing upon the earth and upon

Idealist	Futurist	Historicist	Preterist	Greek / Literal
every nation and tribe and tongue and people,		the Wesleys, Whitefield, Edwards, and Finney),		καὶ ἐπὶ πᾶν ἔθνος καὶ φυλὴν καὶ γλῶσσαν καὶ λαόν, and upon every nation and tribe and tongue and people,
7 saying in a great voice, "Fear God and give to him glory, because the hour of his judgment has come, and worship the one having made heaven and the earth and sea and fountain of waters!"	7 saying in a great voice, "Fear God and give to him glory, because the hour of his judgment has come, and worship the one having made heaven and the earth and sea and fountain of waters!" This eternal gospel of faith in Christ was received by the 144,000 and the Gentile multitudes they evangelized but was rejected by the followers of the beast.	7 saying in a great voice, "Fear God and give to him glory, because the hour of his judgment has come, and worship the one having made heaven and the earth and sea and fountain of waters!" This was the great preaching in England and America that was taking place just prior to God's judgment upon Catholicism on the Continent through the French Revolution.	7 saying in a great voice, "Fear God and give to him glory, because the hour of his judgment has come, and worship the one having made heaven and the earth and sea and fountain of waters!"	14:7 λέγων ἐν φωνῇ μεγάλῃ· saying in a great voice, φοβήθητε τὸν θεὸν καὶ δότε αὐτῷ δόξαν, "Fear God and give to him glory, ὅτι ἦλθεν ἡ ὥρα τῆς κρίσεως αὐτοῦ, because the hour of his judgment has come, καὶ προσκυνήσατε τῷ ποιήσαντι τὸν οὐρανὸν καὶ τὴν γῆν and worship the one having made heaven and the earth καὶ θάλασσαν καὶ πηγὰς ὑδάτων. and sea and fountain of waters!"
8 And another angel, a second one, followed, saying, "Fallen, fallen has Babylon the great (the pagan anti-Christian world and the apostate church), which has made every nation to drink out of the wine of wrath of her immorality."	8 And another angel, a second one, followed, saying, "Fallen, fallen has Babylon the great (literal Babylon to be rebuilt by the Antichrist during the Tribulation period; cf. Rev. 17–18), which has made every nation to drink out of the wine of wrath of her immorality."	8 And another angel, a second one, followed, saying, "Fallen, fallen has Babylon the great (papal Rome; cf. Rev. 16–18), which has made every nation to drink out of the wine of wrath of her immorality."	8 And another angel, a second one, followed, saying, "Fallen, fallen has Babylon (Jerusalem) the great, which has made every nation to drink out of the wine of wrath of her immorality"	14:8 Καὶ ἄλλος ἄγγελος δεύτερος ἠκολούθησεν λέγων· And another angel, a second one, followed, saying, ἔπεσεν ἔπεσεν Βαβυλὼν ἡ μεγάλη "Fallen, fallen has Babylon the great, ἡ ἐκ τοῦ οἴνου τοῦ θυμοῦ τῆς πορνείας αὐτῆς which out of the wine of wrath of her immorality πεπότικεν πάντα τὰ ἔθνη. has made every nation to drink."
9 And another angel, a third, followed them, saying in a great voice, "If anyone worships the beast and his image and receives the mark	9 And another angel, a third, followed them, saying in a great voice, "If anyone worships the beast and his image and receives the mark	9 And another angel, a third, followed them, saying in a great voice, "If anyone worships the beast and his image and receives the mark upon	9 And another angel, a third, followed them, saying in a great voice, "If anyone worships the beast and his image and receives the mark	14:9 Καὶ ἄλλος ἄγγελος τρίτος ἠκολούθησεν αὐτοῖς And another angel, a third, followed them, λέγων ἐν φωνῇ μεγάλῃ· saying in a great voice,

Greek Text and English Translation	Preterist View	Historicist View	Futurist View	Idealist View
εἴ τις προσκυνεῖ τὸ θηρίον καὶ τὴν εἰκόνα αὐτοῦ "If anyone worships the beast and his image	upon his forehead or upon his hand (which Jews did by praying for Caesar and expelling Jewish Christians from their synagogues, thus exposing them to the imperial cult; indeed, the Jewish phylacteries/tephillim [leather boxes with OT Scripture placed on their foreheads and forearms] have become but the mark of the beast on Jews),	his forehead or upon his hand (that is, accepts the pope as "Vicar of the Son of God"),	upon his forehead or upon his hand,	upon his forehead or upon his hand,
καὶ λαμβάνει χάραγμα and receives the mark				
ἐπὶ τοῦ μετώπου αὐτοῦ ἢ ἐπὶ τὴν χεῖρα αὐτοῦ, upon his forehead or upon his hand,				
14:10 καὶ αὐτὸς πίεται ἐκ τοῦ οἴνου τοῦ θυμοῦ τοῦ θεοῦ even he will drink out of the wine of the wrath of God,	10 even he will drink out of the wine of the wrath of God, having been mixed undiluted in the cup of his wrath (the curses of the covenant on disobedient Israel), and he will be tormented by fire and sulfur before the holy angels and before the Lamb.	10 even he will drink out of the wine of the wrath of God, having been mixed undiluted in the cup of his wrath, and he will be tormented by fire and sulfur before the holy angels and before the Lamb.	10 even he will drink out of the wine of the wrath of God, having been mixed undiluted in the cup of his wrath, and he will be tormented by fire and sulfur before the holy angels and before the Lamb.	10 even he will drink out of the wine of the wrath of God, having been mixed undiluted in the cup of his wrath, and he will be tormented by fire and sulfur before the holy angels and before the Lamb.
τοῦ κεκερασμένου ἀκράτου ἐν τῷ ποτηρίῳ τῆς ὀργῆς αὐτοῦ having been mixed undiluted in the cup of his wrath,				
καὶ βασανισθήσεται ἐν πυρὶ καὶ θείῳ and he will be tormented by fire and sulfur				
ἐνώπιον ἀγγέλων ἁγίων καὶ ἐνώπιον τοῦ ἀρνίου. before the holy angels and before the Lamb.				
14:11 καὶ ὁ καπνὸς τοῦ βασανισμοῦ αὐτῶν εἰς αἰῶνας αἰώνων ἀναβαίνει, And the smoke of their torment forever rises,	11 And the smoke of their torment forever rises, and they do not have rest day and night,	11 And the smoke of their torment forever rises, and they do not have rest day and night,	11 And the smoke of their torment forever rises (which testifies to the eternality of hell,	11 And the smoke of their torment forever rises, and they do not have rest day and night,

καὶ οὐκ ἔχουσιν ἀνάπαυσιν ἡμέρας καὶ νυκτός and they do not have rest day and night,			refuting the annihilation theory), and they do not have rest day and night,	
οἱ προσκυνοῦντες τὸ θηρίον καὶ τὴν εἰκόνα αὐτοῦ the ones who worship the beast and his image	the ones who worship the beast and his image—also if anyone receives the mark of his name.	the ones who worship the beast and his image—also if anyone receives the mark of his name.	the ones who worship the beast and his image—also if anyone receives the mark of his name.	the ones who worship the beast and his image—also if anyone receives the mark of his name.
καὶ εἴ τις λαμβάνει τὸ χάραγμα τοῦ ὀνόματος αὐτοῦ. and if anyone receives the mark of his name.				
14:12 Ὧδε ἡ ὑπομονὴ τῶν ἁγίων ἐστίν, Here is the perseverance of the saints,	12 Here is the perseverance of the saints, the ones who keep the commandments of God and the faith of Jesus."	12 Here is the perseverance of the saints, the ones who keep the commandments of God and the faith of Jesus."	12 Here is the perseverance of the saints, the ones who keep the commandments of God and the faith of Jesus."	12 Here is the perseverance of the saints, the ones who keep the commandments of God and the faith of Jesus" (an apt description of all Christians who are killed for their faithfulness to the gospel throughout the church age; thus, the church both reigns in God's kingdom but also suffers the Great Tribulation, from the first to the second comings of Christ).
οἱ τηροῦντες τὰς ἐντολὰς τοῦ θεοῦ καὶ τὴν πίστιν Ἰησοῦ. the ones who keep the commandments of God and the faith of Jesus.				
14:13 Καὶ ἤκουσα φωνῆς ἐκ τοῦ οὐρανοῦ λεγούσης· And I heard a voice out of heaven saying,	13 And I heard a voice out of heaven saying, "Write: Blessed are the dead, the ones who die in the Lord from now on." Indeed, the Spirit says, "In order that they may rest from their labors, for their works follow after them."	13 And I heard a voice out of heaven saying, "Write: Blessed are the dead, the ones who die in the Lord from now on." Indeed, the Spirit says, "In order that they may rest from their labors, for their works follow after them" (though those works are based on God's saving grace and not on the legalism of the Catholic Church).	13 And I heard a voice out of heaven saying, "Write: Blessed are the dead, the ones who die in the Lord from now on." Indeed, the Spirit says, "In order that they may rest from their labors, for their works follow after them." These are those Gentile multitudes that will die during the Tribulation precisely	13 And I heard a voice out of heaven saying, "Write: Blessed are the dead, the ones who die in the Lord from now on." Indeed, the Spirit says, "In order that they may rest from their labors, for their works follow after them," works that are the result of justification by faith and not legalism.
γράψον· μακάριοι οἱ νεκροὶ "Write: Blessed [are] the dead,				
οἱ ἐν κυρίῳ ἀποθνῄσκοντες ἀπ' ἄρτι. the ones who die in the Lord from now on."				
ναί, λέγει τὸ πνεῦμα, ἵνα ἀναπαήσονται ἐκ τῶν κόπων αὐτῶν, Indeed, the Spirit says, "In order that they may rest from their labors,				

REVELATION

Greek Text and English Translation	Preterist View	Historicist View	Futurist View	Idealist View
τὰ γὰρ ἔργα αὐτῶν ἀκολουθεῖ μετ᾽ αὐτῶν. for their works follow after them."			because they will be faithful to Christ.	
14:14 Καὶ εἶδον, καὶ ἰδοὺ νεφέλη λευκή, And I looked, and behold, a white cloud, καὶ ἐπὶ τὴν νεφέλην καθήμενον ὅμοιον υἱὸν ἀνθρώπου, and upon the cloud [I saw] one seated like the Son of Man, ἔχων ἐπὶ τῆς κεφαλῆς αὐτοῦ στέφανον χρυσοῦν having upon his head a gold crown καὶ ἐν τῇ χειρὶ αὐτοῦ δρέπανον ὀξύ. and in his hand a sharp sickle.	14 And I looked, and behold, a white cloud, and upon the cloud I saw one seated like the Son of Man, having upon his head a gold crown and in his hand a sharp sickle. This is the Parousia of Christ, who will return to judge Jerusalem (in A.D. 70; cf. Rev. 1:7).	14 And I looked, and behold, a white cloud, and upon the cloud I saw one seated like the Son of Man, having upon his head a gold crown and in his hand a sharp sickle.	14 And I looked, and behold, a white cloud, and upon the cloud I saw one seated like the Son of Man, having upon his head a gold crown and in his hand a sharp sickle.	14 And I looked, and behold, a white cloud, and upon the cloud I saw one seated like the Son of Man, having upon his head a gold crown and in his hand a sharp sickle.
14:15 καὶ ἄλλος ἄγγελος ἐξῆλθεν ἐκ τοῦ ναοῦ κράζων And another angel came out of the temple crying ἐν φωνῇ μεγάλῃ τῷ καθημένῳ ἐπὶ τῆς νεφέλης· in a great voice to the one seated upon the cloud, πέμψον τὸ δρέπανόν σου καὶ θέρισον, "Send your sickle and reap, ὅτι ἦλθεν ἡ ὥρα θερίσαι, because the hour has come to reap, ὅτι ἐξηράνθη ὁ θερισμὸς τῆς γῆς. because the harvest of the earth became ripe!"	15 And another angel came out of the temple crying in a great voice to the one seated upon the cloud, "Send your sickle and reap in judgment, because the hour has come to reap, because the harvest of the earth became ripe!"	15 And another angel came out of the temple crying in a great voice to the one seated upon the cloud, "Send your sickle and reap, because the hour has come to reap, because the harvest of the earth became ripe!"	15 And another angel came out of the temple crying in a great voice to the one seated upon the cloud, "Send your sickle and reap, because the hour has come to reap, because the harvest of the earth became ripe!"	15 And another angel came out of the temple crying in a great voice to the one seated upon the cloud, "Send your sickle and reap, because the hour has come to reap, because the harvest of the earth became ripe!"
14:16 καὶ ἔβαλεν ὁ καθήμενος ἐπὶ τῆς νεφέλης τὸ δρέπανον αὐτοῦ And the one seated upon the cloud cast his sickle	16 And the one seated upon the cloud cast his	16 And the one seated upon the cloud cast his sickle upon the earth and	16 And the one seated upon the cloud cast his	16 And the one seated upon the cloud cast his

sickle upon the earth and the earth was reaped.	sickle upon the earth and the earth was reaped.	the earth was reaped. This first harvest is the ingathering of the true church at the end of history, when Christ returns.	sickle upon the earth and the earth was reaped.
17 And another angel came out of the temple in heaven also having a sharp sickle.	17 And another angel came out of the temple in heaven also having a sharp sickle.	17 And another angel came out of the temple in heaven also having a sharp sickle.	17 And another angel came out of the temple in heaven also having a sharp sickle.
18 And another angel came out of the altar having authority over the fire, and he cried in a great voice to the one having the sharp sickle, saying, "Send your sharp sickle and gather the clusters of the vine of the earth, because its grapes have ripened!"	18 And another angel came out of the altar having authority over the fire, and he cried in a great voice to the one having the sharp sickle, saying, "Send your sharp sickle and gather the clusters of the vine of the earth, because its grapes have ripened!"	18 And another angel came out of the altar having authority over the fire, and he cried in a great voice to the one having the sharp sickle, saying, "Send your sharp sickle and gather the clusters of the vine of the earth, because its grapes have ripened!"	18 And another angel came out of the altar, having authority over the fire, and he cried in a great voice to the one having the sharp sickle, saying, "Send your sharp sickle and gather the clusters of the vine of the earth (Israel, the vineyard of the Lord; cf. Isa. 5), because its grapes have ripened!"
19 And the angel cast his sickle unto the earth and gathered the vine of the earth and cast it into the winepress of the wrath of the great God.	19 And the angel cast his sickle unto the earth and gathered the vine of the earth and cast it into the winepress of the wrath of the great God. This refers	19 And the angel cast his sickle unto the earth and gathered the vine of the earth and cast it into the winepress of the wrath of the great God.	19 And the angel cast his sickle unto the earth and gathered the vine of the earth and cast it into the winepress of the wrath of the great God.

ἐπὶ τὴν γῆν καὶ ἐθερίσθη ἡ γῆ.
upon the earth and the earth was reaped.

14:17 Καὶ ἄλλος ἄγγελος ἐξῆλθεν ἐκ τοῦ ναοῦ τοῦ ἐν τῷ οὐρανῷ
And another angel came out of the temple in heaven

ἔχων καὶ αὐτὸς δρέπανον ὀξύ.
having also a sharp sickle.

14:18 καὶ ἄλλος ἄγγελος [ἐξῆλθεν] ἐκ τοῦ θυσιαστηρίου
And another angel came out of the altar

[ὁ] ἔχων ἐξουσίαν ἐπὶ τοῦ πυρός,
having authority over the fire,

καὶ ἐφώνησεν φωνῇ μεγάλῃ
and he cried in a great voice

τῷ ἔχοντι τὸ δρέπανον τὸ ὀξὺ λέγων·
to the one having the sharp sickle, saying,

πέμψον σου τὸ δρέπανον τὸ ὀξὺ
"Send your sharp sickle

καὶ τρύγησον τοὺς βότρυας τῆς ἀμπέλου τῆς γῆς,
and gather the clusters of the vine of the earth,

ὅτι ἤκμασαν αἱ σταφυλαὶ αὐτῆς.
because its grapes have ripened!"

14:19 καὶ ἔβαλεν ὁ ἄγγελος τὸ δρέπανον αὐτοῦ εἰς τὴν γῆν
And the angel cast his sickle unto the earth

καὶ ἐτρύγησεν τὴν ἄμπελον τῆς γῆς
and gathered the vine of the earth

Greek Text and English Translation	Preterist View	Historicist View	Futurist View	Idealist View
καὶ ἔβαλεν εἰς τὴν ληνὸν τοῦ θυμοῦ τοῦ θεοῦ τὸν μέγαν. and cast it into the winepress of the wrath of the great God.		This second harvest is the judgment to come upon the papacy and all who adhere to it, from the French Revolution and the Napoleonic Wars and continuing to the end of history.	to the second coming of Christ, when he and his angels will gather the elect unto salvation but pour out judgment upon the followers of the Antichrist (cf. Matt. 24:29–44; Mark 13:24–37; Luke 21:25–33).	This scene pictures the return of Christ at the end of the age, gathering his elect unto salvation but punishing their persecutors (cf. Matt. 24:29–44; Mark 13:24–37; Luke 21:25–33).
14:20 καὶ ἐπατήθη ἡ ληνὸς ἔξωθεν τῆς πόλεως And the winepress was trodden outside the city, καὶ ἐξῆλθεν αἷμα ἐκ τῆς ληνοῦ ἄχρι and blood went out from the winepress τῶν χαλινῶν τῶν ἵππων ἀπὸ σταδίων χιλίων ἑξακοσίων. unto the bridles of the horses for a thousand six hundred stadia.	20 And the winepress was trodden outside the city, and blood went out from the winepress unto the bridles of the horses for a thousand and six hundred stadia, the length of Israel as a Roman province over which blood flowed up to the horse's bridle during the Jewish Revolt (A.D. 66–73).	20 And the winepress was trodden outside the city, and blood went out from the winepress unto the bridles of the horses for a thousand and six hundred stadia, about two hundred miles, the breadth of Italy, the home of Roman Catholicism.	20 And the winepress was trodden outside the city, and blood went out from the winepress unto the bridles of the horses for a thousand and six hundred stadia—about two hundred miles, the length of Israel and centering on the battle of Armageddon (cf. Rev. 16:16).	20 And the winepress was trodden outside the city, and blood went out from the winepress unto the bridles of the horses for a thousand and six hundred stadia. This signifies the perfection of judgment, because 1,600 equals the square of four (the number of the earth, with its four corners) multiplied by the square of ten, referring to completeness. Thus God will perfectly and pervasively judge the earth at the return of Christ.
15:1 Καὶ εἶδον ἄλλο σημεῖον ἐν τῷ οὐρανῷ And I saw another sign in heaven μέγα καὶ θαυμαστόν, ἀγγέλους ἑπτὰ great and wondrous, seven angels	1 This chapter is in preparation for the pouring out of the bowl judgments (Rev. 16–18). And I saw another sign in heaven, great and wondrous, seven angels having the	1 And I saw another sign in heaven, great and wondrous, seven angels having the seven last plagues, because in them the wrath of	1 Revelation 15 is a preface to the last set of judgments—the seven bowl judgments—which will be poured out on the second, and last, three and a half years of the	1 Before John reveals the seven angels with their bowls of wrath (Rev. 16–18), he offers a scene of the church triumphant (cf. Rev. 19–22). Drawing on the

ἔχοντας πληγὰς ἑπτὰ τὰς ἐσχάτας, having the seven last plagues, ὅτι ἐν αὐταῖς ἐτελέσθη ὁ θυμὸς τοῦ θεοῦ. because in them the wrath of God is completed.	seven last plagues, because in them the wrath of God is completed upon Jerusalem in A.D. 70.	God is completed upon the Roman papacy.	Tribulation, the Great Tribulation. And I saw another sign in heaven, great and wondrous, seven angels having the seven last plagues, because in them the wrath of God is completed.	story of the drowning of Pharaoh's host in the Red Sea (Exod. 14:15ff.), John assures the reader that even during the divine judgment of the pagan world, God will preserve a victorious multitude of saints, playing their harps and singing the Song of Moses (Exod. 15) and of the Lamb. The victory over the ancient Egyptians, then, foreshadows the triumph of God's people, the true church, over the beast. And I saw another sign in heaven, great and wondrous, seven angels having the seven last plagues (which, like the trumpet judgments, draw on the Egyptian plagues [Exod. 7–11]), because in them the wrath of God is completed. The vision of the bowl judgments runs parallel to the trumpet (Rev. 8–9) and seal judgments (Rev. 6), covering the entire period between the first and second comings of Christ. Thus for one individual, a particular calamity may be a trumpet judgment, but for another

Greek Text and English Translation	Preterist View	Historicist View	Futurist View	Idealist View
				individual it may be a bowl of wrath. The judgments are simultaneous, though their intensity differs from situation to situation, depending on the depth of depravity of those being punished for their evil deeds. However, in the midst of it all, the true church will be protected by God because the church is the vehicle of the kingdom of God (cf. Rev. 20).
15:2 Καὶ εἶδον ὡς θάλασσαν ὑαλίνην And I saw [something] like a glassy sea,	2 And I saw something like a glassy sea having been mixed with fire and the ones overcoming the beast (Nero, the Antichrist) and his image (a statue of Nero) and the number of his name ("666" = Caesar Nero) standing upon the glassy sea, having harps of God. They overcame Nero's persecution of the church by faithfully dying for Christ (A.D. 64–68).	2 And I saw something like a glassy sea having been mixed with fire (symbolizing the judgment that is about to proceed from the divine throne upon Roman Catholicism) and the ones overcoming the beast and his image and the number of his name (those who follow the pope and not Christ) standing upon the glassy sea, having harps of God.	2 And I saw something like a glassy sea having been mixed with fire (which indicates that the driving force behind God's dispensing of the bowl judgments is his holy anger) and the ones overcoming the beast and his image and the number of his name (the worship of the future Antichrist) standing upon the glassy sea, having harps of God.	2 And I saw something like a glassy sea having been mixed with fire and the ones overcoming the beast and his image and the number of his name standing upon the glassy sea, having harps of God.
μεμιγμένην πυρὶ having been mixed with fire				
καὶ τοὺς νικῶντας ἐκ τοῦ θηρίου and the ones overcoming of the beast				
καὶ ἐκ τῆς εἰκόνος αὐτοῦ καὶ ἐκ τοῦ ἀριθμοῦ τοῦ ὀνόματος αὐτοῦ and of his image and of the number of his name				
ἑστῶτας ἐπὶ τὴν θάλασσαν τὴν ὑαλίνην standing upon the glassy sea				
ἔχοντας κιθάρας τοῦ θεοῦ. having harps of God.				

15:3 καὶ ᾄδουσιν τὴν ᾠδὴν Μωϋσέως τοῦ δούλου τοῦ θεοῦ And they sing the Song of Moses the servant of God καὶ τὴν ᾠδὴν τοῦ ἀρνίου λέγοντες· and the Song of the Lamb, saying, μεγάλα καὶ θαυμαστὰ τὰ ἔργα σου, "Great and wondrous are your works, κύριε ὁ θεὸς ὁ παντοκράτωρ· Lord God Almighty; δίκαιαι καὶ ἀληθιναὶ αἱ ὁδοί σου, righteous and true [are] your ways, ὁ βασιλεὺς τῶν ἐθνῶν· King of the Gentiles.	3 And they sing the Song of Moses, the servant of God, and the Song of the Lamb, saying, "Great and wondrous are your works, Lord God Almighty; righteous and true are your ways, King of the Gentiles.	3 And they sing the Song of Moses, the servant of God, and the Song of the Lamb, saying, "Great and wondrous are your works, Lord God Almighty; righteous and true are your ways, King of the Gentiles.	3 And they sing the Song of Moses, the servant of God, and the Song of the Lamb (these will be Christians converted during the Tribulation period, not the church, which will be raptured to heaven before the beginning of the Tribulation; these tribulation saints sing the Song of the new exodus because the Lamb's death for them [Rev. 5] and their death for him are paradoxically the key to their deliverance in heaven), saying, "Great and wondrous are your works, Lord God Almighty; righteous and true are your ways, King of the Gentiles." This is a divine parody of the Gentile Antichrist who will rule the nations. During the days of the Tribulation, New York, London, and Brussels will no longer be the commercial hubs of the earth. Instead, Babylon will become the commercial capital of the world (see Rev. 17–18) because the Antichrist will move the United Nations center to Babylon to join forces with the European Union already there in his bid to rule the world.	3 And they sing the Song of Moses, the servant of God, and the Song of the Lamb, saying, "Great and wondrous are your works, Lord God Almighty; righteous and true are your ways, King of the Gentiles.

Greek Text and English Translation	Preterist View	Historicist View	Futurist View	Idealist View
15:4 τίς οὐ μὴ φοβηθῇ, κύριε, Who does not fear you, Lord, καὶ δοξάσει τὸ ὄνομά σου; and will glorify your name? ὅτι μόνος ὅσιος, Because [you] alone [are] holy, ὅτι πάντα τὰ ἔθνη ἥξουσιν because all the nations will come καὶ προσκυνήσουσιν ἐνώπιόν σου and will worship before you ὅτι τὰ δικαιώματά σου ἐφανερώθησαν. because your righteous deeds were made manifest.	4 Who does not fear you, Lord, and will glorify your name? Because you alone are holy, because all the nations will come and will worship before you, because your righteous deeds were made manifest." This is the new exodus, God's ultimate deliverance of the martyred Christians during the Neronian persecution.	4 Who does not fear you, Lord, and will glorify your name? Because you alone are holy, because all the nations will come and will worship before you, because your righteous deeds were made manifest." This is the new exodus, the deliverance of the true church.	4 Who does not fear you, Lord, and will glorify your name? Because you alone are holy, because all the nations will come and will worship before you, because your righteous deeds were made manifest."	4 Who does not fear you, Lord, and will glorify your name? Because you alone are holy, because all the nations will come and will worship before you, because your righteous deeds were made manifest."
15:5 Καὶ μετὰ ταῦτα εἶδον, καὶ ἠνοίγη ὁ ναὸς τῆς σκηνῆς And after these things I looked, and the temple of the tent τοῦ μαρτυρίου ἐν τῷ οὐρανῷ, of the witness in heaven was opened,	5 And after these things I looked, and the temple of the tent of the witness in heaven was opened,	5 And after these things I looked, and the temple of the tent (the heavenly tabernacle/temple of which the Roman Catholic Church is the apostate counterpart on earth) of the witness in the heaven was opened,	5 And after these things I looked, and the temple of the tent of the witness in the heaven was opened,	5 And after these things I looked, and the temple of the tent of the witness in the heaven was opened,
15:6 καὶ ἐξῆλθον οἱ ἑπτὰ ἄγγελοι and the seven angels came out [οἱ] ἔχοντες τὰς ἑπτὰ πληγὰς ἐκ τοῦ ναοῦ the ones having the seven plagues out of the temple ἐνδεδυμένοι λίνον καθαρὸν λαμπρὸν having been clothed with clean bright linen,	6 and the seven angels, the ones having the seven plagues, came out of the temple, having been clothed with clean, bright linen and having been girdled around their chests with golden	6 and the seven angels, the ones having the seven plagues, came out of the temple, having been clothed with clean, bright linen and having been girdled	6 and the seven angels, the ones having the seven plagues, came out of the temple, having been clothed with clean, bright linen and having been girdled	6 and the seven angels, the ones having the seven plagues, came out of the temple, having been clothed with clean, bright linen and having been girdled

καὶ περιεζωσμένοι and having been girdled	girdles. This signifies that the Jerusalem temple and the old covenant are about to fall and be replaced forever with the new temple, the church, the body of Christ, and the new covenant, which is based on faith in Christ.	around their chests with golden girdles.	around their chests with golden girdles.	around their chests with golden girdles.
περὶ τὰ στήθη ζώνας χρυσᾶς. around the chests with golden girdles.				
15:7 καὶ ἓν ἐκ τῶν τεσσάρων ζῴων ἔδωκεν τοῖς ἑπτὰ ἀγγέλοις And one of the four living creatures gave to the seven angels	7 And one of the four living creatures gave to the seven angels seven golden bowls being filled with the wrath of God, the one living forever. These seven bowl judgments (Rev. 16–18) will be the climax to the covenantal curses that will fall upon idolatrous Jerusalem for having rejected her Messiah.	7 And one of the four living creatures gave to the seven angels seven golden bowls being filled with the wrath of God, the one living forever. These plagues/bowls will finish off the papacy, beginning from the French Revolution and extending to the future wrap-up of history at the second coming of Christ.	7 And one of the four living creatures gave to the seven angels seven golden bowls being filled with the wrath of God, the one living forever.	7 And one of the four living creatures gave to the seven angels seven golden bowls being filled with the wrath of God, the one living forever.
ἑπτὰ φιάλας χρυσᾶς γεμούσας τοῦ θυμοῦ τοῦ θεοῦ seven golden bowls being filled with the wrath of God				
τοῦ ζῶντος εἰς τοὺς αἰῶνας τῶν αἰώνων. the one living forever.				
15:8 καὶ ἐγεμίσθη ὁ ναὸς καπνοῦ And the temple was filled with smoke	8 And the temple was filled with smoke of the glory of God and of his power, and no one was able to enter into the temple until the seven plagues of the seven angels should be completed. In other words, once the bowl judgments begin, no intercession will be heard any longer in heaven for earthly Jerusalem.	8 And the temple was filled with smoke of the glory of God and of his power, and no one was able to enter into the temple until the seven plagues of the seven angels should be completed with the unfolding of the seven bowl judgments (Rev. 16–18). The time for the papacy to repent will be no more.	8 And the temple was filled with smoke of the glory of God and of his power, and no one was able to enter into the temple until the seven plagues of the seven angels should be completed. The mention of "temple/tent/glory/smoke" recalls the dedication of the Solomonic temple in Jerusalem and the filling of that place with the presence of God, and the rebuilt temple	8 And the temple was filled with smoke of the glory of God and of his power, and no one was able to enter into the temple until the seven plagues of the seven angels should be completed. The second coming of Christ will bring an end to human history, meting out the last dregs of divine wrath. And for all eternity the temple and kingdom of God will dwell with the saints (Rev.
ἐκ τῆς δόξης τοῦ θεοῦ καὶ ἐκ τῆς δυνάμεως αὐτοῦ, of the glory of God and of his power,				
καὶ οὐδεὶς ἐδύνατο εἰσελθεῖν εἰς τὸν ναὸν and no one was able to enter into the temple				
ἄχρι τελεσθῶσιν αἱ ἑπτὰ πληγαὶ τῶν ἑπτὰ ἀγγέλων. until the seven plagues of the seven angels should be completed.				

REVELATION

15:8   **16:1**

Greek Text and English Translation	Preterist View	Historicist View	Futurist View	Idealist View
			in Jerusalem during the future Tribulation period. Though now polluted by the presence of the Antichrist, it will be cleansed and rededicated to God at the return of Christ. And in the Millennium that immediately follows, the restored Jerusalem temple, which is the earthly counterpart to the heavenly temple, will see Christ enthroned in it, reinstituting the OT sacrificial system and ruling the world from Jerusalem, his headquarters. Jerusalem, the city of God, will replace Babylon, the city of the Antichrist.	21–22). But the time of intercession and mercy for the lost will be over.
16:1 Καὶ ἤκουσα μεγάλης φωνῆς And I heard a great voice ἐκ τοῦ ναοῦ λεγούσης τοῖς ἑπτὰ ἀγγέλοις· out of the temple saying to the seven angels, ὑπάγετε καὶ ἐκχέετε τὰς ἑπτὰ φιάλας τοῦ θυμοῦ τοῦ θεοῦ εἰς τὴν γῆν. "Go and pour out the seven bowls of the wrath of God onto the earth!"	1 And I heard a great voice out of the temple saying to the seven angels, "Go and pour out the seven bowls of the wrath of God onto the earth!"	1 The bowl judgments began to be poured out on the papacy in 1789, the beginning of the French Revolution. That year marked the fulfillment of the 1,260 days/years prophecy, which began in A.D. 533 (when Emperor Justinian declared the bishop of Rome to be supreme over all bishops). The French	1 The bowl judgments will be poured out on the world in the last days of the Great Tribulation, right before the second coming of Christ. Like the trumpet judgments, they recall the Egyptian plagues but are more intense, inflicting the whole world. And I heard a great voice out of the temple saying to	1 And I heard a great voice (that of God himself) out of the temple saying to the seven angels, "Go and pour out the seven bowls of the wrath of God onto the earth!"

16:2 Καὶ ἀπῆλθεν ὁ πρῶτος καὶ ἐξέχεεν τὴν φιάλην αὐτοῦ εἰς τὴν γῆν,
And the first [angel] came out and poured out his bowl onto the earth,

καὶ ἐγένετο ἕλκος κακὸν καὶ πονηρὸν
and there came to be bad and evil sores

ἐπὶ τοὺς ἀνθρώπους τοὺς ἔχοντας τὸ χάραγμα τοῦ θηρίου
upon the men having the mark of the beast

καὶ τοὺς προσκυνοῦντας τῇ εἰκόνι αὐτοῦ.
and worshipping his image.

---

2 And the first angel came out and poured out his bowl onto the earth, and there came to be bad and evil sores upon the men having the mark of the beast and worshipping his image. The first bowl judgment recalls the sixth Egyptian plague of boils/sores (Exod. 9:8–12) but ironically is reapplied by John to the Jerusalem of his day, not to ancient Egypt. As such, it is a part of the covenantal curses Moses inveighed against Israel if it should ever leave the worship of Yahweh (Deut. 28:27, 35). This judgment fell on Jerusalem during its siege by the Romans, which caused boils and rashes in the

---

Revolution was aimed at the power of the papacy, killing two million people, including 24,000 priests, in a five-year period and turning 40,000 churches into stables. The power of the papacy in France was shattered. And I heard a great voice out of the temple saying to the seven angels, "Go and pour out the seven bowls of the wrath of God onto the earth!"

2 And the first angel came out and poured out his bowl onto the earth, and there came to be bad and evil sores upon the men having the mark of the beast and worshipping his image; that is, the moral corruption and general dissolution of society spread over those countries that adhered to Roman Catholicism.

---

the seven angels, "Go and pour out the seven bowls of the wrath of God onto the earth!"

2 And the first angel came out and poured out his bowl onto the earth, and there came to be bad and evil sores upon the men having the mark of the beast and worshipping his image. These sores/rashes will be caused by the fallout of radioactivity of the nuclear war of World War III. Nagasaki and Hiroshima pale by comparison to that coming day.

---

2 And the first angel came out and poured out his bowl onto the earth, and there came to be bad and evil sores upon the men having the mark of the beast and worshipping his image. These are the impurities of infections that cannot be cured: AIDS, staph infections, cancer, and so on.

Greek Text and English Translation	Preterist View	Historicist View	Futurist View	Idealist View
	city, where sanitation was lost. With dead bodies piled in rotting heaps throughout Jerusalem, and the streets running with rivers of blood and sewage, diseases of every sort became rampant. The mark of the beast and image of the beast are Nero/the Roman emperor. The Jews, in effect, worshipped the imperial cult when they said to Pilate, "We have no king but Caesar" (John 19:15) and then crucified the real king, Messiah Jesus.			
16:3 Καὶ ὁ δεύτερος ἐξέχεεν τὴν φιάλην αὐτοῦ εἰς τὴν θάλασσαν, And the second poured out his bowl onto the sea, καὶ ἐγένετο αἷμα ὡς νεκροῦ, and there came to be blood like of one dead, καὶ πᾶσα ψυχὴ ζωῆς ἀπέθανεν τὰ ἐν τῇ θαλάσσῃ. and every living soul died, the ones in the sea.	3 And the second poured out his bowl onto the sea, and there came to be blood like of one dead, and every living soul died, the ones in the sea. The second bowl judgment is reminiscent of the first Egyptian plague (Exod. 7:17–21). The bowl judgments intensify the trumpet judgments in that the former signify the destruction of Jerusalem and, with that, the demise of the old covenant. Here the	3 And the second poured out his bowl onto the sea, and there came to be blood like of one dead, and every living soul died, the ones in the sea, an allusion to the destruction of the papal naval fleets in France, Spain, and Portugal. God used the British navy to destroy the Catholic French navy and its allies, from 1793 to 1815. Two hundred French, Spanish, and Dutch ships were destroyed, along with three	3 And the second poured out his bowl onto the sea, and there came to be blood like of one dead, and every living soul died, the ones in the sea. Nuclear fallout will pollute all marine life in both saltwaters and freshwaters.	3 And the second poured out his bowl onto the sea, and there came to be blood like of one dead, and every living soul died, the ones in the sea. The second bowl judgment represents God's judgment on the seas: shipwrecks, naval battles, tsunamis, oil spills, and other sea disasters.

				4 And the third poured out his bowl onto the rivers and the fountains of the waters, and they became blood.
			4 And the third poured out his bowl onto the rivers and the fountains of the waters, and they became blood.	5 And I heard the angel of the waters saying, "You are righteous, the one who is and who was, the holy one, because you judged these things,
	hundred to four hundred frigates and many more smaller vessels.	4 And the third poured out his bowl onto the rivers and the fountains of the waters, and they became blood.	4 And the third poured out his bowl onto the rivers and the fountains of the waters, and they became blood.	5 And I heard the angel of the waters saying, "You are righteous, the one who is and who was, the holy one, because you judged these things,

16:4 Καὶ ὁ τρίτος ἐξέχεεν τὴν φιάλην αὐτοῦ
And the third poured out his bowl

εἰς τοὺς ποταμοὺς καὶ τὰς πηγὰς τῶν ὑδάτων,
onto the rivers and the fountains of the waters,

καὶ ἐγένετο αἷμα.
and they became blood.

16:5 Καὶ ἤκουσα τοῦ ἀγγέλου τῶν ὑδάτων λέγοντος·
And I heard the angel of the waters saying,

δίκαιος εἶ, ὁ ὢν καὶ ὁ ἦν, ὁ ὅσιος,
"You are righteous, the one who is and who was, the holy one,

ὅτι ταῦτα ἔκρινας,
because you judged these things,

---

slaughter of Jewish soldiers by the Roman navy on the Sea of Galilee is alluded to. And the prevalence of blood and death—unclean according to Jewish scruples (Lev. 7:26–27; 15:19–23; etc.)—is a sign that John considers the Israel of his day as unclean before God.

4 And the third poured out his bowl onto the rivers and the fountains of the waters, and they became blood. The second bowl judgment affects the bodies of saltwater, and the third bowl judgment affects the bodies of freshwater (cf. again the first Egyptian plague, Exod. 7:12–21). The third bowl judgment attests to the pollution of Jerusalem's water supply during the Roman siege.

5 And I heard the angel of the waters saying, "You are righteous, the one who is and who was, the holy one, because you judged these things,

---

5 And I heard the angel of the waters saying, "You are righteous, the one who is and who was, the holy one, because you judged these things (this bowl judgment recalls Napoleon's attack on the populations along the rivers of northern Italy),

Greek Text and English Translation	Preterist View	Historicist View	Futurist View	Idealist View
16:6 ὅτι αἷμα ἁγίων καὶ προφητῶν ἐξέχεαν because they poured out the blood of saints and prophets καὶ αἷμα αὐτοῖς [δ]ἐδοκας πιεῖν, ἄξιοί εἰσιν. and you gave them blood to drink; they are worthy [of punishment]."	6 because they poured out the blood of saints and prophets and you gave them blood to drink; they are worthy of punishment."	6 because they poured out the blood of saints and prophets and you gave them blood to drink; they are worthy of punishment." It was in those rivers—the Rhine, the Danube, and the Po—that multitudes of Christians were slaughtered at the command of the popes: Lutherans, Moravians, Hussites, Albigenses, Waldensians, Vaudios, and Huguenots. Napoleon's attack on the papacy in northern Italy was therefore a divine turning of the tables.	6 because they poured out the blood of saints and prophets and you gave them blood to drink; they are worthy of punishment."	6 because they poured out the blood of saints and prophets and you gave them blood to drink; they are worthy of punishment."
16:7 Καὶ ἤκουσα τοῦ θυσιαστηρίου λέγοντος· And I heard the altar saying, ναὶ κύριε ὁ θεὸς ὁ παντοκράτωρ, "Indeed Lord God Almighty, ἀληθιναὶ καὶ δίκαιαι αἱ κρίσεις σου. true and righteous [are] your judgments."	7 And I heard the altar saying, "Indeed Lord God Almighty, true and righteous are your judgments." Thus did Jerusalem kill the prophets of God, including Jesus (see 2 Chron. 36:15–16; Matt. 23:31–36; Luke 13:33–34; indeed, Luke 9–19 as a whole; and Acts 7:52), and God will exact his justice upon the Holy City turned unholy (cf. Matt. 23:31–36).	7 And I heard the altar saying, "Indeed Lord God Almighty, true and righteous are your judgments."	7 And I heard the altar saying, "Indeed Lord God Almighty, true and righteous are your judgments." This shedding of blood will be in retaliation for the killing of the saints by the Antichrist.	7 And I heard the altar saying, "Indeed Lord God Almighty, true and righteous are your judgments."

16:8 Καὶ ὁ τέταρτος ἐξέχεεν τὴν φιάλην αὐτοῦ ἐπὶ τὸν ἥλιον, And the fourth poured out his bowl upon the sun, καὶ ἐδόθη αὐτῷ καυματίσαι τοὺς ἀνθρώπους ἐν πυρί. and there was granted to it to scorch men by fire.	8 And the fourth poured out his bowl upon the sun, and there was granted to it to scorch men by fire.	8 And the fourth poured out his bowl upon the sun, and there was granted to it to scorch men by fire.	8 And the fourth poured out his bowl upon the sun, and there was granted to it to scorch men by fire. This scorching heat of nuclear exchange will radically upset the atmosphere. Global warming today is but a foretaste of that day.	8 And the fourth poured out his bowl upon the sun, and there was granted to it to scorch men by fire.
16:9 καὶ ἐκαυματίσθησαν οἱ ἄνθρωποι καῦμα μέγα And men were scorched with great heat καὶ ἐβλασφήμησαν τὸ ὄνομα τοῦ θεοῦ and they blasphemed the name of God, τοῦ ἔχοντος τὴν ἐξουσίαν ἐπὶ τὰς πληγὰς ταύτας the one having the authority over these plagues καὶ οὐ μετενόησαν δοῦναι αὐτῷ δόξαν. and they did not repent to give him glory.	9 And men were scorched with great heat, and they blasphemed the name of God, the one having the authority over these plagues, and they did not repent to give him glory. This fourth bowl/plague reverses the covenantal blessing that was present in the exodus, when Israel was shielded from the heat of the sun by the Shekinah cloud (see Exod. 13:21–22; cf. Ps. 91:1–6). Thus the scorching of Jerusalemites during the Roman siege is a symbolic reference to the blessing of the covenant turned into a curse (cf. the seventh Egyptian plague; Exod. 9:22–26). Despite God's wrath, the Jerusalemites did not repent.	9 And men were scorched with great heat, and they blasphemed the name of God, the one having the authority over these plagues, and they did not repent to give him glory. The timing of the fourth bowl judgment overlaps with the outpouring of the second and third bowl judgments (the years following the French Revolution). In particular, Napoleon Bonaparte was the "sun" that God used to scorch the papal kingdoms, defeating in the space of eight years every kingdom in Europe, from Naples to Berlin, and from Lisbon to Moscow.	9 And men were scorched with great heat, and they blasphemed the name of God, the one having the authority over these plagues, and they did not repent to give him glory.	9 And men were scorched with great heat, and they blasphemed the name of God, the one having the authority over these plagues, and they did not repent to give him glory. Deaths caused by the sun—cancer, global warming, heat stroke, and so on—constitute the fourth bowl judgment. Yet no repentance comes from sinners.
16:10 Καὶ ὁ πέμπτος ἐξέχεεν τὴν φιάλην αὐτοῦ ἐπὶ τὸν θρόνον τοῦ θηρίου, And the fifth poured out his bowl upon the throne of the beast,	10 And the fifth poured his bowl upon the throne of the beast, and his kingdom became	10 And the fifth poured his bowl upon the throne of the beast, and his kingdom became	10 And the fifth poured his bowl upon the throne of the beast, and his kingdom became	10 And the fifth poured his bowl upon the throne of the beast, and his kingdom became

Greek Text and English Translation	Preterist View	Historicist View	Futurist View	Idealist View
καὶ ἐγένετο ἡ βασιλεία αὐτοῦ ἐσκοτωμένη, and his kingdom became darkened,	darkened, and they gnawed their tongues from the pain,	darkened (Rome and the papacy were thrown into disorder and distress by the invasion of the French in 1797; this began the progressive deterioration of Roman Catholicism until 1866), and they gnawed their tongues from the pain,	darkened, and they gnawed their tongues from the pain (the world-wide darkness will result from the massive loss of power because of the nuclear holocaust, but still men will not repent),	darkened, and they gnawed their tongues from the pain,
καὶ ἐμασῶντο τὰς γλώσσας αὐτῶν ἐκ τοῦ πόνου, and they gnawed their tongues from the pain,				
16:11 καὶ ἐβλασφήμησαν τὸν θεὸν τοῦ οὐρανοῦ and they blasphemed the God of heaven	11 and they blasphemed the God of heaven out of their pain and out of their sores and did not repent from their works. The fifth bowl judgment resembles the ninth Egyptian plague (Exod. 10:21–29) but now turned against Jerusalem. Also, Rome is here included in the purview of divine judgment because it joined with Jews in persecuting Christians. Thus the darkness upon the throne of the beast alludes to the civil war in the Roman Empire caused by Nero's death (A.D. 68). Three men competed for his vacated throne (Galba, Otho, and Vitellius), and each was quickly deposed.	11 and they blasphemed the God of heaven out of their pain and out of their sores and did not repent from their works. So the papacy refused to repent, even expounding two blasphemous declarations: the Immaculate Conception of Mary (1854) and the infallibility of the pope when speaking ex cathedra (1870).	11 and they blasphemed the God of heaven out of their pain and out of their sores and did not repent from their works.	11 and they blasphemed the God of heaven out of their pain and out of their sores and did not repent from their works. Thus all anti-God governments ("the throne of the beast") will fall before God's judgment, and the light of civilizations will go out: Assyria, Babylonia, Persia, Rome, etc.
ἐκ τοῦ πόνου αὐτῶν καὶ ἐκ τῶν ἑλκῶν αὐτῶν out of their pain and out of their sores				
καὶ οὐ μετενόησαν ἐκ τῶν ἔργων αὐτῶν. and did not repent from their works.				

16:12 Καὶ ὁ ἕκτος ἐξέχεεν τὴν φιάλην αὐτοῦ And the sixth poured out his bowl ἐπὶ τὸν ποταμὸν τὸν μέγαν τὸν Εὐφράτην, upon the great river, the Euphrates, καὶ ἐξηράνθη τὸ ὕδωρ αὐτοῦ, and its waters were dried up, ἵνα ἑτοιμασθῇ ἡ ὁδὸς τῶν βασιλέων τῶν ἀπὸ ἀνατολῆς ἡλίου. in order that the way of the kings from the east might be prepared.	"Darkness" and chaos fell over the empire in A.D. 69 until Vespasian (the general leading the Roman army's invasion of Israel) was named Caesar. His son, Titus, then assumed command of the siege of Jerusalem. 12 And the sixth poured out his bowl upon the great river, the Euphrates, and its waters were dried up, in order that the way of the kings from the east might be prepared.	12 And the sixth poured out his bowl upon the great river, the Euphrates, and its waters were dried up, in order that the way of the kings from the east might be prepared. Here we have the rise and the fall of the Turkish Empire. Arising from the eastern Roman Empire, the Turks destroyed Catholicism (Constantinople and beyond) but met their match in October 1917 when they suffered defeat in Palestine at the hands of the British General Edmund Allenby. Thus the Turkish Empire, which had its roots near the Euphrates River, "dried up."	12 And the sixth poured out his bowl upon the great river, the Euphrates, and its waters were dried up, in order that the way of the kings from the east might be prepared.	12 And the sixth poured out his bowl upon the great river, the Euphrates, and its waters were dried up, in order that the way of the kings from the east might be prepared.
16:13 Καὶ εἶδον ἐκ τοῦ στόματος τοῦ δράκοντος And I saw out of the mouth of the dragon καὶ ἐκ τοῦ στόματος τοῦ θηρίου and out of the mouth of the beast	13 And I saw three unclean spirits like frogs come out of the mouth of the dragon and out of the mouth of the beast and out of the mouth	13 And I saw three unclean spirits like frogs come out of the mouth of the dragon and out of the mouth of the beast and out of the mouth	13 And I saw three unclean spirits like frogs come out of the mouth of the dragon (Satan) and out of the mouth of the beast (Antichrist)	13 And I saw three unclean spirits like frogs come out of the mouth of the dragon and out of the mouth of the beast

Greek Text and English Translation	Preterist View	Historicist View	Futurist View	Idealist View
καὶ ἐκ τοῦ στόματος τοῦ ψευδοπροφήτου and out of the mouth of the false prophet	and out of the mouth of the false prophet.	of the false prophet. So Roman Catholicism rose again to prominence, the pope and the priest-hood being empowered by the demonic.	and out of the mouth of the (Antichrist's) false prophet.	and out of the mouth of the false prophet.
πνεύματα τρία ἀκάθαρτα ὡς βάτραχοι· three unclean spirits like frogs.				
16:14 εἰσὶν γὰρ πνεύματα δαιμονίων ποιοῦντα σημεῖα, For they are demonic spirits making signs,	14 For they are demonic spirits making signs, which proceed out upon the kings of the whole inhabited earth to gather them unto the war of the great day of God the Almighty. There was symbolic and his-	14 For they are demonic spirits making signs, which proceed out upon the kings of the whole inhabited earth to gather them unto the war of the great day of God the Almighty.	14 For they are demonic spirits making signs, which proceed out upon the kings of the whole inhabited earth to gather them unto the war of the great day of God the Almighty.	14 For they are demonic spirits making signs, which proceed out upon the kings of the whole inhabited earth to gather them unto the war of the great day of God the Almighty.
ἃ ἐκπορεύεται ἐπὶ τοὺς βασιλεῖς τῆς οἰκουμένης ὅλης which proceed out upon the kings of the whole inhabited earth	torical significance to the sixth bowl judgment. Symbolically, the drying up of the Euphrates before the kings from the east is an allusion			
συναγαγεῖν αὐτοὺς εἰς τὸν πόλεμον to gather them unto the war	to Cyrus the Persian diverting the Euphrates River so that his troops could march into Babylon on the dry riverbed and			
τῆς ἡμέρας τῆς μεγάλης τοῦ θεοῦ τοῦ παντοκράτορος. of the great day of God the Almighty.	conquer the famed city of Nebuchadnezzar in 539 B.C. Thus the fifth bowl judgment figuratively equates Jerusalem with the old pagan Babylon. Jerusalem's defeat at the hands of the Roman army is imminent. Historically,			

this judgment alludes to General Titus's reinforcing his Roman legions with thousands of troops from the region of the Euphrates. The three frogs recall the second Egyptian plague (Exod. 8:1–7) and symbolize the demonic empowerment of Satan (dragon)/beast (Nero, Roman caesar, Antichrist)/false prophet (Roman imperial priesthood) in attacking Jerusalem. Just as God used evil, demonic nations (Assyria, Babylonia) to judge Israel in the OT, so he uses the Roman Empire and its imperial cult to judge Jerusalem. But one day, just as God judged Assyria and Babylonia, so will he judge Rome (which indeed he did in A.D. 476).

15 "Behold, I come as a thief. Blessed is the one who is alert and keeping his garments in order that he may not walk naked and men see his shame."

15 "Behold, I come as a thief. Blessed is the one who is alert and keeping his garments in order that he may not walk naked and men see his shame."

15 "Behold, I come as a thief. Blessed is the one who is alert and keeping his garments in order that he may not walk naked and men see his shame."

15 "Behold, I come as a thief. Blessed is the one who is alert and keeping his garments in order that he may not walk naked and men see his shame."

16:15 Ἰδοὺ ἔρχομαι ὡς κλέπτης.
"Behold, I come as a thief.

μακάριος ὁ γρηγορῶν καὶ τηρῶν τὰ ἱμάτια αὐτοῦ,
Blessed [is] the one who is alert and keeping his garments,

ἵνα μὴ γυμνὸς περιπατῇ καὶ βλέπωσιν τὴν ἀσχημοσύνην αὐτοῦ.
in order that he may not walk naked and men see his shame."

REVELATION

Greek Text and English Translation	Preterist View	Historicist View	Futurist View	Idealist View
16:16 Καὶ συνήγαγεν αὐτοὺς εἰς τὸν τόπον And he gathered them to the place τὸν καλούμενον Ἑβραϊστὶ ʿΑρμαγεδδών. being called in Hebrew "Harmageddon."	16 And he gathered them to the place being called in Hebrew "Harmageddon" (= mountain of Megiddo). Megiddo was the scene of many significant battles, including the defeat of the Canaanites by judges Deborah and Barak (Judg. 5:19) and the death of the godly young king of Judah, Josiah, at the hands of the Egyptian army (2 Chron. 35:20–25). The battle of Armageddon is therefore not to be understood as some future, end-time World War III but rather is an allusion to Israel's climactic loss to the Romans, much as Waterloo was for Napoleon or Gettysburg was for the Confederacy. It was at the "Armageddon" of Jerusalem's loss to the Romans that Christ came like a thief to destroy that apostate city.	16 And he gathered them to the place being called in Hebrew "Harmageddon." Thus the Roman Empire under the auspices of the papacy will one day precipitate the final, end-time war at Megiddo.	16 And he gathered them to the place being called in Hebrew "Harmageddon." In other words, three armies will converge in Megiddo, Israel, to fight each other for control of Jerusalem and the world: the Chinese army (the kings of the east; Rev. 16:12); the Antichrist and the revived Roman Empire, which will move the headquarters of the United Nations and the European Union to New Babylon (Rev. 17:12–18); and Russia and its Muslim ally, Iran (Ezek. 38–39). These three will position themselves in the Middle East to take over Israel. But just before they do, Christ will return in power and glory on the Mount of Olives (Zech. 14; Acts 1:9–11) and defeat the three enemy empires at Armageddon.	16 And he gathered them to the place being called in Hebrew "Harmageddon." The historical background for the sixth bowl was the first-century expectation/fear that the Parthians would cross the Euphrates River from the East and attack the West—Rome, led by Nero revived, no less. That potential invasion will spell the "Armageddon" of Rome. This historical situation is repeated in history; God topples one anti-God nation after the next.
16:17 Καὶ ὁ ἕβδομος ἐξέχεεν τὴν φιάλην αὐτοῦ ἐπὶ τὸν ἀέρα, And the seventh poured out his bowl upon the air,	17 And the seventh poured out his bowl upon the air, and there came	17 And the seventh poured out his bowl upon the air, and there came	17 And the seventh poured out his bowl upon the air, and there came	17 And the seventh poured out his bowl upon the air, and there came

a great voice out of the temple from the throne, saying, "It has happened!"	a great voice out of the temple from the throne, saying, "It has happened!"	a great voice out of the temple from the throne, saying, "It has happened!"	a great voice out of the temple from the throne, saying, "It has happened!" The seventh bowl judgment (cf. the seventh Egyptian plague) will be the grand finale of the fall of Jerusalem to Rome.	καὶ ἐξῆλθεν φωνὴ μεγάλη — and there came a great voice; ἐκ τοῦ ναοῦ ἀπὸ τοῦ θρόνου — out of the temple from the throne, λέγουσα· γέγονεν. — saying, "It has happened!"
18 And there were lightnings and voices and thunders, and there was a great earthquake such as had never been since man had happened upon the earth, so great an earthquake was it.	18 And there were lightnings and voices and thunders, and there was a great earthquake such as had never been since man had happened upon the earth, so great an earthquake was it.	18 And there were lightnings and voices and thunders, and there was a great earthquake such as had never been since man had happened upon the earth, so great an earthquake was it.	18 And there were lightnings and voices and thunders, and there was a great earthquake such as had never been since man had happened upon the earth, so great an earthquake was it.	16:18 καὶ ἐγένοντο ἀστραπαὶ καὶ φωναὶ καὶ βρονταί — And there were lightnings and voices and thunders, καὶ σεισμὸς ἐγένετο μέγας, — and there was a great earthquake, οἷος οὐκ ἐγένετο ἀφ᾽ οὗ ἄνθρωπος ἐγένετο — such as had never been since man had happened ἐπὶ τῆς γῆς τηλικοῦτος σεισμὸς οὕτω μέγας. — upon the earth, so great an earthquake [was it].
19 And the great city fell into three parts, and the cities of the nations fell. And Babylon the great was remembered before God to give her the cup of the wine of the anger of his wrath.	19 And the great city (New Babylon) fell into three parts, and the cities of the nations fell. And Babylon the great was remembered before God to give her the cup of the wine of the anger of his wrath.	19 And the great city fell into three parts, and the cities of the nations fell. And Babylon the great was remembered before God to give her the cup of the wine of the anger of his wrath.	19 And the great city fell into three parts, and the cities of the nations fell. And Babylon the great was remembered before God to give her the cup of the wine of the anger of his wrath. The fall of Jerusalem was made possible by a political shake-up/"earthquake" in that city. Thus the Jews divided into three opposing parties, with people following either Eleazer, John, or Simon. Such internal strife depleted Israel's ability to withstand the	16:19 καὶ ἐγένετο ἡ πόλις ἡ μεγάλη εἰς τρία μέρη — And the great city [fell] into three parts καὶ αἱ πόλεις τῶν ἐθνῶν ἔπεσαν. — and the cities of the nations fell. καὶ Βαβυλὼν ἡ μεγάλη ἐμνήσθη — And Babylon the great was remembered ἐνώπιον τοῦ θεοῦ δοῦναι αὐτῇ τὸ ποτήριον τοῦ οἴνου — before God to give her the cup of the wine τοῦ θυμοῦ τῆς ὀργῆς αὐτοῦ. — of the anger of his wrath.

Greek Text and English Translation	Preterist View	Historicist View	Futurist View	Idealist View
	Romans. This was a part of the covenantal curses unleashed on the Jews in A.D. 70 (cf. Ezekiel's prophecy of the fate of Jerusalem at the hands of the Babylonians when he spoke of those burned, killed by the sword, and scattered; Ezek. 5).			
16:20 καὶ πᾶσα νῆσος ἔφυγεν καὶ ὄρη οὐχ εὑρέθησαν. And every island fled and mountains were not found.	20 And every island fled, and mountains were not found.	20 And every island fled, and mountains were not found.	20 And every island fled, and mountains were not found.	20 And every island fled, and mountains were not found.
16:21 καὶ χάλαζα μεγάλη ὡς ταλαντιαία καταβαίνει And great hail weighing about a talent descends	21 And great hail weighing about a talent descends out of heaven upon men, and men blasphemed God because of the plague of hail, because exceedingly great is its plague. The islands fleeing, the mountains being leveled, and the hail stones falling are allusions to the Romans engineering the leveling of hills and islands with their machines like the catapult, which hurled hundred-pound stones into Jerusalem, decimating the city. But still, the Jews did	21 And great hail weighing about a talent descends out of heaven upon men, and men blasphemed God because of the plague of hail, because exceedingly great is its plague. Such will be the final defeat of the Roman papacy, the new Babylon. This is still forthcoming in history, awaiting the return of Christ.	21 And great hail weighing about a talent descends out of heaven upon men, and men blasphemed God because of the plague of hail, because exceedingly great is its plague. This will all happen at the second coming of Christ (cf. Rev. 19).	21 And great hail weighing about a talent descends out of heaven upon men, and men blasphemed God because of the plague of hail, because exceedingly great is its plague. At the end of history, the final judgment of God will be poured out on the pagan world, illustrated in the seventh bowl plague. After that, Christ will return to establish the eternal state (see Rev. 19; 21–22).
ἐκ τοῦ οὐρανοῦ ἐπὶ τοὺς ἀνθρώπους, out of heaven upon men,				
καὶ ἐβλασφήμησαν οἱ ἄνθρωποι τὸν θεὸν and men blasphemed God				
ἐκ τῆς πληγῆς τῆς χαλάζης, because of the plague of hail,				
ὅτι μεγάλη ἐστὶν ἡ πληγὴ αὐτῆς σφόδρα. because exceedingly great is its plague.				

			1 And one of the seven angels having the seven bowls came and spoke with me, saying, "Come, I will show you the judgment of the great harlot sitting upon many waters,
		1 And one of the seven angels having the seven bowls came and spoke with me, saying, "Come, I will show you the judgment of the great harlot sitting upon many waters,	
	1 And one of the seven angels having the seven bowls came and spoke with me, saying, "Come, I will show you the judgment of the great harlot sitting upon many waters,		
			2 with whom the kings of the earth committed fornication and the inhabitants of the earth
		2 with whom the kings of the earth committed fornication and the inhabitants of the earth were	
	2 with whom the kings of the earth committed fornication and the inhabitants of the earth		

not repent. While the Romans hurled their stones of destruction on the "Holy" City, they sarcastically cried out, "The Son cometh" (see Josephus, *Jewish Wars* 5:6:3). In saying this, the Roman soldiers unknowingly were affirming that the Parousia of Christ was indeed his coming to judge Jerusalem through the Romans!

(**Editor's note**: At this point in the book of Revelation, many preterists see both Rome and Jerusalem as under the indictment of Rev. 17.)

1 And one of the seven angels having the seven bowls came and spoke with me, saying, "Come, I will show you the judgment of the great harlot sitting upon many waters,

2 with whom the kings of the earth committed fornication and the inhabitants of the earth

17:1 Καὶ ἦλθεν εἷς ἐκ τῶν ἑπτὰ ἀγγέλων τῶν ἐχόντων τὰς ἑπτὰ φιάλας
And one of the seven angels having the seven bowls came

καὶ ἐλάλησεν μετ᾽ ἐμοῦ λέγων·
and spoke with me, saying,

δεῦρο, δείξω σοι τὸ κρίμα
"Come, I will show you the judgment

τῆς πόρνης τῆς μεγάλης τῆς καθημένης ἐπὶ ὑδάτων πολλῶν,
of the great harlot sitting upon many waters,

17:2 μεθ᾽ ἧς ἐπόρνευσαν οἱ βασιλεῖς τῆς γῆς
with whom the kings of the earth committed fornication

Greek Text and English Translation	Preterist View	Historicist View	Futurist View	Idealist View
καὶ ἐμεθύσθησαν οἱ κατοικοῦντες τὴν γῆν and the ones inhabiting the earth were made drunk ἐκ τοῦ οἴνου τῆς πορνείας αὐτῆς. by the wine of her harlotry."	were made drunk by the wine of her harlotry." The angel thereby showed John the imminent punishment of Roma, goddess of Rome, whose political and economic alliances with the nations polluted them with idolatry.	were made drunk by the wine of her harlotry." This is a vision of the upcoming punishment of the church of Rome, whose political and economic liaisons with the nations have corrupted the church spiritually.	made drunk by the wine of her harlotry." This is the imminent destruction of literal, new Babylon, whose political and economic rule advance the cause of the Antichrist.	were made drunk by the wine of her harlotry." This is the anti-Christ world system and the harlot (the apostate church).
17:3 καὶ ἀπήνεγκέν με εἰς ἔρημον ἐν πνεύματι. And he carried me into the desert by the Spirit. Καὶ εἶδον γυναῖκα καθημένην ἐπὶ θηρίον κόκκινον, And I saw a woman sitting upon the beast in scarlet γέμον[τα] ὀνόματα βλασφημίας, being filled with blasphemous names, ἔχον κεφαλὰς ἑπτὰ καὶ κέρατα δέκα. having seven heads and ten horns.	3 And he carried me into the desert by the Spirit. And I saw a woman sitting upon the beast in scarlet being filled with blasphemous names, having seven heads and ten horns.	3 And he carried me into the desert by the Spirit. And I saw a woman sitting upon the beast in scarlet being filled with blasphemous names, having seven heads and ten horns.	3 And he carried me into the desert by the Spirit. And I saw a woman sitting upon the beast in scarlet being filled with blasphemous names, having seven heads and ten horns.	3 And he carried me into the desert by the Spirit. And I saw a woman sitting upon the beast in scarlet being filled with blasphemous names, having seven heads and ten horns.
17:4 καὶ ἡ γυνὴ ἦν περιβεβλημένη πορφυροῦν καὶ κόκκινον And the woman was clothed in purple and scarlet καὶ κεχρυσωμένη χρυσίῳ καὶ λίθῳ τιμίῳ καὶ μαργαρίταις, and being gilded in gold and precious stones and pearls, ἔχουσα ποτήριον χρυσοῦν ἐν τῇ χειρὶ αὐτῆς having a golden cup in her hand	4 And the woman was clothed in purple and scarlet and being gilded in gold and precious stones and pearls, having a golden cup in her hand being filled with abominations and impurities of her fornication.	4 And the woman was clothed in purple and scarlet and being gilded in gold and precious stones and pearls, having a golden cup in her hand being filled with abominations and impurities of her fornication.	4 And the woman was clothed in purple and scarlet and being gilded in gold and precious stones and pearls, having a golden cup in her hand being filled with abominations and impurities of her fornication.	4 And the woman was clothed in purple and scarlet and being gilded in gold and precious stones and pearls, having a golden cup in her hand being filled with abominations and impurities of her fornication.

Greek / Literal			

γέμον βδελυγμάτων καὶ τὰ ἀκάθαρτα τῆς πορνείας αὐτῆς
being filled with abominations and impurities of her fornication

17:5 καὶ ἐπὶ τὸ μέτωπον αὐτῆς ὄνομα γεγραμμένον,
and upon her forehead a name having been written,

μυστήριον, Βαβυλὼν ἡ μεγάλη,
"Mystery, Babylon the great,

ἡ μήτηρ τῶν πορνῶν καὶ τῶν βδελυγμάτων τῆς γῆς.
the mother of harlots and abominations of the earth."

17:6 καὶ εἶδον τὴν γυναῖκα μεθύουσαν
And I saw the woman being drunk

ἐκ τοῦ αἵματος τῶν ἁγίων
from the blood of the saints

καὶ ἐκ τοῦ αἵματος τῶν μαρτύρων Ἰησοῦ.
and from the blood of the martyrs of Jesus.

Καὶ ἐθαύμασα ἰδὼν αὐτὴν θαῦμα μέγα.
And I was amazed with a great amazement, seeing her.

Column 2

5 And upon her forehead was a name having been written, "Mystery, Babylon the great, the mother of harlots and abominations of the earth."

6 And I saw the woman being drunk from the blood of the saints and from the blood of Jesus. And I was greatly amazed seeing her. This vision was of Rome, the new Babylon, seen as Roma dressed expensively as a harlot with her scarlet and purple attire and gaudy jewelry. She personified Rome and its empire—the beast, including Nero and Domitian. Their demand to be worshipped oozed of blasphemy. The ten kings did their bidding. Roma and the beast plunged the world into spiritual immorality. Her name, Roma, is a mystery—amor (love)

Column 3

5 And upon her forehead was a name having been written, "Mystery, Babylon the great, the mother of harlots and abominations of the earth."

6 And I saw the woman being drunk from the blood of the saints and from the blood of the martyrs of Jesus. And I was greatly amazed seeing her. So the desert is the Campagna (the low plain surrounding the city of Rome). The harlot is the pope, whose scarlet and purple robes and lavish jewelry bespeak the corruption of the ornate Roman church. The beast is the Roman church, which embodies the syncretistic alliance of Christianity and paganism (e.g., mother-goddess worship, idolatrous rites, anti-Christ sacrifice of the masses, indulgences). The Roman

---

Column 4

5 And upon her forehead was a name having been written, "Mystery, Babylon the great, the mother of harlots and abominations of the earth."

6 And I saw the woman being drunk from the blood of the saints and from the blood of the martyrs of Jesus. And I was greatly amazed seeing her. So the angel showed John literal Babylon in the eastern Arabian desert, situated on the Euphrates River and its canals. Babylon will be the new home of the revived Roman Empire/European Union (the beast), led by the Antichrist (the harlot). The Antichrist will be powerful, rich, and blasphemous. The "mystery" of Babylon is that the city of Babylon will be the end-time capital of the kingdom of the Antichrist, revived from

---

Column 5

5 And upon her forehead was a name having been written, "Mystery, Babylon the great, the mother of harlots and abominations of the earth."

6 And I saw the woman being drunk from the blood of the saints and from the blood of the martyrs of Jesus. And I was greatly amazed seeing her. Thus the angel carried John to the desert, a symbol for the dwelling place of demons. There John saw Babylon, the symbol for any pleasure—mad, luxurious, blasphemous society, which seduces many in the church (from OT Babylon to NT Rome to modern Las Vegas) and seduces the world with its godless philosophy and persecutes true Christians because they refuse to bow before Babylon's idolatry. The mystery of Babylon is the

Greek Text and English Translation	Preterist View	Historicist View	Futurist View	Idealist View
	spelled backwards. She inspired the beast (Nero, then Domitian) to persecute Christians because they worshipped Jesus, not Caesar.	Catholic Church mercilessly persecutes the followers of the Protestant Reformation, the true church. The seven heads/hills represent the seven forms of government under the Roman Empire throughout its existence. The ten horns are subordinate kingdoms that comprise the Roman Empire, and culminate in the Roman papacy. The mystery of Babylon is that the spirit of Antichrist persecutes the church.	its defeat by Cyrus in 539 B.C. New Babylon will oppose Christ and his spiritual kingdom like no other kingdom in history. Many Tribulation saints will die at the hands of the Antichrist and his coalition.	mystery of evil that permeates any society and turns it against Christ.
17:7 Καὶ εἶπέν μοι ὁ ἄγγελος· διὰ τί ἐθαύμασας; And the angel said to me, "Why were you amazed?	7 And the angel said to me, "Why were you amazed? I will tell you the mystery of the woman and of the beast carrying her, having the seven heads and the ten horns.	7 And the angel said to me, "Why were you amazed? I will tell you the mystery of the woman and of the beast carrying her, having the seven heads and the ten horns.	7 And the angel said to me, "Why were you amazed? I will tell you the mystery of the woman and of the beast carrying her, having the seven heads and the ten horns.	7 And the angel said to me, "Why were you amazed? I will tell you the mystery of the woman and of the beast carrying her, having the seven heads and the ten horns.
ἐγὼ ἐρῶ σοι τὸ μυστήριον τῆς γυναικὸς καὶ τοῦ θηρίου τοῦ βαστάζοντος αὐτὴν I will tell you the mystery of the woman and of the beast carrying her				
τοῦ ἔχοντος τὰς ἑπτὰ κεφαλὰς καὶ τὰ δέκα κέρατα. having the seven heads and the ten horns.				
17:8 Τὸ θηρίον ὃ εἶδες ἦν καὶ οὐκ ἔστιν The beast which you saw was and is not	8 The beast which you saw was and is not and is about to rise out of the abyss and goes to destruction, and the inhabitants of the earth	8 The beast which you saw was and is not and is about to rise out of the abyss and goes to destruction, and the inhabitants of the earth will be	8 The beast which you saw was and is not and is about to rise out of the abyss and goes to destruction, and the inhabitants of the earth	8 The beast which you saw was and is and is about to rise out of the abyss and goes to destruction, and the inhabitants of the earth will be

Greek / Literal				
17:8 καὶ μέλλει ἀναβαίνειν ἐκ τῆς ἀβύσσου καὶ εἰς ἀπώλειαν ὑπάγει, and is about to rise out of the abyss and goes to destruction, καὶ θαυμασθήσονται οἱ κατοικοῦντες ἐπὶ τῆς γῆς, and those inhabiting the earth will be amazed, ὧν οὐ γέγραπται τὸ ὄνομα ἐπὶ τὸ βιβλίον τῆς ζωῆς the ones whose names have not been written in the book of life ἀπὸ καταβολῆς κόσμου, from the foundation of the world, βλεπόντων τὸ θηρίον ὅτι ἦν καὶ οὐκ ἔστιν καὶ παρέσται· seeing the beast that was and is not and is present.	will be amazed, the ones whose names have not been written in the book of life from the foundation of the world, seeing the beast that was and is present. In other words, the beast who was and is not was Nero, but he will be revived and sent from hell to stir up civil war in the Roman Empire.	amazed, the ones whose names have not been written in the book of life from the foundation of the world, seeing the beast that was and is not and is present. Thus, because John needed more information, the angel further explained the vision: the beast that was and disappeared and returns is the papacy, which was first the Antichrist spirit that drove the Roman Empire and then was later made visible in the popes who held the world spellbound.	will be amazed, the ones whose names have not been written in the book of life from the foundation of the world, seeing the beast that was and is not and is present. So the angel clarified the situation: the beast who was, is not, and will be is Rome and the revived Roman Empire. This one, the Antichrist, will deceive the nations.	amazed, the ones whose names have not been written in the book of life from the foundation of the world, seeing the beast that was and is present. Thus John was puzzled about the beast who was, is not, and is, is the Antichrist, who is manifested in John's day through Rome but will culminate in a future attempt to rule the world.
17:9 ὧδε ὁ νοῦς ὁ ἔχων σοφίαν. Αἱ ἑπτὰ κεφαλαὶ ἑπτὰ ὄρη εἰσίν, Here is the mind having wisdom: the seven heads are seven mountains, ὅπου ἡ γυνὴ κάθηται ἐπ᾽ αὐτῶν. on which the the woman is seated on them, καὶ βασιλεῖς ἑπτά εἰσιν· and they are seven kings.	9 Here is the mind having wisdom: the seven heads are seven mountains on which the woman is seated, and they are seven kings.	9 Here is the mind having wisdom: the seven heads are seven mountains on which the woman is seated, and they are seven kings.	9 Here is the mind having wisdom: the seven heads are seven mountains on which the woman is seated, and they are seven kings.	9 Here is the mind having wisdom: the seven heads are seven mountains on which the woman is seated, and they are seven kings.
17:10 οἱ πέντε ἔπεσαν, ὁ εἷς ἔστιν, ὁ ἄλλος οὔπω ἦλθεν, Five have fallen, the one is, the other has not yet come, καὶ ὅταν ἔλθῃ ὀλίγον αὐτὸν δεῖ μεῖναι. and when he comes he must remain a little while.	10 Five have fallen, the one is, the other has not yet come, and when he comes he must remain a little while.	10 Five have fallen, the one is, the other has not yet come, and when he comes he must remain a little while.	10 Five have fallen, the one is, the other has not yet come, and when he comes he must remain a little while.	10 Five have fallen, the one is, the other has not yet come, and when he comes he must remain a little while.
17:11 καὶ τὸ θηρίον ὃ ἦν καὶ οὐκ ἔστιν And the beast which was and is not	11 And the beast which was and is not, he is also	11 And the beast which was and is not, he is also	11 And the beast which was and is not, he is also	11 And the beast which was and is not, he is also

Greek Text and English Translation	Preterist View	Historicist View	Futurist View	Idealist View
καὶ αὐτὸς ὄγδοός ἐστιν καὶ ἐκ τῶν ἑπτά ἐστιν, and he is an eighth and is out of the seven, καὶ εἰς ἀπώλειαν ὑπάγει. and he goes unto destruction.	an eighth and is out of the seven, and he goes unto destruction. In other words, the seven heads are the first-century Roman caesars: Augustus, Tiberius, Caligula (Gaius), Claudius, Nero (the five who have fallen), Vespasian (the one who is), and Titus. The one who was is Nero; the one who is to come briefly is Titus. The eighth is Domitian, who is Nero Redivivus. The seven hills are the hills upon which Rome is located: Capitoline, Aventine, Caelian, Esquiline, Quirinal, Viminal, and Palatine.	an eighth and is out of the seven, and he goes unto destruction. More specifically, the seven heads/hills represent the forms of Roman government, five of which had fallen by John's day (kings, consuls, dictators, decemvirs, military tribunes). The sixth in John's day comprised the caesars. The seventh would be Diocletian, the most infamous persecutor of early Christians. The eighth is the worst persecutor of all, the Roman papacy, which persecuted Wycliffe, Luther, Tyndale, and countless millions of true Christians, followers of the Reformation.	an eighth and is out of the seven, and he goes unto destruction. More particularly, the seven heads/hills are world empires. Five had fallen by John's day: Egypt, Assyria, Babylon, Persia, and Greece. The sixth (the one who is) was Rome in John's day. The seventh, the one to come briefly, will be the remainder of the Roman caesars, until the fall of the Roman Empire. The eighth, the beast who was, is not, and will be, will be the revived Roman Empire/European Union at the end of history, led by the Antichrist from New Babylon, his capital city.	an eighth and is out of the seven, and he goes unto destruction. So the seven heads/hills are godless empires. Five had fallen by John's day: ancient Babylonia, Assyria, new Babylonia, Medo-Persia, and Greece. The one in John's day (the sixth) was Rome. The seventh will be all governments, from the fall of Rome to the Antichrist. The Antichrist will be the eighth and final godless society.
17:12 Καὶ τὰ δέκα κέρατα ἃ εἶδες δέκα βασιλεῖς εἰσιν, And the ten horns which you saw are ten kings, οἵτινες βασιλείαν οὔπω ἔλαβον, who have not yet received a kingdom, ἀλλὰ ἐξουσίαν ὡς βασιλεῖς μίαν ὥραν λαμβάνουσιν μετὰ τοῦ θηρίου. but they will have authority as kings for one hour with the beast.	12 And the ten horns which you saw are ten kings who have not yet received a kingdom, but they will have authority like kings for one hour with the beast.	12 And the ten horns which you saw are ten kings who have not yet received a kingdom, but they will have authority like kings for one hour with the beast.	12 And the ten horns which you saw are ten kings who have not yet received a kingdom, but they will have authority like kings for one hour with the beast.	12 And the ten horns which you saw are ten kings who have not yet received a kingdom, but they will have authority like kings for one hour with the beast.

Greek	Translation 1	Translation 2	Translation 3	Translation 4
17:13 οὖ τοι μίαν γνώμην ἔχουσιν καὶ τὴν δύναμιν / These have one mind and power / καὶ ἐξουσίαν αὐτῶν τῷ θηρίῳ διδόασιν. / and they give their authority to the beast.	13 These have one mind and power, and they give their authority to the beast.	13 These have one mind and power, and they give their authority to the beast.	13 These have one mind and power, and they give their authority to the beast.	13 These have one mind and power, and they give their authority to the beast.
17:14 οὖτοι μετὰ τοῦ ἀρνίου πολεμήσουσιν / These will make war with the Lamb, / καὶ τὸ ἀρνίον νικήσει αὐτούς, / and the Lamb will overcome them, / ὅτι κύριος κυρίων ἐστὶν καὶ βασιλεὺς βασιλέων / because he is Lord of Lords and King of Kings / καὶ οἱ μετ᾽ αὐτοῦ κλητοὶ καὶ ἐκλεκτοὶ καὶ πιστοί. / and the ones with him [are] called and chosen and faithful.	14 These will make war with the Lamb, and the Lamb will overcome them, because he is Lord of Lords and King of Kings, and the ones with him are called and chosen and faithful." The ten horns are the ten client kings appointed by Rome to be puppet governments who will join with the beast to fight the approaching army of the Messiah—the Lamb and his followers.	14 These will make war with the Lamb, and the Lamb will overcome them, because he is Lord of Lords and King of Kings, and the ones with him are called and chosen and faithful." Thus the ten horns are the ten subordinate kingdoms that comprised the Roman Empire up until A.D. 532: Anglo-Saxons, Franks, Alleman-Franks, Burgundic-Franks, Visigoths, Suevi, Vandals, Ostrogoths, Bavarians, and Lombards. After that the papacy emerged. These warred against the Lamb.	14 These will make war with the Lamb, and the Lamb will overcome them, because he is Lord of Lords and King of Kings, and the ones with him are called and chosen and faithful." Thus the Antichrist (the beast) and the harlot (the revived Roman Empire/Babylon) will marshal their forces against Russia and its Muslim-led confederation to descend on Jerusalem to take control of that city.	14 These will make war with the Lamb, and the Lamb will overcome them, because he is Lord of Lords and King of Kings, and the ones with him are called and chosen and faithful." The ten horns, then, is a symbolic number representing all anti-Christian powers on earth, who wage war against the true church; but they will fail miserably.
17:15 Καὶ λέγει μοι· τὰ ὕδατα ἃ εἶδες / And he says to me, "The waters which you saw, / οὗ ἡ πόρνη κάθηται, λαοὶ καὶ ὄχλοι εἰσὶν / where the harlot sits, are peoples and crowds / καὶ ἔθνη καὶ γλῶσσαι. / and nations and tongues.	15 And he says to me, "The waters which you saw, where the harlot sits, are peoples and crowds and nations and tongues.	15 And he says to me, "The waters which you saw, where the harlot sits, are peoples and crowds and nations and tongues.	15 And he says to me, "The waters which you saw, where the harlot sits, are peoples and crowds and nations and tongues.	15 And he says to me, "The waters which you saw, where the harlot sits, are peoples and crowds and nations and tongues.
17:16 καὶ τὰ δέκα κέρατα ἃ εἶδες καὶ τὸ θηρίον / And the ten horns which you saw and the beast / οὗτοι μισήσουσιν τὴν πόρνην / these will hate the harlot	16 And the ten horns which you saw and the beast, these will hate the harlot and will make her desolated and naked, and they will consume	16 And the ten horns which you saw and the beast, these will hate the harlot and will make her desolated and naked, and they will consume	16 And the ten horns which you saw and the beast, these will hate the harlot and will make her desolated and naked, and they will consume	16 And the ten horns which you saw and the beast, these will hate the harlot and will make her desolated and naked, and they will consume

Greek Text and English Translation	Preterist View	Historicist View	Futurist View	Idealist View
καὶ ἠρημωμένην ποιήσουσιν αὐτὴν καὶ γυμνὴν and they will make her desolated and naked καὶ τὰς σάρκας αὐτῆς φάγονται καὶ αὐτὴν κατακαύσουσιν ἐν πυρί. and they will consume her flesh and they will burn her up with fire.	her flesh, and they will burn her with fire.	her flesh, and they will burn her with fire.	her flesh, and they will burn her with fire.	her flesh, and they will burn her with fire.
17:17 ὁ γὰρ θεὸς ἔδωκεν εἰς τὰς καρδίας αὐτῶν ποιῆσαι τὴν γνώμην For God gave into their hearts to do his mind αὐτοῦ καὶ ποιῆσαι μίαν γνώμην and to do one mind καὶ δοῦναι τὴν βασιλείαν αὐτῶν and to give their kingdom τῷ θηρίῳ ἄχρι τελεσθήσονται οἱ λόγοι τοῦ θεοῦ. to the beast until the words of God will have been completed.	17 For God gave into their hearts to do his intent and to act with one mind and to give their kingdom to the beast until the words of God will have been completed.	17 For God gave into their hearts to do his intent and to act with one mind and to give their kingdom to the beast until the words of God will have been completed.	17 For God gave into their hearts to do his intent and to act with one mind and to give their kingdom to the beast until the words of God will have been completed.	17 For God gave into their hearts to do his intent and to act with one mind and to give their kingdom to the beast until the words of God will have been completed.
17:18 καὶ ἡ γυνὴ ἣν εἶδες ἐστιν ἡ πόλις ἡ μεγάλη And the woman which you saw is the great city ἡ ἔχουσα βασιλείαν ἐπὶ τῶν βασιλέων τῆς γῆς. having a kingdom over the kings of the earth."	18 And the woman which you saw is the great city having a kingdom over the kings of the earth." The ten horns are the Parthian client kings led by Nero Redivivus for the purpose of turning on Rome and destroying it. Domitian, however, will broker a peace pact with the Parthians and enlist them to fight the Lamb. Behind all of this is God,	18 And the woman which you saw is the great city having a kingdom over the kings of the earth." So the fall of the godless Roman church is certain. Foreshadowed by the burning of Rome by the Goths in the fifth and sixth centuries and intensified by the bowl judgments of the French Revolution (eighteenth century), the Romish	18 And the woman which you saw is the great city having a kingdom over the kings of the earth." In other words, along the way, the Antichrist will betray and destroy the Russian-led Muslim army in a bid to conquer the world. All that will stand in his way is Jerusalem. But Christ will return and annihilate the Antichrist and the European Union.	18 And the woman which you saw is the great city having a kingdom over the kings of the earth." Eventually, all earthly godless powers (the beast) turn against their religious orientation (the harlot) and destroy it, but without replacing it with the true worship of God and Christ.

who will engineer the destruction of the Roman Empire at the hands of the Messianic army. Moreover, Jerusalem, which was in cahoots with Rome, now experiences Rome's turning on the "Holy" City to destroy it. This is so because Jerusalem was filled with the blood of the prophets.

(**Editor's note:** There are two camps of biblical preterists regarding Revelation 17–18—those who equate Babylon of Revelation 17–18 with the fall of Jerusalem in A.D. 70 and those who equate it with the fall of Rome in A.D. 476. Both views are incorporated in the interpretation given here. The former event—the fall of Jerusalem—happened shortly before or after Revelation was written, while the latter event—the fall of Rome—happened much later than when John supposed it would. But his prophecy eventually was indeed fulfilled. There was OT precedent for John equating Babylon with both Jerusalem and Rome, for just as God used Babylon as his instrument for punishing apostate Jerusalem [587 B.C.], so

system will soon receive its just deserts.

Greek Text and English Translation	Preterist View	Historicist View	Futurist View	Idealist View
	God used Rome to punish apostate Jerusalem in A.D. 70; but God would one day destroy Rome for destroying his people as well [A.D. 476], just as He used Persia to destroy ancient Babylon... The allusions to the two cities—Jerusalem and Rome—are interspersed throughout Revelation 18.)			
18:1 Μετὰ ταῦτα εἶδον ἄλλον ἄγγελον After these things I saw another angel καταβαίνοντα ἐκ τοῦ οὐρανοῦ descending out of heaven ἔχοντα ἐξουσίαν μεγάλην, καὶ ἡ γῆ ἐφωτίσθη ἐκ τῆς δόξης αὐτοῦ. having great authority, and the earth was illumined by his glory.	1 After these things I saw another angel descending out of heaven having great authority, and the earth was illumined by his glory.	1 After these things I saw another angel descending out of heaven having great authority, and the earth was illumined by his glory.	1 After these things I saw another angel descending out of heaven having great authority, and the earth was illumined by his glory.	1 After these things I saw another angel descending out of heaven having great authority, and the earth was illumined by his glory.
18:2 καὶ ἔκραξεν ἐν ἰσχυρᾷ φωνῇ λέγων· And he cried in a strong voice saying, ἔπεσεν ἔπεσεν Βαβυλὼν ἡ μεγάλη, "Fallen, fallen has Babylon the great!" καὶ ἐγένετο κατοικητήριον δαιμονίων And it became a habitation of demons καὶ φυλακὴ παντὸς πνεύματος ἀκαθάρτου and a lair of every unclean spirit	2 And he cried in a strong voice, saying, "Fallen, fallen has Babylon the great!" (Even though Jerusalem and Rome may not yet have fallen in John's day, it was certain that they would.) And it became a habitation of demons and a lair of every unclean spirit and a lair of every	2 And he cried in a strong voice, saying, "Fallen, fallen has Babylon the great!" (Papal Rome is as good as fallen). And it became a habitation of demons and a lair of every unclean spirit (cf. Jer. 51:7) and a lair of every unclean bird (cf. Isa. 13:21–22) and a lair of every unclean and hated beast,	2 And he cried in a strong voice, saying, "Fallen, fallen has New Babylon the great!" (which is as good as dead; this will occur at the second coming of Christ at the end of the Great Tribulation. Revelation 17 records New Babylon's future religious fall, while Revelation 18 records its future commercial	2 And he cried in a strong voice, saying, "Fallen, fallen has Babylon the great!" And it became a habitation of demons and a lair of every unclean spirit and a prison of every unclean bird and a prison of every unclean and hated beast,

καὶ φυλακὴ παντὸς ὀρνέου ἀκαθάρτου and a lair of every unclean bird [καὶ φυλακὴ παντὸς θηρίου ἀκαθάρτου] καὶ μεμισημένου, and a lair of every unclean and hated beast, **18:3** ὅτι ἐκ τοῦ οἴνου τοῦ θυμοῦ τῆς πορνείας αὐτῆς πέπωκαν πάντα τὰ ἔθνη because out of the wine of wrath of her fornication all nations have drunk καὶ οἱ βασιλεῖς τῆς γῆς μετ' αὐτῆς ἐπόρνευσαν and the kings of the earth fornicated with her καὶ οἱ ἔμποροι τῆς γῆς ἐκ τῆς δυνάμεως τοῦ στρήνους αὐτῆς ἐπλούτησαν. and the merchants of the earth became rich from the power of her luxury.	unclean and hated beast (apostate Jerusalem was overrun by demons, just as Jesus prophesied [Matt. 12:38–45; 24:2]!), 3 because out of the wine of wrath of her fornica-tion all nations have drunk, and kings of the earth fornicated with her, and the merchants of the earth became rich from the power of her luxury. Ancient Rome was well known for its luxury (cf. Aelius Aristides' descrip-tion referred to below).	demise; both describe the same event but from dif-ferent perspectives). And it became a habitation of demons and a lair of every unclean spirit and a lair of every unclean bird and a lair of every unclean and hated beast, 3 because out of the wine of wrath of her fornication all nations have drunk, and kings of the earth fornicated with her (that is, com-mitted spiritual adultery with the Antichrist), and the merchants of the earth became rich from the power of her luxury (materialism).	3 because out of the wine of wrath of her fornica-tion all nations have drunk, and kings of the earth fornicated with her, and the merchants of the earth became rich from the power of her luxury. Babylon represents the worldly city or center of wickedness that allures, tempts, and draws people away from God (cf. Ezek. 27–28). Babylon is the pleasure-mad, ar-rogant world with all its seductive luxuries and pleasures, with its anti-Christian philosophy and culture, and with its teeming multitudes that have forsaken God and have lived according to the lusts of the flesh and the desires of the mind. In the first century, Babylon was Rome. Two generations ago it was Berlin. Today, perhaps, it is Las Vegas ("What happens in Vegas stays in

Greek Text and English Translation	Preterist View	Historicist View	Futurist View	Idealist View
				Vegas!") or even a university campus. Babylon can be found everywhere throughout the history of the world. It is the center of anti-Christian seduction any time in history. Babylon can even be the world in the church, as it once infiltrated ancient Israel (see Rev. 2:9 and the "synagogue of Satan").
18:4 Καὶ ἤκουσα ἄλλην φωνὴν ἐκ τοῦ οὐρανοῦ λέγουσαν· And I heard another voice out of heaven saying, ἐξέλθατε ὁ λαός μου ἐξ αὐτῆς "Come out, my people, from her, ἵνα μὴ συγκοινωνήσητε ταῖς ἁμαρτίαις αὐτῆς, in order that you may not have fellowship with her sins καὶ ἐκ τῶν πληγῶν αὐτῆς ἵνα μὴ λάβητε, and so that you might not receive any of her plagues	4 And I heard another voice out of heaven saying, "Come out, my people, from her, in order that you may not have fellowship with her sins and that you might not receive any of her plagues	4 And I heard another voice out of heaven saying, "Come out, my people (cf. Isa. 48:20; Jer. 51:6, 45; which happened with the Protestant Reformation), from her, in order that you may not have fellowship with her sins and that you might not receive any of her plagues (which applies to all who do not leave Roman Catholicism)	4 And I heard another voice out of heaven saying, "Come out, my people (those few true Christians who will survive martyrdom at the hands of the Antichrist), from her, in order that you may not have fellowship with her sins and that you might not receive any of her plagues	4 And I heard another voice out of heaven saying, "Come out, my people, from her, in order that you may not have fellowship with her sins and that you might not receive any of her plagues (cf. Isa. 51:11; Jer. 51:45; 2 Cor. 6:17; this admonition is addressed to the church of all periods)
18:5 ὅτι ἐκολλήθησαν αὐτῆς αἱ ἁμαρτίαι ἄχρι τοῦ οὐρανοῦ because her sins have clung together as far as the sky καὶ ἐμνημόνευσεν ὁ θεὸς τὰ ἀδικήματα αὐτῆς. and God has remembered her misdeeds!	5 because her sins have clung together as far as the sky and God has remembered her misdeeds!	5 because her sins have clung together as far as the sky and God has remembered her misdeeds!	5 because her sins have clung together as far as the sky (like the Tower of Babel [Gen. 11:5–9], where Babylon had its beginning), and God has remembered her misdeeds!	5 because her sins have clung together as far as the sky (like the Tower of Babel in Gen. 11) and God has remembered her misdeeds!

18:6 ἀπόδοτε αὐτῇ ὡς καὶ αὐτὴ ἀπέδοκεν — Give back to her as also she gave back, καὶ διπλώσατε τὰ διπλᾶ κατὰ τὰ ἔργα αὐτῆς, — and double the double according to her works; ἐν τῷ ποτηρίῳ ᾧ ἐκέρασεν — in the cup in which she mixed, κεράσατε αὐτῇ διπλοῦν, — mix double for her;	6 Give back to her as also she gave back, and double the double according to her works; in the cup in which she mixed, mix double for her;	6 Give back to her as also she gave back, and double the double according to her works; in the cup in which she mixed, mix double for her;	6 Give back to her as also she gave back, and double the double according to her works; in the cup in which she mixed, mix double for her;	6 Give back to her as also she gave back, and double the double according to her works; in the cup in which she mixed, mix double for her;
18:7 ὅσα ἐδόξασεν αὐτὴν καὶ ἐστρηνίασεν, — by as much as she glorified herself and luxuriated, τοσοῦτον δότε αὐτῇ βασανισμὸν καὶ πένθος. — by so much give to her torment and sorrow, ὅτι ἐν τῇ καρδίᾳ αὐτῆς λέγει ὅτι κάθημαι βασίλισσα — because in her heart she says that 'I sit like a queen καὶ χήρα οὐκ εἰμι καὶ πένθος οὐ μὴ ἴδω. — and I am not a widow and I never ever behold sorrow.'	7 by as much as she glorified herself and luxuriated, by so much give to her torment and sorrow, because in her heart she says that 'I sit like a queen and am not a widow and never ever behold sorrow.'	7 by as much as she glorified herself and luxuriated, by so much give to her torment and sorrow, because in her heart she says that 'I sit like a queen [the supposed Queen Mother of the church = Mary and Mariology] and am not a widow and never ever behold sorrow.'	7 by as much as she glorified herself and luxuriated, by so much give to her torment and sorrow, because in her heart she says that 'I sit like a queen and am not a widow and never ever behold sorrow.'	7 by as much as she glorified herself and luxuriated, by so much give to her torment and sorrow, because in her heart she says that 'I sit like a queen and am not a widow and never ever behold sorrow.' The judgment of Babylon in every generation causes the unrighteous to mourn, but the righteous to rejoice.
18:8 διὰ τοῦτο ἐν μιᾷ ἡμέρᾳ ἥξουσιν αἱ πληγαὶ αὐτῆς, — Because of this, in one day her plagues will come, θάνατος καὶ πένθος καὶ λιμός, — death and sorrow and famine, καὶ ἐν πυρὶ κατακαυθήσεται, — and by fire she will be consumed, ὅτι ἰσχυρὸς κύριος ὁ θεὸς ὁ κρίνας αὐτήν. — because the Lord God, the one judging her, is strong.	8 Because of this, in one day her plagues will come, death and sorrow and famine, and by fire she will be consumed, because the Lord God, the one judging her, is strong. These allusions to OT oracles against Babylon, Tyre, Sodom, and Jerusalem (see, for example, Isa. 48:20; Jer. 50:8; 51:6; Ezek. 18:21) apply again to both	8 Because of this, in one day her plagues will come, death and sorrow and famine, and by fire she will be consumed, because the Lord God, the one judging her, is strong.	8 Because of this, in one day her plagues will come, death and sorrow and famine, and by fire she will be consumed, because the Lord God, the one judging her, is strong. Jeremiah 50–51 predicts that Babylon will utterly fall, never to rise again. This prophecy was not actually fulfilled in 539 B.C., when Cyrus the Persian defeated Babylon, as many interpreters	8 Because of this, in one day her plagues will come, death and sorrow and famine, and by fire she will be consumed, cause the Lord God, the one judging her, is strong.

Greek Text and English Translation	Preterist View	Historicist View	Futurist View	Idealist View
	Jerusalem in A.D. 70 and Rome in A.D. 476.		mistakenly assume. Rather, Babylon was defeated only temporarily at that time. Indeed, Sadaam Hussein began the rebuilding of Babylon, which will blossom again and one day serve as the home of the Antichrist. But when Christ returns, he will finally destroy Babylon, thereby fulfilling Jeremiah 50–51.	
18:9 Καὶ κλαύσουσιν καὶ κόψονται ἐπ᾽ αὐτὴν οἱ βασιλεῖς τῆς γῆς οἱ μετ᾽ αὐτῆς πορνεύσαντες καὶ στρηνιάσαντες, And the kings of the earth, the ones having fornicated and luxuriated with her, will weep and wail over her	9 And the kings of the earth, the ones having fornicated and luxuriated with her (Rome), will weep and wail over her when they see the smoke of her burning,	9 And the kings of the earth, the ones having fornicated and luxuriated with her, will weep and wail over her when they see the smoke of her burning,	9 And the kings of the earth, the ones having fornicated and luxuriated with her, will weep and wail over her when they see the smoke of her burning,	9 And the kings of the earth, the ones having fornicated and luxuriated with her, will weep and wail over her when they see the smoke of her burning,
ὅταν βλέπωσιν τὸν καπνὸν τῆς πυρώσεως αὐτῆς, when they see the smoke of her burning,				
18:10 ἀπὸ μακρόθεν ἑστηκότες and standing from afar	10 and standing from afar because of the fear of her torment, saying,	10 and standing from afar because of the fear of her torment, saying,	10 and standing from afar because of the fear of her torment, saying,	10 and standing from afar because of the fear of her torment, saying,
διὰ τὸν φόβον τοῦ βασανισμοῦ αὐτῆς λέγοντες· because of the fear of her torment, saying,	'Woe, woe, the great city, Babylon the strong city, because in one hour your judgment has come.' (Jerusalem fell in A.D. 70 in a short time; Rome, in A.D. 476, took longer.)	'Woe, woe, the great city, Babylon the strong city, because in one hour your judgment has come.'	'Woe, woe, the great city, Babylon the strong city (rebuilt by the Antichrist to exceed even its former glory under King Nebuchadnezzar), because in one hour your judgment has come.'	'Woe, woe, the great city, Babylon the strong city, because in one hour your judgment has come.'
οὐαὶ οὐαί, ἡ πόλις ἡ μεγάλη, Βαβυλὼν ἡ πόλις ἡ ἰσχυρά, 'Woe, woe, the great city, Babylon the strong city,				
ὅτι μιᾷ ὥρᾳ ἦλθεν ἡ κρίσις σου. because in one hour your judgment has come.'				

18:11 Καὶ οἱ ἔμποροι τῆς γῆς κλαίουσιν καὶ πενθοῦσιν ἐπ᾽ αὐτήν, And the merchants of the earth weep and sorrow over her,	11 And the merchants of the earth weep and sorrow over her, because no one buys their cargo any longer,	11 And the merchants of the earth weep and sorrow over her, because no one buys their cargo any longer,	11 And the merchants of the earth weep and sorrow over her, because no one buys their cargo any longer,	11 And the merchants of the earth weep and sorrow over her, because no one buys their cargo any longer,
ὅτι τὸν γόμον αὐτῶν οὐδεὶς ἀγοράζει οὐκέτι because no one buys their cargo any longer,					
18:12 γόμον χρυσοῦ καὶ ἀργύρου καὶ λίθου τιμίου cargo of gold and silver and valuable stone	12 cargo of gold and silver and valuable stone and of pearls and of fine linen and of purple and of silk and of scarlet, and all costly wood and every ivory vessel and most valuable vessel of wood and of bronze and of iron and of marble,	12 cargo of gold and silver and valuable stone and of pearls and of fine linen and of purple and of silk and of scarlet, and all costly wood and every ivory vessel and every most valuable vessel of wood and of bronze and of iron and of marble,	12 cargo of gold and silver and valuable stone and of pearls and of fine linen and of purple and of silk and of scarlet, and all costly wood and every ivory vessel and every most valuable vessel of wood and of bronze and of iron and of marble,	12 cargo of gold and silver and valuable stone and of pearls and of fine linen and of purple and of silk and of scarlet, and all costly wood and every ivory vessel and every most valuable vessel of wood and of bronze and of iron and of marble,
καὶ μαργαριτῶν καὶ βυσσίνου and of pearls and of fine linen					
καὶ πορφύρας καὶ σιρικοῦ καὶ κοκκίνου, and of purple and of silk and of scarlet,					
καὶ πᾶν ξύλον θύϊνον καὶ πᾶν σκεῦος ἐλεφάντινον and all costly wood and every ivory vessel					
καὶ πᾶν σκεῦος ἐκ ξύλου τιμιοτάτου and every most valuable vessel of wood					
καὶ χαλκοῦ καὶ σιδήρου καὶ μαρμάρου, and of bronze and of iron and of marble,					
18:13 καὶ κιννάμωμον καὶ ἄμωμον καὶ θυμιάματα καὶ μύρον and cinnamon and spice and incense and ointment	13 and cinnamon and spice and incense and ointment and frankincense and wine and oil and fine meal and grain and beasts of burden and sheep, and of horses and of carriages and of bodies and souls of men.	13 and cinnamon and spice and incense and ointment and frankincense and wine and oil and fine meal and grain and beasts of burden and sheep, and of horses and of carriages and of bodies and souls of men.	13 and cinnamon and spice and incense and frankincense and wine and oil and fine meal and grain and beasts of burden and sheep, and of horses and of carriages and of bodies and souls of men. These twenty-eight items parade the opulence and affluence that will characterize the new Babylon to be rebuilt by the Antichrist.	13 and cinnamon and spice and incense and frankincense and wine and oil and fine meal and grain and beasts of burden and sheep, and of horses and of carriages and of bodies and souls of men. This recalls the great number of slaves, prostitutes, and victims of the amphitheater that fed ancient
καὶ λίβανον καὶ οἶνον καὶ ἔλαιον καὶ σεμίδαλιν καὶ σῖτον and frankincense and wine and oil and fine meal and grain					
καὶ κτήνη καὶ πρόβατα, καὶ ἵππων καὶ ῥεδῶν and beasts of burden and sheep and of horses and of carriages					

Greek Text and English Translation	Preterist View	Historicist View	Futurist View	Idealist View
καὶ σωμάτων, καὶ ψυχὰς ἀνθρώπων. and of bodies and souls of men.				Rome's thirst for pleasure, entertainment, and gore.
18:14 καὶ ἡ ὀπώρα σου τῆς ἐπιθυμίας τῆς ψυχῆς ἀπῆλθεν ἀπὸ σοῦ, And the fruit of your soul's lust departed from you, καὶ πάντα τὰ λιπαρὰ καὶ τὰ λαμπρὰ ἀπώλετο ἀπὸ σοῦ and all the sumptuous things and the bright things perished from you, καὶ οὐκέτι οὐ μὴ αὐτὰ εὑρήσουσιν. and they will never find them any longer.	14 And the fruit of your soul's lust departed from you, and all the sumptuous things and the bright things perished from you, and they will never find them any longer.	14 And the fruit of your soul's lust departed from you, and all the sumptuous things and the bright things perished from you, and they will never find them any longer.	14 And the fruit of your soul's lust departed from you, and all the sumptuous things and the bright things perished from you, and they will never find them any longer.	14 And the fruit of your soul's lust departed from you, and all the sumptuous things and the bright things perished from you, and they will never find them any longer.
18:15 Οἱ ἔμποροι τούτων οἱ πλουτήσαντες ἀπ' αὐτῆς The merchants of these, the ones having been made rich from her, ἀπὸ μακρόθεν στήσονται διὰ τὸν φόβον τοῦ βασανισμοῦ from afar will stand because of the fear of the torment αὐτῆς κλαίοντες καὶ πενθοῦντες λέγοντες· of her weeping and sorrowing, saying,	15 The merchants of these, the ones having been made rich from her, from afar will stand because of the fear of the torment of her weeping and sorrowing,	15 The merchants of these, the ones having been made rich from her, from afar will stand because of the fear of the torment of her weeping and sorrowing,	15 The merchants of these, the ones having been made rich from her, from afar will stand because of the fear of the torment of her weeping and sorrowing,	15 The merchants of these, the ones having been made rich from her, from afar will stand because of the fear of the torment of her weeping and sorrowing,
18:16 οὐαὶ οὐαί, ἡ πόλις ἡ μεγάλη, 'Woe, woe, the great city, ἡ περιβεβλημένη βύσσινον καὶ πορφυροῦν καὶ κόκκινον having been clothed with fine linen and purple and scarlet,	16 saying, 'Woe, woe, the great city, having been clothed with fine linen and purple and scarlet, and having been gilded with gold and valuable stone and pearl,	16 saying, 'Woe, woe, the great city, having been clothed with fine linen and purple and scarlet, and having been gilded with gold and valuable stone and pearl (cf. Ezek. 27–28	16 saying, 'Woe, woe, the great city, having been clothed with fine linen and purple and scarlet, and having been gilded with gold and valuable stone and pearl,	16 saying, 'Woe, woe, the great city, having been clothed with fine linen and purple and scarlet, and having been gilded with gold and valuable stone and pearl,

καὶ κεχρυσωμένη [ἐν] χρυσίῳ καὶ λίθῳ τιμίῳ καὶ μαργαρίτῃ, / and having been gilded with gold and valuable stone and pearl,		of ancient Tyre, now applied to the Vatican, which is believed to own one-third of Europe's real estate, thanks to the formation of the European Economic Community by the Treaty of Rome in 1957),		
18:17 ὅτι μιᾷ ὥρᾳ ἠρημώθη ὁ τοσοῦτος πλοῦτος. / because in one hour such great wealth was made desolate.'	17 because in one hour such great wealth. was made desolate.' And every steersman and every one sailing to a place and sailors and as many as work the sea, stood from afar	17 because in one hour such great wealth was made desolate.' The beginning of the end of the papacy began with the Protestant Reformation in 1517; in God's timing, the Vatican's ruin will be complete. And every steersman and every one sailing to a place and sailors and as many as work the sea, stood from afar	17 because in one hour such great wealth was made desolate.' And every steersman and every one sailing to a place and sailors and as many as work the sea, stood from afar	17 because in one hour such great wealth was made desolate.' And every steersman and every one sailing to a place and sailors and as many as work the sea, stood from afar
Καὶ πᾶς κυβερνήτης καὶ πᾶς ὁ ἐπὶ τόπον πλέων καὶ ναῦται / And every steersman and every one sailing to a place and sailors				
καὶ ὅσοι τὴν θάλασσαν ἐργάζονται, ἀπὸ μακρόθεν ἔστησαν / and as many as work the sea, stood from afar				
18:18 καὶ ἔκραζον βλέποντες τὸν καπνὸν τῆς πυρώσεως αὐτῆς λέγοντες· / and cried out, seeing the smoke of her burning, saying,	18 and cried out, seeing the smoke of her burning, saying, 'Who is like the great city?' (cf. Aristides' description of luxurious second-century A.D. Rome; Oratio 26, A.D. 155).	18 and cried out, seeing the smoke of her burning, saying, 'Who is like the great city?'	18 and cried out, seeing the smoke of her burning, saying, 'Who is like the great city?'	18 and cried out, seeing the smoke of her burning, saying, 'Who is like the great city?'
τίς ὁμοία τῇ πόλει τῇ μεγάλῃ; / 'Who [is] like the great city?'				
18:19 καὶ ἔβαλον χοῦν ἐπὶ τὰς κεφαλὰς αὐτῶν / And they cast dust on their heads	19 And they cast dust on their heads and cried out, weeping and wailing, saying, "Woe, woe, the great city, in which all the ones having the ships in the sea became	19 And they cast dust on their heads and cried out, weeping and wailing, saying, "Woe, woe, the great city, in which all the ones having the ships in the sea became	19 And they cast dust on their heads and cried out, weeping and wailing, saying, "Woe, woe, the great city, in which all the ships in the sea became	19 And they cast dust on their heads and cried out, weeping and wailing, saying, "Woe, woe, the great city, in which all the ones having the ships in the sea became rich from
καὶ ἔκραζον κλαίοντες καὶ πενθοῦντες λέγοντες, / and cried out, weeping and wailing, saying,				

Greek Text and English Translation	Preterist View	Historicist View	Futurist View	Idealist View
οὐαὶ οὐαί, ἡ πόλις ἡ μεγάλη, 'Woe, woe, the great city, ἐν ᾗ ἐπλούτησαν πάντες οἱ ἔχοντες τὰ πλοῖα ἐν τῇ θαλάσσῃ ἐκ τῆς τιμιότητος αὐτῆς, in which all the ones having the ships in the sea became rich from her worth, ὅτι μιᾷ ὥρᾳ ἠρημώθη. because in one hour she was made desolate.'	rich from her worth, because in one hour she was made desolate."	rich from her worth, because in one hour she was made desolate."	rich from her worth, because in one hour she was made desolate."	her worth, because in one hour she was made desolate" (cf. Ezek. 27).
18:20 Εὐφραίνου ἐπ᾽ αὐτῇ, οὐρανὲ καὶ οἱ ἅγιοι Be glad over her, O heaven and saints καὶ οἱ ἀπόστολοι καὶ οἱ προφῆται, and apostles and prophets, ὅτι ἔκρινεν ὁ θεὸς τὸ κρίμα ὑμῶν ἐξ αὐτῆς, because God judged your judgment against her."	20 Be glad over her, O heaven and saints and apostles and prophets, because God judged your judgment against her." (Cf. the Jewish Sibylline Oracles' gloating over the eventual fall of Rome [3:350–68].)	20 Be glad over her, O heaven and saints and apostles and prophets, because God judged your judgment against her." In other words, the biblical apostles—Peter, Paul, and the others—will rejoice in heaven when the Vatican is fully defeated, because then the idolatrous worship of their names will stop.	20 Be glad over her, O heaven and saints and apostles and prophets, because God judged your judgment against her."	20 Be glad over her, O heaven and saints and apostles and prophets, because God judged your judgment against her."
18:21 Καὶ ἦρεν εἷς ἄγγελος ἰσχυρὸς λίθον ὡς μύλινον μέγαν And one strong angel raised a stone like a great millstone, καὶ ἔβαλεν εἰς τὴν θάλασσαν λέγων· and cast [it] into the sea, saying, οὕτως ὁρμήματι βληθήσεται Βαβυλὼν ἡ μεγάλη πόλις· "Thus with a rush Babylon the great city will be thrown	21 And one strong angel raised a stone like a great millstone and cast it into the sea, saying, "Thus with a rush Babylon the great city will be thrown and never ever be found any longer.	21 And one strong angel raised a stone like a great millstone and cast it into the sea, saying, "Thus with a rush Babylon the great city will be thrown and never ever be found any longer (cf. Jer. 51:63–64).	21 And one strong angel raised a stone like a great millstone and cast it into the sea, saying, "Thus with a rush Babylon the great city will be thrown and never ever be found any longer.	21 And one strong angel raised a stone like a great millstone and cast it into the sea, saying, "Thus with a rush Babylon the great city will be thrown and never ever be found any longer.

κοὶ οὐ μὴ εὑρεθῇ ἔτι. and never be found any longer.				
18:22 κοὶ φωνὴ κιθαρῳδῶν κοὶ μουσικῶν κοὶ αὐλητῶν κοὶ σαλπιστῶν And the sound of harpers and of musicians and of flutists and of trumpeters	22 And the sound of harpers and of musicians and of flutists and of trumpeters will never ever be heard in	22 And the sound of harpers and of musicians and of flutists and of trumpeters will never ever be heard in	22 And the sound of harpers and of musicians and of flutists and of trumpeters will never ever be heard in	22 And the sound of musicians and of flutists and of trumpeters will never ever be heard in
οὐ μὴ ἀκουσθῇ ἐν σοὶ ἔτι, will never ever be heard in you again,	you again, and every craftsman of every craft will never ever be found in you again, and a sound of a mill will never ever be heard in you again,	you again, and every craftsman of every craft will never ever be found in you again, and a sound of a mill will never ever be heard in you again,	you again, and every craftsman of every craft will never ever be found in you again, and a sound of a mill will never ever be heard in you again,	you again, and every craftsman of every craft will never ever be found in you again, and a sound of a mill will never ever be heard in you again,
κοὶ πᾶς τεχνίτης πάσης τέχνης οὐ μὴ εὑρεθῇ ἐν σοὶ ἔτι, and every craftsman of every craft will never ever be found in you again,				
κοὶ φωνὴ μύλου οὐ μὴ ἀκουσθῇ ἐν σοὶ ἔτι, and a sound of a mill will never ever be heard in you again,	23 and light of a lamp will never ever shine in you again, and a voice of a bridegroom and of bride will never ever be heard in you again, because your merchants were the great ones of the earth, because by your sorcery all the nations were deceived,	23 and light of a lamp will never ever shine in you again, and a voice of a bridegroom and of bride will never ever be heard in you again, because your merchants were the great ones of the earth, because by your sorcery all the nations were deceived,	23 and light of a lamp will never ever shine in you again, and a voice of a bridegroom and of bride will never ever be heard in you again, because your merchants were the great ones of the earth, because by your sorcery all the nations were deceived,	23 and light of a lamp will never ever shine in you again, and a voice of a bridegroom and of bride will never ever be heard in you again, because your merchants were the great ones of the earth, because by your sorcery all the nations were deceived,
18:23 κοὶ φῶς λύχνου οὐ μὴ φάνῃ ἐν σοὶ ἔτι, and light of a lamp will never ever shine in you again,				
κοὶ φωνὴ νυμφίου κοὶ νύμφης οὐ μὴ ἀκουσθῇ ἐν σοὶ ἔτι· and a voice of a bridegroom and of a bride will never ever be heard in you again,				
ὅτι οἱ ἔμποροί σου ἦσαν οἱ μεγιστᾶνες τῆς γῆς, because your merchants were the great ones of the earth,		deceived by the supposed sacerdotal powers of the priesthood together with its indulgences,		
ὅτι ἐν τῇ φαρμακείᾳ σου ἐπλανήθησαν πάντα τὰ ἔθνη, because by your sorcery all the nations were deceived,				
18:24 κοὶ ἐν αὐτῇ αἷμα προφητῶν κοὶ ἁγίων εὑρέθη and by her the blood of the prophets and of the saints was found	24 and by her the blood of the prophets and of the saints was found (in Jerusalem) and of the saints (in Rome, shed	24 and by her the blood of the prophets and of the saints was found and of all the ones having	24 and by her the blood of the prophets and of the saints was found and of all the ones	24 and by her the blood of the prophets and the saints was found and

Greek Text and English Translation	Preterist View	Historicist View	Futurist View	Idealist View
18:24 καὶ πάντων τῶν ἐσφαγμένων ἐπὶ τῆς γῆς." and of all the ones having been slain on the earth."	by Nero) was found and of all the ones having been slain on the earth."	been slain on the earth because of the Vatican's oppressive policies."	having been slain on the earth." The martyred Tribulation Christians will be vindicated when Christ returns visibly to destroy the Antichrist and all anti-God forces.	of all the ones having been slain on the earth."
19:1 Μετὰ ταῦτα ἤκουσα ὡς φωνὴν After these things I heard [something] like a great voice	1 After these things I heard something like a great voice of a numerous crowd in heaven saying, "Halleluia: salvation and glory and power to our God,	1 After these things I heard something like a great voice of a numerous crowd in heaven saying, "Halleluia: salvation and glory and power to our God,	1 After these things I heard something like a great voice of a numerous crowd in heaven saying, "Halleluia: salvation and glory and power to our God,	1 After these things I heard a great voice of a numerous crowd in heaven saying, "Halleluia: salvation and glory and power to our God,
μεγάλην ὄχλου πολλοῦ ἐν τῷ οὐρανῷ λεγόντων· of a numerous crowd in heaven saying,				
ἀλληλουϊά· ἡ σωτηρία καὶ ἡ δόξα καὶ ἡ δύναμις τοῦ θεοῦ ἡμῶν, "Halleluia: salvation and glory and power to our God,				
19:2 ὅτι ἀληθιναὶ καὶ δίκαιαι αἱ κρίσεις αὐτοῦ· because his judgments [are] true and righteous,	2 because his judgments are true and righteous, because he judged the great harlot (Jerusalem and, one day, Rome) who defiled the earth by her fornication, and he avenged the blood of his servants by her hand."	2 because his judgments are true and righteous, because he judged the great harlot (the papacy) who defiled the earth by her fornication, and he avenged the blood of his servants by her hand."	2 because his judgments are true and righteous, because he judged the great harlot (the Antichrist, whose headquarters will be New Babylon) who defiled the earth by her fornication, and he avenged the blood of his servants (the Tribulation saints) by her hand."	2 because his judgments are true and righteous, because he judged the great harlot (the godless world) who defiled the earth by her fornication, and he avenged the blood of his servants (Christians throughout the history of the church) by her hand."
ὅτι ἔκρινεν τὴν πόρνην τὴν μεγάλην because he judged the great harlot				
ἥτις ἔφθειρεν τὴν γῆν ἐν τῇ πορνείᾳ αὐτῆς, who defiled the earth by her fornication,				
καὶ ἐξεδίκησεν τὸ αἷμα τῶν δούλων αὐτοῦ ἐκ χειρὸς αὐτῆς. and he avenged the blood of his servants by her hand."				
19:3 καὶ δεύτερον εἴρηκαν· ἀλληλουϊά· And a second time they said, "Halleluia:	3 And a second time they said, "Halleluia: and her smoke rises forever."	3 And a second time they said, "Halleluia: and her smoke rises forever."	3 And a second time they said, "Halleluia: and her smoke rises forever."	3 And a second time they said, "Halleluia: and her smoke rises forever."

Greek	Translation 1	Translation 2	Translation 3	Translation 4
καὶ ὁ καπνὸς αὐτῆς ἀναβαίνει εἰς τοὺς αἰῶνας τῶν αἰώνων. / and her smoke rises forever."				
19:4 καὶ ἔπεσαν οἱ πρεσβύτεροι οἱ εἴκοσι τέσσαρες καὶ τὰ τέσσαρα ζῷα καὶ προσεκύνησαν τῷ θεῷ / And the twenty-four elders and the four living creatures fell and worshipped God	4 And the twenty-four elders and the four living creatures fell and worshipped God, who is seated upon the throne, saying, "Amen, Halleluia."	4 And the twenty-four elders and the four living creatures fell and worshipped God, who is seated upon the throne, saying, "Amen, Halleluia."	4 And the twenty-four elders and the four living creatures fell and worshipped God, who is seated upon the throne, saying, "Amen, Halleluia."	4 And the twenty-four elders and the four living creatures fell and worshipped God, who is seated upon the throne, saying, "Amen, Halleluia."
τῷ καθημένῳ ἐπὶ τῷ θρόνῳ λέγοντες· ἀμὴν ἀλληλουϊά, / who is seated upon the throne, saying, "Amen, Halleluia."				
19:5 Καὶ φωνὴ ἀπὸ τοῦ θρόνου ἐξῆλθεν λέγουσα· / And a voice came out from the throne, saying,	5 And a voice came out from the throne, saying, "Praise our God, all his servants and those who fear him, the small and great."	5 And a voice came out from the throne, saying, "Praise our God, all his servants and those who fear him, the small and great."	5 And a voice came out from the throne, saying, "Praise our God, all his servants and those who fear him, the small and great."	5 And a voice came out from the throne, saying, "Praise our God, all his servants and those who fear him, the small and great."
αἰνεῖτε τῷ θεῷ ἡμῶν πάντες οἱ δοῦλοι αὐτοῦ / "Praise our God, all his servants				
[καὶ] οἱ φοβούμενοι αὐτόν, οἱ μικροὶ καὶ οἱ μεγάλοι. / and those who fear him, small and great."				
19:6 Καὶ ἤκουσα ὡς φωνὴν ὄχλου πολλοῦ / And I heard [something] like a voice of a numerous crowd	6 And I heard something like a voice of a numerous croid and like a voice of many waters and as a thunderous, strong voice, saying, "Halleluia, because our Lord God the Almighty has reigned.	6 And I heard something like a voice of a numerous crowd and like a voice of many waters and like a thunderous, strong voice, saying, "Halleluia, because our Lord God the Almighty has reigned (through the true church).	6 And I heard something like a voice of many crowds and like a voice of many waters and like a thunderous, strong voice, saying, "Halleluia, because our Lord God the Almighty has reigned.	6 And I heard something like a voice of many crowds and like a voice of many waters and like a thunderous, strong voice, saying, "Halleluia, because our Lord God the Almighty has reigned (because it is the second coming of Christ, at the end of history, that will finally vindicate his kingdom, which has been present through the church in the midst of history; cf. Rev. 6:12ff.; 11:15ff.; 14:14ff.; 16:17ff.).
καὶ ὡς φωνὴν ὑδάτων πολλῶν καὶ ὡς φωνὴν βροντῶν ἰσχυρῶν λεγόντων· / and like a voice of many waters and like a voice of strong thunders saying,				
ἀλληλουϊά, ὅτι ἐβασίλευσεν κύριος ὁ θεὸς [ἡμῶν] ὁ παντοκράτωρ. / "Halleluia, because our Lord God the Almighty has reigned.				

Greek Text and English Translation	Preterist View	Historicist View	Futurist View	Idealist View
19:7 χαίρωμεν καὶ ἀγαλλιῶμεν καὶ δώσομεν τὴν δόξαν αὐτῷ, Let us rejoice and let us us exult and let us give glory to him, ὅτι ἦλθεν ὁ γάμος τοῦ ἀρνίου because the marriage of the Lamb has come καὶ ἡ γυνὴ αὐτοῦ ἡτοίμασεν ἑαυτήν and his wife has prepared herself."	7 Let us rejoice, and let us exult, and let us give glory to him, because the marriage of the Lamb has come and his wife has prepared herself." The marriage of the church of Christ (cf. Rev. 11:15–19) is the counterpart to God's divorce of Israel because of the latter's spiritual adultery.	7 Let us rejoice, and let us exult, and let us give glory to him, because the marriage of the Lamb has come and his wife has prepared herself."	7 Let us rejoice, and let us exult, and let us give glory to him, because the marriage of the Lamb has come and his wife has prepared herself." At the Rapture the church was united to Christ as his bride in heaven (see John 14:1–6), but at the second coming the church will be publicly proclaimed on earth to be Christ's bride.	7 Let us rejoice, and let us exult, and let us give glory to him, because the marriage of the Lamb has come and his wife (the true church) has prepared herself."
19:8 καὶ ἐδόθη αὐτῇ ἵνα περιβάληται βύσσινον λαμπρὸν καθαρόν· And to her was given that she might be clothed in white, clean linen, τὸ γὰρ βύσσινον τὰ δικαιώματα τῶν ἁγίων ἐστίν. for the linen is the righteousness of the saints.	8 And to her was given that she might be clothed in white, clean linen, for the linen is the righteousness of the saints (cf. Eph. 5:25–29; 2 Cor.11:2–3).	8 And to her was given that she might be clothed in white, clean linen, for the linen is the righteousness of the saints.	8 And to her was given that she might be clothed in white, clean linen, for the linen is the righteousness of the saints.	8 And to her was given that she might be clothed in white, clean linen, for the linen is the righteousness of the saints.
19:9 Καὶ λέγει μοι· γράψον· And he says to me, "Write, μακάριοι οἱ εἰς τὸ δεῖπνον τοῦ γάμου τοῦ ἀρνίου κεκλημένοι. 'Blessed are the ones who have been called to the marriage supper of the Lamb.'" καὶ λέγει μοι· οὗτοι οἱ λόγοι ἀληθινοὶ τοῦ θεοῦ εἰσιν. And he says to me, "These words of God are true."	9 And he says to me, "Write, 'Blessed are the ones who have been called to the marriage supper of the Lamb.'" And he says to me, "These words of God are true."	9 And he says to me, "Write, 'Blessed are the ones who have been called to the marriage supper of the Lamb.'" And he says to me, "These words of God are true."	9 And he says to me, "Write, 'Blessed are the ones who have been called to the marriage supper of the Lamb.'" These are the wedding guests, which consist of both the OT and Tribulation saints. This identification preserves the distinction between Israel and the church, which is the central theme of Revelation,	9 And he says to me, "Write, 'Blessed are the ones who have been called to the marriage supper of the Lamb'" (the church, which is brought to faith in Christ by the effectual call of God). And he says to me, "These words of God are true."

19:10 καὶ ἔπεσα ἔμπροσθεν τῶν ποδῶν αὐτοῦ προσκυνῆσαι αὐτῷ. And I fell before his feet to worship him. καὶ λέγει μοι· ὅρα μή And he says to me, "See [that] you [do] not [do this]! σύνδουλός σού εἰμι καὶ τῶν ἀδελφῶν σου I am your fellow servant and one of your brothers τῶν ἐχόντων τὴν μαρτυρίαν Ἰησοῦ· τῷ θεῷ προσκύνησον. having the witness of Jesus; worship God!" ἡ γὰρ μαρτυρία Ἰησοῦ ἐστιν τὸ πνεῦμα τῆς προφητείας. For the witness of Jesus is the spirit of prophecy.	10 And I fell before his feet to worship him. And he says to me, "See that you do not do this! I am your fellow servant and one of your brothers having the witness of Jesus; worship God!" For the witness of Jesus is the spirit of prophecy.	10 And I fell before his feet to worship him. And he says to me, "See that you do not do this! (Neither should Christians worship popes, saints, relics, Mary, etc.) I am your fellow servant and one of your brothers having the witness of Jesus; worship God!" For the witness of Jesus is the spirit of prophecy (the message of the Reformers—justification by faith alone).	as Christ reveals the future to John. And he says to me, "These words of God are true." 10 And I fell before his feet to worship him. And he says to me, "See that you do not do this! I am your fellow servant and one of your brothers having the witness of Jesus; worship God!" For the witness of Jesus is the spirit of prophecy.	10 And I fell before his feet to worship him. And he says to me, "See that you do not do this! I am your fellow servant and one of your brothers having the witness of Jesus; worship God!" For the witness of Jesus is the spirit of prophecy.
19:11 Καὶ εἶδον τὸν οὐρανὸν ἠνεῳγμένον, And I saw the heaven having been opened, καὶ ἰδοὺ ἵππος λευκὸς καὶ ὁ καθήμενος ἐπ᾽ αὐτὸν and behold, a white horse and the one sitting upon it [καλούμενος] πιστὸς καὶ ἀληθινός, being called faithful and true, καὶ ἐν δικαιοσύνῃ κρίνει καὶ πολεμεῖ. and in righteousness he judges and makes war.	11 And I saw the heaven having been opened, and behold, there was a white horse and the one sitting upon it being called faithful and true, and in righteousness he judges and makes war against Jerusalem through the Romans in A.D. 70. So this is not a supposed second coming of Christ, at the end of history.	11 And I saw the heaven having been opened, and behold, there was a white horse and the one sitting upon it being called faithful and true, and in righteousness he judges and makes war on the works-salvation agenda of Catholicism.	11 And I saw the heaven having been opened to reveal the second coming of Christ at the end of the Great Tribulation (Rev. 6–18) to now establish the Millennium (Rev. 20), and behold, there was a white horse and the one sitting upon it being called faithful and true, and in righteousness he judges and makes war.	11 And I saw the heaven having been opened, and behold, there was a white horse and the one sitting upon it being called faithful and true, and in righteousness he judges and makes war. This will happen at the second coming of Christ.
19:12 οἱ δὲ ὀφθαλμοὶ αὐτοῦ [ὡς] φλὸξ πυρός, But his eyes [are] like flaming fire,	12 But his eyes are like flaming fire, and upon his head are many diadems,	12 But his eyes are like flaming fire, and upon his head are many diadems,	12 But his eyes are like flaming fire, and upon his head are many diadems,	12 But his eyes are like flaming fire, and upon his head are many diadems,

Greek Text and English Translation	Preterist View	Historicist View	Futurist View	Idealist View
καὶ ἐπὶ τὴν κεφαλὴν αὐτοῦ διαδήματα πολλά, and upon his head [are] many diadems, ἔχων ὄνομα γεγραμμένον ὃ οὐδεὶς οἶδεν εἰ μὴ αὐτός, having a name written which no one knows except he himself;	having a name written which no one knows except he himself;	having a name written which no one knows except he himself;	having a name written which no one knows except he himself;	having a name written which no one knows except he himself;
19:13 καὶ περιβεβλημένος ἱμάτιον βεβαμμένον αἵματι, and having been clothed with a garment having been dipped in blood, καὶ κέκληται τὸ ὄνομα αὐτοῦ ὁ λόγος τοῦ θεοῦ. and his name has been called the Word of God.	13 and having been clothed with a garment having been dipped in blood, and his name has been called the Word of God.	13 and having been clothed with a garment having been dipped in blood, and his name has been called the Word of God. It is this message of justification that defeats the papacy.	13 and having been clothed with a garment having been dipped in blood, and his name has been called the Word of God.	13 and having been clothed with a garment having been dipped in blood, and his name has been called the Word of God.
19:14 Καὶ τὰ στρατεύματα [τὰ] ἐν τῷ οὐρανῷ ἠκολούθει αὐτῷ And the armies in heaven followed him ἐφ᾽ ἵπποις λευκοῖς, ἐνδεδυμένοι βύσσινον λευκὸν καθαρόν. upon white horses, being clothed in white, clean linen.	14 And the armies in heaven followed him upon white horses, being clothed in white, clean linen.	14 And the armies in heaven followed him upon white horses, being clothed in white, clean linen, which is the righteousness of Christ received by faith alone.	14 And the armies in heaven (the raptured church) followed him upon white horses, being clothed in white, clean linen.	14 And the armies in heaven (the departed saints) followed him upon white horses, being clothed in white, clean linen.
19:15 καὶ ἐκ τοῦ στόματος αὐτοῦ ἐκπορεύεται ῥομφαία ὀξεῖα, And out of his mouth proceeds a sharp sword, ἵνα ἐν αὐτῇ πατάξῃ τὰ ἔθνη, in order that by it he might smite the nations, καὶ αὐτὸς ποιμανεῖ αὐτοὺς ἐν ῥάβδῳ σιδηρᾷ, and he will shepherd them with a rod of iron,	15 And out of his mouth proceeds a sharp sword, in order that by it he might smite the nations, and he will shepherd them with a rod of iron, and he treads the winepress of the wine of the anger of the wrath of God the almighty. Christ	15 And out of his mouth proceeds a sharp sword, in order that by it he might smite the nations, and he will shepherd them with a rod of iron, and he treads the winepress of the wine of the anger of the wrath of God the almighty.	15 And out of his mouth proceeds a sharp sword, in order that by it he might smite the nations, and he will shepherd them with a rod of iron (as the Davidic Messiah-King), and he treads the winepress of the wine of	15 And out of his mouth proceeds a sharp sword, in order that by it he might smite the nations, and he will shepherd them with a rod of iron, and he treads the winepress of the wine of the anger of the wrath of God the almighty.

καὶ αὐτὸς πατεῖ τὴν ληνὸν τοῦ οἴνου / and he treads the winepress of the wine τοῦ θυμοῦ τῆς ὀργῆς τοῦ θεοῦ τοῦ παντοκράτορος. / of the anger of the wrath of God the almighty.	does this through the church's preaching of the gospel. This preaching of the gospel will bring about the transformation of society and thereby the establishment of the kingdom of God (see Rev. 20). This is a postmillennial reading of things (see again Rev. 20).		the anger of the wrath of God the almighty.	
19:16 καὶ ἔχει ἐπὶ τὸ ἱμάτιον καὶ ἐπὶ τὸν μηρὸν αὐτοῦ ὄνομα γεγραμμένον· / And he has upon his garment and upon his thigh a name having been written, Βασιλεὺς βασιλέων καὶ κύριος κυρίων. / "King of Kings and Lord of Lords."	16 And he has upon his garment and upon his thigh a name having been written, "King of Kings and Lord of Lords."	16 And he has upon his garment and upon his thigh a name having been written, "King of Kings and Lord of Lords."	16 And he has upon his garment and upon his thigh a name having been written, "King of Kings and Lord of Lords."	16 And he has upon the garment and upon his thigh a name having been written, "King of Kings and Lord of Lords."
19:17 Καὶ εἶδον ἕνα ἄγγελον ἑστῶτα ἐν τῷ ἡλίῳ / And I saw one angel standing in the sun, καὶ ἔκραξεν [ἐν] φωνῇ μεγάλῃ λέγων / and he cried in a great voice, saying πᾶσιν τοῖς ὀρνέοις τοῖς πετομένοις ἐν μεσουρανήματι· / to all the birds flying in the midheaven, Δεῦτε συνάχθητε εἰς τὸ δεῖπνον τὸ μέγα τοῦ θεοῦ / "Come, be gathered together unto the great supper of God	17 And I saw one angel standing in the sun, and he cried in a great voice, saying to all the birds flying in the midheaven, "Come, be gathered together unto the great supper of God (the counterpart of the marriage of the church and Christ [Rev. 19:1–10])	17 And I saw one angel standing in the sun, and he cried in a great voice, saying to all the birds flying in the midheaven, "Come, be gathered together unto the great supper of God	17 And I saw one angel standing in the sun, and he cried in a great voice, saying to all the birds flying in the midheaven, "Come, be gathered together unto the great supper of God at the battle of Armageddon	17 And I saw one angel standing in the sun, and he cried in a great voice, saying to all the birds flying in the midheaven, "Come, be gathered together unto the great supper of God
19:18 ἵνα φάγητε σάρκας βασιλέων / in order that you might eat the fleshes of kings καὶ σάρκας χιλιάρχων καὶ σάρκας ἰσχυρῶν / and the fleshes of chiliarchs and the fleshes of the strong	18 in order that you might eat the fleshes of kings and the fleshes of chiliarchs and the fleshes of the strong and the fleshes of horses and of the ones sitting upon	18 in order that you might eat the fleshes of kings and the fleshes of chiliarchs and the fleshes of the strong and the fleshes of horses and of the ones sitting upon	18 in order that you might eat the fleshes of kings and the fleshes of chiliarchs and the fleshes of the strong and the fleshes of horses and of the ones sitting upon	18 in order that you might eat the fleshes of kings and the fleshes of chiliarchs and the fleshes of horses and of the ones sitting upon

Greek Text and English Translation	Preterist View	Historicist View	Futurist View	Idealist View
καὶ σάρκας ἵππων καὶ τῶν καθημένον ἐπ᾽ αὐτῶν and the fleshes of horses and of the ones sitting upon them	the fleshes of both free and servants and great!"	them and the fleshes of both free and servants and small and great!"	them and the fleshes of both free and servants and small and great!"	them and the fleshes of both free and servants and small and great!"
καὶ σάρκας πάντων ἐλευθέρων τε καὶ δούλων καὶ μικρῶν καὶ μεγάλων. and the fleshes of both free and servants and small and great!"				
19:19 Καὶ εἶδον τὸ θηρίον καὶ τοὺς βασιλεῖς τῆς γῆς And I saw the beast and the kings of the earth	19 And I saw the beast and the kings of the earth and their armies, having been gathered to make war with the one sitting on the horse and with his army.	19 And I saw the beast and the kings of the earth and their armies, having been gathered to make war with the one sitting on the horse and with his army.	19 And I saw the beast (the Antichrist) and the kings of the earth and their armies (China, Russia, Iran, etc.), having been gathered to make war with the one sitting on the horse and with his army. While the intention of the Antichrist will be at first to destroy China, Russia, Iran, and other nations that contend for the rulership of the world, he and his enemies will unite forces to fight the descending Christ.	19 And I saw the beast (anti-Christian society seen politically) and the kings of the earth and their armies, having been gathered to make war with the one sitting on the horse and with his army. These are the enemies of God's final assault on Christ and his church.
καὶ τὰ στρατεύματα αὐτῶν συνηγμένα and their armies having been gathered				
ποιῆσαι τὸν πόλεμον μετὰ τοῦ καθημένου ἐπὶ τοῦ ἵππου to make war with the one sitting on the horse				
καὶ μετὰ τοῦ στρατεύματος αὐτοῦ. and with his army.				
19:20 καὶ ἐπιάσθη τὸ θηρίον καὶ μετ᾽ αὐτοῦ ὁ ψευδοπροφήτης And the beast was seized and with him the false prophet,	20 And the beast was seized and with him the false prophet, the one having made signs before him, by which he deceived those having received the mark of the beast and those worshipping his image.	20 And the beast (the pope/Antichrist) was seized and with him the false prophet (the sacerdotal priesthood), the one having made signs before him, by which he deceived those having received the mark of	20 And the beast was seized and with him the false prophet, the one having made signs before him, by which he deceived those having received the mark of the beast and those worshipping his image.	20 And the beast was seized and with him the false prophet (the religious syncretism of the anti-Christian society), the one having made signs before him, by which he deceived those having received
ὁ ποιήσας τὰ σημεῖα ἐνώπιον αὐτοῦ, the one having made signs before him,				

Greek / Literal translation	Preterist	Historicist	Idealist	Futurist
ἐν οἷς ἐπλάνησεν τοὺς λαβόντας τὸ χάραγμα τοῦ θηρίου by which he deceived those having received the mark of the beast καὶ τοὺς προσκυνοῦντας τῇ εἰκόνι αὐτοῦ· and those worshipping his image. ζῶντες ἐβλήθησαν οἱ δύο εἰς τὴν λίμνην τοῦ πυρὸς τῆς καιομένης ἐν θείῳ. The two were cast alive into the lake of fire burning with sulfur.	The two were cast alive into the lake of fire burning with sulfur.	the beast and those worshipping his image (veneration of the pope as the "Vicar of Christ"). The two were cast alive into the lake of fire burning with sulfur. The Protestant Reformation was thus the beginning of the end of Roman Catholicism. Beyond that, Christ conquers the world through the true church's preaching of the gospel. And, then, at Christ's second coming, he will wrap up human history, making visible his present lordship over all.	The two were cast alive into the lake of fire burning with sulfur.	the mark of the beast and those worshipping his image. The two were cast alive into the lake of fire burning with sulfur.
19:21 καὶ οἱ λοιποὶ ἀπεκτάνθησαν ἐν τῇ ῥομφαίᾳ And the rest were killed by the sword τοῦ καθημένου ἐπὶ τοῦ ἵππου τῇ ἐξελθούσῃ ἐκ τοῦ στόματος αὐτοῦ, of the one sitting upon the horse proceeding out of his mouth, καὶ πάντα τὰ ὄρνεα ἐχορτάσθησαν ἐκ τῶν σαρκῶν αὐτῶν. and all the birds were filled by their fleshes.	21 And the rest were killed by the sword of the one sitting upon the horse, proceeding out of his mouth, and all the birds were filled by their fleshes. (Editor's note: The preterist interpretation of Revelation 20 falls into two camps. The one, consistent with the view that the "second	21 And the rest were killed by the sword of the one sitting upon the horse, proceeding out of his mouth, and all the birds were filled by their fleshes (the unclean birds symbolize the curse of the covenant [see Deut. 28:26, 49] now having befallen Jerusalem in A.D. 70 for her apostasy). (Editor's note: The historicist position takes the amillennial approach to Revelation 20, as does the idealist school of thought. According to the amillennial position, there will be no literal Millennium. Rather, it is the reign of the church in the kingdom of God between the first coming and second coming of Christ. Christ bound Satan in his	21 And the rest were killed by the sword of the one sitting upon the horse, proceeding out of his mouth, and all the birds were filled by their fleshes. This "banquet" is the counterpart to the marriage supper of the Lamb (Rev. 19:1–10). (Editor's note: The futurist position is premillennial in perspective, meaning that Christ will return a second time, before the literal Millennium to be established on earth. In fact, Christ's Parousia will establish his reign in Jerusalem for one thousand years.)	21 And the rest were killed by the sword of the one sitting upon the horse, proceeding out of his mouth, and all the birds were filled by their fleshes. After this comes the eternal state. (Editor's note: Similar to the historicist position [but without equating the beast with a revived Roman papacy], the idealist school of interpretation takes an amillennial approach to Revelation 20. Thus there will be no literal one-thousand-year reign of Christ on the earth. Rather, Christ rules now spiritually

Greek Text and English Translation	Preterist View	Historicist View	Futurist View	Idealist View
	coming" of Christ took place at the fall of Jerusalem in A.D. 70, posits no future advent of Christ. The other camp within the preterist school holds to a future return of Christ, portrayed in Revelation 20:7–15; this latter viewpoint espouses the postmillennial interpretation, that Christ will return after the Millennium.)	life, death, and resurrection so that the devil could not deceive the nations wholesale. But in the future, Satan will be released for a brief last stand against Christ and the church, only to be finally defeated at the return of Christ, at the end of history. Then will come the eternal state [Rev. 21–22].)		through the church, both in heaven and on earth, and there will be no literal kingdom in Jerusalem for one thousand years. Instead, Christ's kingdom manifests itself through the church between his first and second advents. After that will come the eternal state [Rev. 21–22].)
20:1 Καὶ εἶδον ἄγγελον καταβαίνοντα ἐκ τοῦ οὐρανοῦ And I saw an angel descending out of heaven,	1 And I saw an angel descending out of heaven, having the key of the abyss (bottomless pit) and a great chain in his hand.	1 And I saw an angel descending out of heaven, having the key of the abyss and a great chain in his hand.	1 And I saw an angel descending out of heaven (at the second coming of Christ), having the key of the abyss and a great chain in his hand.	1 And I saw an angel descending out of heaven, having the key of the abyss and a great chain in his hand.
ἔχοντα τὴν κλεῖν τῆς ἀβύσσου having the key of the abyss				
καὶ ἅλυσιν μεγάλην ἐπὶ τὴν χεῖρα αὐτοῦ. and a great chain in his hand.				
20:2 καὶ ἐκράτησεν τὸν δράκοντα, ὁ ὄφις ὁ ἀρχαῖος, And he grabbed the dragon, the serpent of old,	2 And he grabbed the dragon, the serpent of old, who is the Devil and the Satan, and bound him for a thousand years	2 And he grabbed the dragon, the serpent of old, who is the Devil and the Satan, and bound him for a thousand years	2 And he grabbed the dragon, the serpent of old, who is the Devil and the Satan, and bound him literally for a thousand years	2 And he grabbed the dragon, the serpent of old, who is the Devil and the Satan, and bound him for a thousand years
ὅς ἐστιν Διάβολος καὶ ὁ Σατανᾶς, who is the Devil and the Satan,				
καὶ ἔδησεν αὐτὸν χίλια ἔτη and bound him for a thousand years				

20:3 καὶ ἔβαλεν αὐτὸν εἰς τὴν ἄβυσσον καὶ ἔκλεισεν καὶ ἐσφράγισεν ἐπάνω αὐτοῦ, and threw him into the abyss and shut and sealed [it] over him, ἵνα μὴ πλανήσῃ ἔτι τὰ ἔθνη in order that he might not deceive the nations any longer ἄχρι τελεσθῇ τὰ χίλια ἔτη. until the thousand years are completed. μετὰ ταῦτα δεῖ λυθῆναι αὐτὸν μικρὸν χρόνον. After these [years] it is necessary that he be loosed for a little time.	3 and threw him into the abyss and shut and sealed it over him in order that he might not deceive the nations until the thousand years are completed. So, the binding of Satan began during Jesus' ministry on earth (Matt. 12:24–29) and was secured at Christ's death and resurrection (Luke 10:18; John 12:31–32; Col. 2:15; Heb. 2:14–15). This began the Millennium ("1,000 years"), a number to be interpreted figuratively as the presence of the kingdom of God on earth through the church now, beginning with the first coming of Christ. It will continue forever, along the way building momentum and transforming the world into righteousness. The nations, beginning with first-century Judaism, one by one collapse before the advance of the gospel/kingdom of God. Christians rule in this kingdom now (Rev. 1:6; Eph. 2:6; Col. 3:1–4). After these years it is necessary that he (Satan) be loosed for a little time.	3 and threw him into the abyss and shut and sealed it over him in order that he might not deceive the nations until the thousand years are completed. This all happened at the first coming of Christ. After these years it is necessary that he (Satan) be loosed for a little time.	3 and threw him into the abyss and shut and sealed it over him in order that he might not deceive the nations any longer until the thousand years are completed. The result is that the millennial kingdom of Christ will be established on earth, with Jerusalem being its headquarters. The rebuilt temple will be rededicated to God, and the OT sacrificial system will be reinstated, all of which are types of the one perfect sacrifice of Christ on the cross. After these years it is necessary that he (Satan) be loosed for a little time.	3 and threw him into the abyss and shut and sealed it over him in order that he might not deceive the nations until the thousand years are completed (which took place at the first coming of Christ). After these years it is necessary that he be loosed for a little time.

Greek Text and English Translation	Preterist View	Historicist View	Futurist View	Idealist View
20:4 Καὶ εἶδον θρόνους καὶ ἐκάθισαν ἐπ᾿ αὐτοὺς And I saw thrones and [those who] sat upon them καὶ κρίμα ἐδόθη αὐτοῖς, καὶ τὰς ψυχὰς τῶν πεπελεκισμένων and judgment was given to them, and the souls of those having been beheaded διὰ τὴν μαρτυρίαν Ἰησοῦ because of the witness of Jesus καὶ διὰ τὸν λόγον τοῦ θεοῦ and because of the Word of God καὶ οἵτινες οὐ προσεκύνησαν τὸ θηρίον οὐδὲ τὴν εἰκόνα αὐτοῦ and those who did not worship the beast nor his image καὶ οὐκ ἔλαβον τὸ χάραγμα and did not receive the mark ἐπὶ τὸ μέτωπον καὶ ἐπὶ τὴν χεῖρα αὐτῶν. upon the forehead and upon their hand. καὶ ἔζησαν καὶ ἐβασίλευσαν μετὰ τοῦ Χριστοῦ χίλια ἔτη. And they came to life and ruled with Christ for a thousand years.	4 And I saw thrones and those who sat upon them, and judgment was given to them (all Christians ruling with Christ now in the Millennium, that is, in the kingdom of God); and the souls of those having been beheaded because of the witness of Jesus and because of the Word of God (martyred Christians throughout the centuries who reign with Christ in heaven); and those who did not worship the beast nor his image and did not receive the mark upon the forehead and upon their hands (living Christians who reign with Christ on earth). And they came to life (were converted to life spiritually; cf. John 5:24–29; Rom. 6:4–14; Eph. 2:5–6; Col. 3:1) and ruled with Christ for the thousand years.	4 And I saw thrones and those who sat upon them, and judgment was given to them (all Christians ruling now with Christ in his kingdom through the church); and the souls of those having been beheaded because of the witness of Jesus and because of the Word of God (martyred Christians ruling with Christ in the heavenly kingdom); and those who did not worship the beast nor his image and did not receive the mark upon the forehead and upon their hands (living Christians ruling with Christ on earth in his kingdom). And they came to life (at their spiritual conversion) and ruled with Christ for the thousand years.	4 And I saw thrones (of all Christians, but with special honor given to Israel now converted to its Messiah and the martyred saints of the Tribulation) and those who sat upon them, and judgment was given to them; and the souls of those having been beheaded because of the witness of Jesus and because of the Word of God; and those who did not worship the beast nor his image and did not receive the mark upon the forehead and upon their hands. And they came to life (Christians alone will receive resurrection bodies in order to reign in the Millennium. Thus they will join those Christians from the Rapture who had already received their resurrection bodies seven years before. Together they will rule with Christ from Jerusalem) and ruled with Christ for the thousand years.	4 And I saw thrones and those who sat upon them, and judgment was given to them; and the souls of those having been beheaded because of the witness of Jesus and because of the Word of God; and those who did not worship the beast nor his image and did not receive the mark upon the forehead and upon their hands. Thus the martyred Christian rules with Christ now in heaven, while the Christian alive on earth rules with Christ spiritually. And they came to life (at their conversion) and ruled with Christ for the thousand years.

20:5 οἱ λοιποὶ τῶν νεκρῶν οὐκ ἔζησαν ἄχρι τελεσθῇ τὰ χίλια ἔτη. And the rest of the dead did not come to life until the thousand years were completed. Αὕτη ἡ ἀνάστασις ἡ πρώτη. This is the first resurrection.	5 And the rest of the dead did not come to life until the thousand years were completed. This is the first resurrection (that is, salvation).	5 And the rest of the dead did not come to life until the thousand years were completed. This is the first resurrection (that is, salvation).	5 And the rest of the dead did not come to life until the thousand years were completed. (These are dead non-Christians killed by Christ at his Parousia, and who will be resurrected at the end of the one thousand years in order to be tormented for eternity.) This is the first resurrection (the resurrection of believers at the second coming of Christ for the purpose of ruling in the Millennium).	5 And the rest of the dead did not come to life until the thousand years were completed. This is the first resurrection (that is, salvation).
20:6 μακάριος καὶ ἅγιος ὁ ἔχων μέρος ἐν τῇ ἀναστάσει τῇ πρώτῃ· Blessed and holy [is] the one having part in the first resurrection; ἐπὶ τούτων ὁ δεύτερος θάνατος οὐκ ἔχει ἐξουσίαν, over these the second death does not have authority, ἀλλ' ἔσονται ἱερεῖς τοῦ θεοῦ καὶ τοῦ Χριστοῦ but they will be priests of God and of Christ καὶ βασιλεύσουσιν μετ' αὐτοῦ [τὰ] χίλια ἔτη. and will rule with him for the thousand years.	6 Blessed and holy is the one having part in the first resurrection; over these the second death (eternal punishment in the lake of fire for not accepting Christ; see vv. 14–15) does not have authority, but they will be priests of God and of Christ and will rule with him for the thousand years. At this time the "second" (not explicitly called such but implied) resurrection will occur, that is, the physical resurrection from the grave (the first "death," not explicitly called such but implied) Christians (see vv. 12–13; John 5:28–29; 6:38–50, 54; 11:24–25; Rom. 8:11; 1 Thess. 4:14–17).	6 Blessed and holy is the one having part in the first resurrection; over these the second death (eternal punishment in the lake of fire for not accepting Christ) does not have authority, but they will be priests of God and of Christ and will rule with him for the thousand years (a figurative number for the kingdom of God ruling in the true church now).	6 Blessed and holy is the one having part in the first resurrection; over these the second death (the Great White Throne judgment leading to eternal torment [see vv. 12–15]) does not have authority, but they will be priests of God and of Christ and will rule with him for the thousand years, during which time they will perform the sacrificial offerings like the OT priesthood did.	6 Blessed and holy is the one having part in the first resurrection; over these the second death (eternal punishment in the lake of fire for not accepting Christ) does not have authority, but they will be priests of God and of Christ and will rule with him for the thousand years, a figurative number for the reign of the kingdom of God in the true church now.

Greek Text and English Translation	Preterist View	Historicist View	Futurist View	Idealist View
20:7 Καὶ ὅταν τελεσθῇ τὰ χίλια ἔτη, And when the thousand years might be completed, λυθήσεται ὁ σατανᾶς ἐκ τῆς φυλακῆς αὐτοῦ the Satan will be loosed from his prison,	7 And when the thousand years might be completed, the Satan will be loosed from his prison for one last battle against Christ,	7 And when the thousand years might be completed, the Satan will be loosed from his prison,	7 And when the thousand years might be completed, the Satan will be literally loosed from his prison,	7 And when the thousand years might be completed, the Satan will be loosed from his prison,
20:8 καὶ ἐξελεύσεται πλανῆσαι τὰ ἔθνη and he will go forth to deceive the nations τὰ ἐν ταῖς τέσσαρσιν γωνίαις τῆς γῆς, τὸν Γὼγ καὶ Μαγώγ, that are in the four corners of the earth, the Gog and Magog, συναγαγεῖν αὐτοὺς εἰς τὸν πόλεμον, to gather them to war, ὧν ὁ ἀριθμὸς αὐτῶν ὡς ἡ ἄμμος τῆς θαλάσσης. of whom their number of them is like the sand of the sea.	8 and he will go forth to deceive the nations that are in the four corners of the earth, the Gog and Magog (the end-time enemy of God), to gather them to war, whose number is like the sand of the sea.	8 and he will go forth to deceive the nations that are in the four corners of the earth, the Gog and Magog (the revived Roman papacy in the end times), to gather them to war, whose number is like the sand of the sea.	8 and he will go forth to deceive the nations that are in the four corners of the earth (composed of the children of believers in the Millennium, who only pay lip service to Christ, not heartfelt worship), the Gog and Magog, to gather them to war, whose number is like the sand of the sea. Gog and Magog will be the revived Russian-led coalition (cf. Ezek. 38–39), since New Babylon will have been destroyed at the second coming of Christ one thousand years earlier.	8 and he will go forth to deceive the nations that are in the four corners of the earth, the Gog and Magog, to gather them to war, whose number is like the sand of the sea. Gog and Magog is a label from Ezekiel 38–39 describing the enemies of ancient Israel, now applied to the enemies of church at the end of history.
20:9 καὶ ἀνέβησαν ἐπὶ τὸ πλάτος τῆς γῆς And they went up over the breadth of the earth καὶ ἐκύκλευσαν τὴν παρεμβολὴν τῶν ἁγίων and circled the camp of the saints καὶ τὴν πόλιν τὴν ἠγαπημένην, and the city of the beloved,	9 And they went up over the breadth of the earth and circled the camp of the saints and the city of the beloved, and fire descended out of heaven and consumed them.	9 And they went up over the breadth of the earth and circled the camp of the saints and the city of the beloved, and fire descended out of heaven and consumed them.	9 And they went up over the breadth of the earth and circled the camp of the saints and the city of the beloved (Jerusalem), and fire descended out of heaven from God and consumed them.	9 And they went up over the breadth of the earth and circled the camp of the saints and the city of the beloved, and fire descended out of heaven and consumed them. This will happen at the second

Greek / Literal translation	Interpretation	Interpretation
καὶ κατέβη πῦρ ἐκ τοῦ οὐρανοῦ καὶ κατέφαγεν αὐτούς. and fire descended out of heaven and consumed them.		
20:10 καὶ ὁ διάβολος ὁ πλανῶν αὐτοὺς And the devil, the one who deceives them,	10 And the devil, the one who deceives them, was cast into the lake of fire and sulfur, where also the beast (the antichrist pope, the Antichrist) who will rule revived Rome at the end of time) and the false prophet (the spirit of the first-century imperial cult revived at the end of history) are, and they will be tormented day and night forever.	10 And the devil, the one who deceives them, was cast into the lake of fire and sulfur, where also the beast (the antichrist pope, the Antichrist) who will rule revived Rome at the end of time) and the false prophet (the sacerdotal powers of the Catholic priesthood) are, and they will be tormented day and night forever. This will happen at the second coming of
ἐβλήθη εἰς τὴν λίμνην τοῦ πυρὸς καὶ θείου was cast into the lake of fire and sulfur		
ὅπου καὶ τὸ θηρίον καὶ ὁ ψευδοπροφήτης [are], where also the beast and the false prophet [are],		
καὶ βασανισθήσονται ἡμέρας καὶ νυκτὸς εἰς τοὺς αἰῶνας τῶν αἰώνων. and they will be tormented day and night forever.		

10 And the devil, the one who deceives them, was cast into the lake of fire and sulfur, where also the beast (the anti-Christ the beast (the anti-Christ government throughout the history of the church, opposing it but now centralized into one final stand against Christians) and the false prophet (the religious dimension of paganism's attempt to dethrone God between

coming of Christ, at the end of history. Christ's kingdom will be advanced by the church and the gospel between his first and second comings, all the while being persecuted by anti-God, anti-Christ systems. This is the already/not yet prophetic tension characterizing the church: it already reigns with Christ, but it is not yet completely triumphant, as evidenced by paganism's constant attack on the church. This attack will culminate at the end of history, right before the second coming of Christ (Satan will be loosed for a little time). But at that time Christ will destroy forever his enemies (cf. Rev. 20:7–15 with Rev. 19:11–21).

Greek Text and English Translation	Preterist View	Historicist View	Futurist View	Idealist View
		Christ, at the end of history (cf. 2 Thess. 1:7–10).		the first and second comings of Christ, but centralized right before the Parousia) are, and they will be tormented day and night forever.
20:11 Καὶ εἶδον θρόνον μέγαν λευκὸν καὶ τὸν καθήμενον ἐπ᾽ αὐτόν, And I saw a great white throne and the one seated upon it,	11 And I saw a great white throne and the one seated upon it, from whose presence the earth and heaven fled, and place was not found for them.	11 And I saw a great white throne and the one seated upon it, from whose presence the earth and heaven fled, and place was not found for them.	11 And I saw a great white throne and the one seated upon it, from whose presence the earth and heaven fled, and place was not found for them.	11 And I saw a great white throne and the one seated upon it, from whose presence the earth and heaven fled, and place was not found for them.
οὗ ἀπὸ τοῦ προσώπου ἔφυγεν ἡ γῆ καὶ ὁ οὐρανὸς of whom from the presence the earth and the heaven fled,				
καὶ τόπος οὐχ εὑρέθη αὐτοῖς. and place was not found for them.				
20:12 καὶ εἶδον τοὺς νεκρούς, τοὺς μεγάλους καὶ τοὺς μικρούς, ἑστῶτας ἐνώπιον τοῦ θρόνου. And I saw the dead, the great and the small, standing before the throne.	12 And I saw the dead, the great and the small, standing before the throne. And books were opened, and another book was opened, which is the Book of Life, and the dead were judged out of what was written in those books according to their works.	12 And I saw the dead, the great and the small, standing before the throne, having been raised in bodies prepared to live eternally in heaven or in the lake of fire, depending on whether they have been faithful to Christ by rejecting the worship of the papacy. This is the general resurrection. And books were opened, and another book was opened, which is the Book of Life, and the dead were	12 And I saw the dead, the great and the small, standing before the throne. These are both the resurrected righteous at the Rapture and those seven years later at the second coming of Christ who will have ruled with Jesus during the Millennium, along with the dead non-Christians during the Millennium. And books were opened, and another book was opened, which is the Book of Life, and the	12 And I saw the dead, the great and the small, standing before the throne. This will be the physical resurrection of Christians and non-Christians (which happens only at the second coming of Christ; it is the general resurrection of all humanity). And books were opened, and another book was opened, which is the Book of Life, and the dead were judged out of what was
καὶ βιβλία ἠνοίχθησαν, καὶ ἄλλο βιβλίον ἠνοίχθη, And books were opened, and another book was opened,				
ὅ ἐστιν τῆς ζωῆς, which is [the Book] of Life,				
καὶ ἐκρίθησαν οἱ νεκροὶ ἐκ τῶν γεγραμμένων and the dead were judged out of what was written				
ἐν τοῖς βιβλίοις κατὰ τὰ ἔργα αὐτῶν. in those books according to their works.				

20:13 καὶ ἔδωκεν ἡ θάλασσα τοὺς νεκροὺς τοὺς ἐν αὐτῇ And the sea gave [up] the dead in it, καὶ ὁ θάνατος καὶ ὁ ἄδης ἔδωκαν τοὺς νεκροὺς τοὺς ἐν αὐτοῖς, and death and hades gave [up] the dead in them, καὶ ἐκρίθησαν ἕκαστος κατὰ τὰ ἔργα αὐτῶν. and each one was judged according to their works. 20:14 καὶ ὁ θάνατος καὶ ὁ ἄδης ἐβλήθησαν εἰς τὴν λίμνην τοῦ πυρός. And death and hades were cast into the lake of fire. οὗτος ὁ θάνατος ὁ δεύτερός ἐστιν, ἡ λίμνη τοῦ πυρός. This is the second death, the lake of fire. 20:15 καὶ εἴ τις οὐχ εὑρέθη ἐν τῇ βίβλῳ τῆς ζωῆς γεγραμμένος, And if one was not found in the book of life having been written, ἐβλήθη εἰς τὴν λίμνην τοῦ πυρός. [then] he was cast into the lake of fire.	13 And the sea gave up the dead in it, and death and hades gave up the dead in them, and each one was judged according to their works. 14 And death and hades were cast into the lake of fire. This is the second death, the lake of fire. 15 And if one was not found having been written in the Book of Life, then he was cast into the lake of fire. Thus God's kingdom and his saints will finally prevail. (**Editor's note**: One camp within the preterist viewpoint sees in vv. 7–15	judged out of what was written in those books according to their works. 13 And the sea gave up the dead in it, and death and hades gave up the dead in them, and each one was judged according to their works. 14 And death and hades were cast into the lake of fire. This is the second death, the lake of fire. 15 And if one was not found having been written in the Book of Life, then he was cast into the lake of fire. (**Editor's note**: The historicist perspective matches the idealist interpretation of Revelation 21–22, except that the former portrays	dead were judged out of what was written in those books according to their works, whether those works showed their faith in Christ by serving him or showed that they did not believe in Christ but rather worshipped the evil trinity. 13 And the sea gave up the dead in it, and death and hades gave up the dead in them, and each one was judged according to their works. 14 And death and hades were cast into the lake of fire. This is the second death, the lake of fire, which is eternal bodily torment, not soul annihilation. 15 And if one was not found having been written in the Book of Life (which is a record of believers in Jesus), then he was cast into the lake of fire. (**Editor's note**: The futurist position interprets Revelation 21–22 literally	written in those books according to their works. 13 And the sea gave up the dead in it, and death and hades gave up the dead in them, and each one was judged according to their works. 14 And death and hades were cast into the lake of fire. This is the second death, the lake of fire. 15 And if one was not found having been written in the Book of Life, then he was cast into the lake of fire. Thus the Christian (the one who is faithful to Christ) will be raised in an immortal body to enjoy eternity with God and Christ, while the non-Christian

Greek Text and English Translation	Preterist View	Historicist View	Futurist View	Idealist View
	another return of Christ, at the end of history, to be distinguished from his Parousia at the fall of Jerusalem in A.D. 70; other scholars think it describes the coming of Christ to judge Rome in A.D. 476. This position is the postmillennial view: the gospel so transforms society that the world becomes the kingdom of God [Rev. 20:1–6], which in turn will be the catalyst for the second coming of Christ, at the end of history [Rev. 20:7–15]. Therefore, Christ returns after the Millennium [the church's reign in the kingdom]. At Christ's return, Satan and his followers [Ezek. 38–39] will be destroyed [Rev. 20:7–11]. The Great White Throne judgment of all humanity will then follow, with the wicked being physically resurrected to eternal torment and the righteous physically resurrected to eternal bliss [Rev. 20:12–15].) (**Editor's note**: The Preterist position interprets Revelation 21–22	the true church in contrast to Roman Catholicism.)	as the future eternal state of both Israel and the church.)	(the one who worshipped God's enemies) will be raised physically to suffer eternally in the lake of fire (cf. Matt. 25:31–46). (**Editor's note**: The idealist position interprets Revelation 21–22 both figuratively [the new Jerusalem is the church now] and as depicting the literal eternal state in the future.)

	figuratively as the church now and not some future eternal state.)		
	(**Introduction:** The church is the new creation, the new Jerusalem, the new temple, and the new covenant.)	(**Introduction:** The true church, not Roman Catholicism, is the new Jerusalem now and in the eternal state.)	(**Introduction:** A literal new heaven and a new earth in the eternal state after the temporal Millennium in which Israel and the church will have separate roles as the peoples of God.)
21:1 Καὶ εἶδον οὐρανὸν καινὸν καὶ γῆν καινήν. And I saw a new heaven and a new earth.	1 And I saw a new heaven and a new earth. For the first heaven and the first earth passed away and the sea is no more. The OT speaks of a literal new heaven and a new earth in Isaiah 65:17 and 66:22. But in the NT that promise is reapplied figuratively to the Christian and to the church (see 2 Cor. 5:17; Gal. 6:15; Eph. 2:10).	1 And I saw a new heaven and a new earth. For the first heaven and the first earth passed away and the sea is no more. The church is the new creation in Christ now and in the future eternal state at the second coming of Christ.	1 And I saw a new heaven and a new earth. For the first heaven and the first earth passed away and the sea is no more. The old heaven and earth were destroyed by fire (see Rev. 20:9; 2 Pet. 3:6–13).
ὁ γὰρ πρῶτος οὐρανὸς καὶ ἡ πρώτη γῆ ἀπῆλθαν For the first heaven and the first earth passed away			
καὶ ἡ θάλασσα οὐκ ἔστιν ἔτι. and the sea is no more.			
21:2 καὶ τὴν πόλιν τὴν ἁγίαν Ἰερουσαλὴμ καινὴν And the Holy City, New Jerusalem,	2 And I saw the Holy City, the new Jerusalem, descending out of heaven from God, having been prepared like a bride having been adorned for her husband. The church is the new Jerusalem, which replaced the old Jerusalem in A.D. 70 (contrast Rev. 21:9–22:9 with 17:1–19:10).	2 And I saw the Holy City, the new Jerusalem, descending out of heaven from God, having been prepared like a bride having been adorned for her husband. This is in contrast to Roman Catholicism, the spiritual harlot of Revelation 17–18.	2 And I saw the Holy City, the new Jerusalem (converted Israel), descending out of heaven from God having been prepared like a bride (the church), having been adorned for her husband. This indicates that both peoples of God—OT Israel and the NT church—will have their respective, separate roles in the eternal state.
εἶδον καταβαίνουσαν ἐκ τοῦ οὐρανοῦ I saw descending out of heaven			
ἀπὸ τοῦ θεοῦ ἡτοιμασμένην from God, having been prepared			
ὡς νύμφην κεκοσμημένην τῷ ἀνδρὶ αὐτῆς. like a bride having been adorned for her husband.			

Additional column (right):

(**Introduction:** The church is the new Jerusalem now and in the eternal state. This is the already/not yet eschatological tension at work.)

1 And I saw a new heaven and a new earth. For the first heaven and the first earth passed away and the sea is no more. The church is already the new creation in Christ (see 2 Cor. 5:17; Gal. 6:15; Eph. 2:10), but it has not yet reached its final goal—inhabiting the new Jerusalem, the eternal state, which is heaven revealed (cf. v. 2).

2 And I saw the Holy City, the new Jerusalem (symbolizing the truth that the church is the new Israel; a separate role for Israel of the OT is finished in the plan of God), descending out of heaven from God, having been prepared like a bride, having been adorned for her husband. Thus the church as Christ's bride

Greek Text and English Translation	Preterist View	Historicist View	Futurist View	Idealist View
			The first will express its faith in Christ by observing the Mosaic law, especially the sacrificial system. The second will express its faith in Christ by not observing the Mosaic law.	has replaced Israel as the wife of Yahweh. So the eternal state begun at the second coming of Christ, the new Jerusalem, will be inhabited by the one people of God—the church.
21:3 καὶ ἤκουσα φωνῆς μεγάλης ἐκ τοῦ θρόνου λεγούσης· And I heard a great voice out of the throne saying,	3 And I heard a great voice out of the throne saying, "Behold! The tabernacle of God is with men, and he will dwell with them, and they will be his people, and God himself will be with them as their God (the church is the new covenant, which replaced Israel, the old covenant [cf. v. 7; 2 Sam. 7:14; Jer. 31; 2 Cor. 6:18]; and the church is the new temple of God, which replaced the old Jerusalem temple [cf. Rev. 21:22; 1 Cor. 3:16; 6:19; 2 Cor. 6:16; Eph. 2:19–22; Heb. 8:13; 9:11, 24; 12:18–28; 1 Pet. 2:5],	3 And I heard a great voice out of the throne saying, "Behold! The tabernacle of God [is] with men, and he will dwell with them, and they will be his people, and God himself will be with them as their God (so the true church is the new covenant of Christ's blood, not the papacy and its sacrilegious mass),	3 And I heard a great voice out of the throne saying, "Behold! The tabernacle of God is with men, and he will dwell with them, and they will be his people, and God himself will be with them as their God (both Israel and the church in the eternal state will enjoy the blessings of the new covenant: the presence of God [v. 3], life [vv. 4–6], and sonship [v. 7]),	3 And I heard a great voice out of the throne saying, "Behold! The tabernacle of God [is] with men, and he will dwell with them, and they will be his people, and God himself will be with them as their God (the OT covenant formula is now applied to the church, the new covenant, but it awaits its full realization at the Parousia and the eternal state,
ἰδοὺ ἡ σκηνὴ τοῦ θεοῦ μετὰ τῶν ἀνθρώπων, "Behold! The tabernacle of God [is] with men,				
καὶ σκηνώσει μετ᾽ αὐτῶν, καὶ αὐτοὶ λαοὶ αὐτοῦ ἔσονται, and he will dwell with them, and they will be his people,				
καὶ αὐτὸς ὁ θεὸς μετ᾽ αὐτῶν ἔσται [αὐτῶν θεός], and God himself will be with them as their God,				
21:4 καὶ ἐξαλείψει πᾶν δάκρυον ἐκ τῶν ὀφθαλμῶν αὐτῶν, and he will wipe every tear from their eyes,	4 and he will wipe every tear from their eyes, and death will be no more, nor sorrow, nor crying, nor pain	4 and he will wipe every tear from their eyes, and death will be no more, nor sorrow, nor crying, nor pain	4 and he will wipe every tear from their eyes, and death will be no more, nor sorrow, nor crying, nor pain	4 and he will wipe every tear from their eyes, and death will be no more, nor sorrow, nor crying, nor pain

will be any longer, because the former things have passed away."	will be any longer, because the former things have passed away."	will be any longer, because the former things have passed away."	will be any longer, because the former things have passed away."	καὶ ὁ θάνατος οὐκ ἔσται ἔτι οὔτε πένθος and death will be no more, nor sorrow οὔτε κραυγὴ οὔτε πόνος οὐκ ἔσται ἔτι, nor crying, nor pain will not be any longer, [ὅτι] τὰ πρῶτα ἀπῆλθαν. because the former things have passed away".
5 And the one sitting upon the throne said, "Behold! I make all things new." And he says, "Write! Because these words are faithful and true."	5 And the one sitting upon the throne said, "Behold! I make all things new." And he says, "Write! Because these words are faithful and true."	5 And the one sitting upon the throne said, "Behold! I make all things new." And he says, "Write! Because these words are faithful and true."	5 And the one sitting upon the throne said, "Behold! I make all things new." And he says, "Write! Because these words are faithful and true."	21:5 Καὶ εἶπεν ὁ καθήμενος ἐπὶ τῷ θρόνῳ· And the one sitting upon the throne said, ἰδοὺ καινὰ ποιῶ πάντα καὶ λέγει· "Behold! I make all things new." And he says, γράψον, ὅτι οὗτοι οἱ λόγοι πιστοὶ καὶ ἀληθινοί εἰσιν. Write! Because these words are faithful and true."
6 And he said to me, "It has happened. I am the Alpha and the Omega, the beginning and the end. I myself will give to the one thirsting out of the fountain of water of life freely.	6 And he said to me, "It has happened. I am the Alpha and the Omega, the beginning and the end. I myself will give to the one thirsting out of the fountain of water of life freely.	6 And he said to me, "It has happened. I am the Alpha and the Omega, the beginning and the end. I myself will give to the one thirsting out of the fountain of water of life freely.	6 And he said to me, "It has happened. I am the Alpha and the Omega, the beginning and the end. I myself will give to the one thirsting out of the fountain of water of life freely.	21:6 καὶ εἶπέν μοι· γέγοναν. And he said to me, "It has happened. ἐγώ [εἰμι] τὸ ἄλφα καὶ τὸ ὦ, ἡ ἀρχὴ καὶ τὸ τέλος. I am the Alpha and the Omega, the beginning and the end. ἐγὼ τῷ διψῶντι δώσω ἐκ τῆς πηγῆς τοῦ ὕδατος τῆς ζωῆς δωρεάν. I myself will give to the one thirsting out of the fountain of water of life freely.
7 The one who overcomes will inherit these things, and I will be his God, and he himself will be my son. (Thus the church already enjoys the blessings of the new covenant, but their final fulfillment will occur only in the eternal state:	7 The one who overcomes will inherit these things, and I will be his God, and he himself will be my son.	7 The one who overcomes will inherit these things, and I will be his God, and he himself will be my son. (The church presently enjoys the blessings of the new covenant—the presence of God [see v. 3]; eternal life based on justification by faith in Christ	7 The one who overcomes will inherit these things, and I will be his God, and he himself will be my son. The blessings of the new covenant—that is, the gift of eternal life—belong to the church.	21:7 ὁ νικῶν κληρονομήσει ταῦτα The one who overcomes will inherit these things, καὶ ἔσομαι αὐτῷ θεὸς καὶ αὐτὸς ἔσται μοι υἱός. and I will be God to him, and he himself will be a son to me.

Greek Text and English Translation	Preterist View	Historicist View	Futurist View	Idealist View
				the presence of God in his temple, the church [v. 3]; eternal life [v. 4–6]; and sonship [v. 7].)
		alone [see vv. 4–6]; sonship from God [see v. 7].)		
21:8 τοῖς δὲ δειλοῖς καὶ ἀπίστοις But for the cowardly and the unfaithful καὶ ἐβδελυγμένοις καὶ φονεῦσιν καὶ πόρνοις and those having become abominable and murderers and fornicators καὶ φαρμάκοις καὶ εἰδολολάτραις καὶ πᾶσιν τοῖς ψευδέσιν and sorcerers and idolaters and all liars, τὸ μέρος αὐτῶν ἐν τῇ λίμνῃ τῇ καιομένῃ πυρὶ καὶ θείῳ, their part [will be] in the lake burning with fire and sulfur, ὅ ἐστιν ὁ θάνατος ὁ δεύτερος. which is the second death."	8 But for the cowardly and the unfaithful and those having become abominable and murderers and fornicators and sorcerers and idolaters and all liars, their part will be in the lake burning with fire and sulfur, which is the second death." The curses of the old covenant remain on ancient Israel; that is, death (for the blessings and curses of the old covenant, see Deut. 28–30). **(Editor's note:** Revelation 21:9–22:9 is the description of the new Jerusalem; 21:9–21 is the external description. The internal description of the New Jerusalem is given in 21:22–22:9.)	8 But for the cowardly and the unfaithful and those having become abominable and murderers and fornicators and sorcerers and idolaters and all liars (sins that beset the papacy throughout its history), their part will be in the lake burning with fire and sulfur, which is the second death" (eternal torment in the lake of fire), which is in no way to be equated with the Catholic doctrine of purgatory; the differences between the two are obvious: **LAKE OF FIRE** **PURGATORY** Judgment Purgation Non-Christian Christian Eternal Temporary	8 But for the cowardly and the unfaithful and those having become abominable and murderers and fornicators and sorcerers and idolaters and all liars, their part will be in the lake burning with fire and sulfur, which is the second death." Thus the saints will enjoy eternal bliss in the new heaven and new earth, while the lost will endure the eternal torment of the curses of the covenant in the lake of fire. The latter broke the laws of God and must pay for doing so. Above all, they did not believe in Jesus Christ.	8 But for the cowardly and the unfaithful and those having become abominable and murderers and fornicators and sorcerers and idolaters and all liars, their part will be in the lake burning with fire and sulfur, which is the second death." Those outside Christ will suffer the ultimate curse of the covenant—eternal torment in the lake of fire. These people disobey God's Ten Commandments, thereby revealing their lack of faith in Christ.
21:9 Καὶ ἦλθεν εἷς ἐκ τῶν ἑπτὰ ἀγγέλων And there came one of the seven angels	9 And one of the seven angels having the seven bowls being filled with the seven last plagues	9 And one of the seven angels having the seven bowls being filled with the seven last plagues	9 And one of the seven angels having the seven bowls being filled with the seven last plagues	9 And one of the seven angels having the seven bowls being filled with the seven last plagues

τῶν ἐχόντων τὰς ἑπτὰ φιάλας τῶν γεμόντων τῶν ἑπτὰ πληγῶν τῶν ἐσχάτων having the seven bowls being filled with the seven last plagues καὶ ἐλάλησεν μετ᾽ ἐμοῦ λέγων· and spoke with me, saying, δεῦρο, δείξω σοι τὴν νύμφην τὴν γυναῖκα τοῦ ἀρνίου. "Come! I will show you the bride, the wife of the Lamb."	came and spoke with me, saying, "Come! I will show you the bride, the wife of the Lamb." The church as the bride of Christ (see Eph. 5:22–32) has replaced Israel, the unfaithful wife of Yahweh.	came and spoke with me, saying, "Come! I will show you the bride, the wife of the Lamb." The true church is faithful to Christ, but the Roman Catholic "church" is unfaithful because it is apostate.	came and spoke with me, saying, "Come! I will show you the bride, the wife of the Lamb."	came and spoke with me, saying, "Come! I will show you the bride, the wife of the Lamb." The church is the faithful bride of Christ, replacing Israel, the unfaithful wife of Yahweh.
21:10 καὶ ἀπήνεγκέν με ἐν πνεύματι ἐπὶ ὄρος μέγα καὶ ὑψηλόν, And he carried me in the Spirit unto a great and high mountain, καὶ ἔδειξέν μοι τὴν πόλιν τὴν ἁγίαν Ἰερουσαλὴμ and he showed me the city, the holy Jerusalem, καταβαίνουσαν ἐκ τοῦ οὐρανοῦ ἀπὸ τοῦ θεοῦ descending out of heaven from God,	10 And he carried me in the Spirit unto a great and high mountain, and he showed me the city, the holy Jerusalem, descending out of heaven from God,	10 And he carried me in the Spirit unto a great and high mountain, and he showed me the city (not Rome), the holy Jerusalem (in contrast to impure Rome), descending out of heaven from God,	10 And he carried me in the Spirit unto a great and high mountain, and he showed me the city, the holy Jerusalem (to be interpreted literally), descending out of heaven from God,	10 And he carried me in the Spirit unto a great and high mountain, and he showed me the city, the holy Jerusalem, descending out of heaven from God (the manifestation of the heavenly status of the church),
21:11 ἔχουσαν τὴν δόξαν τοῦ θεοῦ, having the glory of God. ὁ φωστὴρ αὐτῆς ὅμοιος λίθῳ τιμιωτάτῳ ὡς λίθῳ ἰάσπιδι κρυσταλλίζοντι. Her light [is] like a most valuable stone, like a stone [of] jasper being clear as crystal,	11 having the glory of God. Her light is like a most valuable stone, like a stone of jasper being clear as crystal (the church displays the brilliant, glorious presence of God as the light of the world; cf. Matt. 5:14–16),	11 having the glory of God's presence. Her light is like a most valuable stone, like a stone of jasper being clear as crystal,	11 having the glory of God. Her light is like a most valuable stone, like a stone of jasper being clear as crystal,	11 having the glory of God. Her light is like a most valuable stone, like a stone of jasper being clear as crystal (the church will display the brilliant presence of God),
21:12 ἔχουσα τεῖχος μέγα καὶ ὑψηλόν, having a great and high wall, ἔχουσα πυλῶνας δώδεκα καὶ ἐπὶ τοῖς πυλῶσιν ἀγγέλους δώδεκα having twelve gates and at the gates twelve angels,	12 having a great and high wall (that is, the church is impregnable and the gates of hell shall not prevail against it; cf. Matt. 16:18), having twelve gates and at the	12 having a great and high wall, having twelve gates and at the gates twelve angels, having names written, which are the names	12 having a great and high wall, having twelve gates and at the gates twelve angels, having names written, which are the names	12 having a great and high wall (the church is impregnable), having twelve gates and at the gates twelve angels, having names written, which are the names

Greek Text and English Translation	Preterist View	Historicist View	Futurist View	Idealist View
καὶ ὀνόματα ἐπιγεγραμμένα, and having names written, ἅ ἐστιν [τὰ ὀνόματα] τῶν δώδεκα φυλῶν υἱῶν Ἰσραήλ· which are the names of the twelve tribes of the sons of Israel;	gates twelve angels, and having names written, which are the names of the twelve tribes of the sons of Israel;	of the twelve tribes of the sons of Israel;	of the twelve tribes of the sons of Israel;	of the twelve tribes of the sons of Israel;
21:13 ἀπὸ ἀνατολῆς πυλῶνες τρεῖς καὶ ἀπὸ βορρᾶ πυλῶνες τρεῖς on the east three gates and on the north three gates καὶ ἀπὸ νότου πυλῶνες τρεῖς καὶ ἀπὸ δυσμῶν πυλῶνες τρεῖς. and on the south three gates and on the west three gates.	13 and on the east three gates and on the north three gates and on the south three gates and on the west three gates. That is to say, the twelve gates are the twelve tribes of Israel, symbolizing the truth that the promise of the restoration of Israel from exile (see Isa. 49:5–6; 56:1–8; Jer. 31:10; Ezek. 34, 37, etc.) is fulfilled in the church.	13 and on the east three gates and on the north three gates and on the south three gates and on the west three gates. Thus the Protestant Reformation is the true successor to old Israel, not Roman Catholicism.	13 and on the east three gates and from on north three gates and on the south three gates and on the west three gates. The twelve gates indicate that Israel will be restored to its Messiah and will inhabit a new, literal Jerusalem. The three gates on each side signify that the holy city will be accessible on all sides. The high walls signify that the city will be protected by God.	13 and on the east three gates and on the north three gates and on the south three gates and on the west three gates (the church is the true Israel).
21:14 καὶ τὸ τεῖχος τῆς πόλεως ἔχον θεμελίους δώδεκα And the wall of the city having twelve foundations, καὶ ἐπ' αὐτῶν δώδεκα ὀνόματα and upon them twelve names τῶν δώδεκα ἀποστόλων τοῦ ἀρνίου. of the twelve apostles of the Lamb.	14 And the wall of the city has twelve foundations, and upon them twelve names of the twelve apostles of the Lamb.	14 And the wall of the city has twelve foundations, and upon them twelve names of the twelve apostles of the Lamb. The true church—Protestantism—is founded on the twelve apostles and not, as Catholicism says, on the primacy of Peter.	14 And the wall of the city has twelve foundations, and upon them twelve names of the twelve apostles of the Lamb. So the new Jerusalem will also be inhabited by the church and its twelve apostles.	14 And the wall of the city has twelve foundations, and upon them twelve names of the twelve apostles of the Lamb (once again, the church is the true Israel).

21:15 Καὶ ὁ λαλῶν μετ᾽ ἐμοῦ εἶχεν μέτρον κάλαμον χρυσοῦν, And the one speaking with me had a golden measuring reed, ἵνα μετρήσῃ τὴν πόλιν in order that he might measure the city καὶ τοὺς πυλῶνας αὐτῆς καὶ τὸ τεῖχος αὐτῆς. and its gates and its walls.	Rather it is Peter's confession, with the other apostles', that Christ is Messiah and Lord that is the foundation of the church (Matt. 16:13–20). 15 And the one speaking with me had a golden measuring reed, in order that he might measure the city and its gates and its wall.	15 And the one speaking with me had a golden measuring reed, in order that he might measure the city and its gates and its wall.	15 And the one speaking with me had a golden measuring reed, in order that he might measure the city and its gates and its wall.	15 And the one speaking with me had a golden measuring reed, in order that he might measure the city and its gates and its wall.
21:16 καὶ ἡ πόλις τετράγωνος κεῖται καὶ τὸ μῆκος αὐτῆς ὅσον [καὶ] τὸ πλάτος. And the city lies foursquare and its length [is] as much as its breadth. καὶ ἐμέτρησεν τὴν πόλιν τῷ καλάμῳ ἐπὶ σταδίων δώδεκα χιλιάδων, And he measured the city with the reed at twelve thousand stadia, τὸ μῆκος καὶ τὸ πλάτος καὶ τὸ ὕψος αὐτῆς ἴσα ἐστίν. the length and the breadth and the height of it are equal.	16 And the city lies foursquare, and its length is as much as its breadth. And he measured the city with the reed at twelve thousand stadia; its length and breadth and height are equal.	16 And the city lies foursquare, and its length is as much as its breadth. This cubed shape of the new Jerusalem alludes to the reality that the church, not the Vatican, is the true temple, the Holy of Holies. And he measured the city with the reed at twelve thousand stadia; its length and breadth and height are equal.	16 And the city lies foursquare, and its length is as much as its breadth. And he measured the city with the reed at twelve thousand stadia; its length and breadth and height are equal. In other words, the new Jerusalem will be a terrestrial city shaped like a cube—1,500 miles in each direction.	16 And the city lies foursquare, and its length is as much as its breadth. And he measured the city with the reed at twelve thousand stadia; its length and breadth and height are equal.
21:17 καὶ ἐμέτρησεν τὸ τεῖχος αὐτῆς ἑκατὸν τεσσεράκοντα τεσσάρων πηχῶν And he measured its walls, a hundred forty-four cubits, μέτρον ἀνθρώπου, ὅ ἐστιν ἀγγέλου. a measure of a man, which is [that] of an angel.	17 And he measured its walls, a hundred and forty-four cubits, a measure of a man, which is that of an angel. In other words, the cubed shape of the church conveys the truth that the church	17 And he measured its walls, a hundred and forty-four cubits, a measure of a man, which is that of an angel.	17 And he measured its walls, a hundred and forty-four cubits, a measure of a man, which is that of an angel. The wall will be only 216 feet tall; that way it will	17 And he measured its walls, a hundred and forty-four cubits, a measure of a man, which is that of an angel. The cubed shape and size of the city/church conveys the conviction

Greek Text and English Translation	Preterist View	Historicist View	Futurist View	Idealist View
	is perfect in Christ and is pervasive in its influence over the world for righteousness' sake. It is the ultimate fulfillment of Ezekiel's prophecy of the establishment of the end-time temple of God (Ezek. 40).		not obscure the glory of God in the city.	that the church is perfect in Christ and pervades the universe.
21:18 καὶ ἡ ἐνδόμησις τοῦ τείχους αὐτῆς ἴασπις And the texture of its wall [was] jasper καὶ ἡ πόλις χρυσίον καθαρὸν ὅμοιον ὑάλῳ καθαρῷ. and the city [was] pure gold like clean glass.	18 And the texture of the city's wall was jasper and the city was pure gold like clean glass.	18 And the texture of the city's wall was jasper and the city was pure gold like clean glass.	18 And the texture of the city's wall was jasper and the city was pure gold like clean glass. Thus the new Jerusalem will be paved literally with gold!	18 And the texture of the city's wall was jasper and the city was pure gold like clean glass.
21:19 οἱ θεμέλιοι τοῦ τείχους τῆς πόλεος παντὶ λίθῳ τιμίῳ κεκοσμημένοι· And the foundations of the wall of the city having been adorned with every valuable stone. ὁ θεμέλιος ὁ πρῶτος ἴασπις, The first foundation [was] jasper, ὁ δεύτερος σάπφιρος, ὁ τρίτος χαλκηδών, ὁ τέταρτος σμάραγδος, the second sapphire, the third chalcedon, the fourth emerald,	19 And the foundations of the wall of the city were adorned with every precious stone. The first foundation was jasper, the second sapphire, the third chalcedon, the fourth emerald,	19 And the foundations of the wall of the city were adorned with every precious stone. The first foundation was jasper, the second sapphire, the third chalcedon, the fourth emerald,	19 And the foundations of the wall of the city were adorned with every precious stone. The first foundation was jasper, the second sapphire, the third chalcedon, the fourth emerald,	19 And the foundations of the wall of the city were adorned with every precious stone. The first foundation was jasper, the second sapphire, the third chalcedon, the fourth emerald,
21:20 ὁ πέμπτος σαρδόνυξ, ὁ ἕκτος σάρδιον, the fifth sardonyx, the sixth sardius, ὁ ἕβδομος χρυσόλιθος, ὁ ὄγδοος βήρυλλος, the seventh chrysolite, the eighth beryl,	20 the fifth sardonyx, the sixth sardonyx, the seventh chrysolite, the eighth beryl, the ninth topaz, the tenth chrysoprase,	20 the fifth sardonyx, the sixth sardius, the seventh chrysolite, the eighth beryl, the ninth topaz, the tenth chrysoprase, the eleventh hyacinth, the	20 the fifth sardonyx, the sixth sardius, the seventh chrysolite, the eighth beryl, the ninth topaz, the tenth chrysoprase, the eleventh hyacinth,	20 the fifth sardonyx, the sixth sardius, the seventh chrysolite, the eighth beryl, the ninth topaz, the tenth chrysoprase, the eleventh hyacinth, the

ὁ ἔνατος τοπάζιον, ὁ δέκατος χρυσόπρασος, the ninth topaz, the tenth chrysoprase, ὁ ἑνδέκατος ὑάκινθος, ὁ δωδέκατος ἀμέθυστος, the eleventh hyacinth, the twelfth amethyst.	the eleventh hyacinth, the twelfth amethyst.	twelfth amethyst. These twelve precious stones recall the twelve stones of the breastplate of the Jewish high priest and signify that every believer is a priest having direct access to God's presence, the Holy of Holies. There is no need here whatsoever for a priesthood of the elite that characterizes Roman Catholicism.	the twelfth amethyst. These remind one of the twelve stones on the breastplate of the Jewish high priest. This tells the reader that the new Jerusalem will be the new, true Holy of Holies.	twelfth amethyst. These twelve precious stones recall the twelve stones of the breastplate of the Jewish high priest, signifying once again that the church is the true Israel, the new temple; that is, the Holy of Holies.
21:21 καὶ οἱ δώδεκα πυλῶνες δώδεκα μαργαρῖται, And the twelve gates [are] twelve pearls, ἀνὰ εἷς ἕκαστος τῶν πυλώνων ἦν ἐξ ἑνὸς μαργαρίτου. one of each of the gates was out of one pearl. καὶ ἡ πλατεῖα τῆς πόλεως χρυσίον καθαρὸν ὡς ὕαλος διαυγής. And the street of the city [was] pure gold like clear glass.	21 And the twelve gates are twelve pearls; one of each of the gates was out of one pearl. So these twelve precious stones recall the twelve stones on the breastplate of the Jewish high priest (Exod. 39:9–14) and signify that Jesus Christ is the new high priest and that his church is the new spiritual priesthood (see Heb. 7–9). And the street of the city was pure gold like clear glass. (The golden color reminded John of the yellow sandstone out of which old Jerusalem was constructed. Apocalyptic Judaism expected the end-time Jerusalem to be built out of gold [see, for example, Tob. 13:16–17;	21 And the twelve gates are literally twelve pearls, one of each of the gates was out of one pearl (this despite the fact that no oysters are large enough to produce such huge pearls). And the street of the city was pure gold like clear glass.	21 And the twelve gates are twelve pearls, one of each of the gates was out of one pearl. And the street of the city was pure gold like clear glass.	

Greek Text and English Translation	Preterist View	Historicist View	Futurist View	Idealist View
	11Q Temple 36:11; 39:3; 41:15]. The church now has that place of honor.)			
21:22 Καὶ ναὸν οὐκ εἶδον ἐν αὐτῇ, And I saw no temple in it,	22 And I saw no temple in it, for the Lord God the Almighty is its temple (the church as indwelled by God is the true temple), and the Lamb.	22 And I saw no temple in it, for the Lord God the Almighty is its temple, and the Lamb. The church as the people of God, not the ornate buildings of the Vatican, is the temple of God!	22 And I saw no temple in it, for the Lord God the Almighty is its temple, and the Lamb. God's presence replaces the temple and the Holy of Holies.	22 And I saw no temple in it, for the Lord God the Almighty is its temple, and the Lamb.
ὁ γὰρ κύριος ὁ θεὸς ὁ παντοκράτωρ ναὸς αὐτῆς ἐστιν καὶ τὸ ἀρνίον. for the Lord God Almighty is its temple, and the Lamb.				
21:23 καὶ ἡ πόλις οὐ χρείαν ἔχει τοῦ ἡλίου οὐδὲ τῆς σελήνης And the city does not have need of the sun nor of the moon	23 And the city does not have need of the sun nor of the moon in order that they might give light in it, for the glory of God illumined it, and its lamp is the Lamb.	23 And the city does not have need of the sun nor of the moon in order that they might give light in it, for the glory of God illumined it, and its lamp is the Lamb.	23 And the city does not have need of the sun nor of the moon in order that they might give light in it, for the glory of God illumined it, and its lamp is the Lamb.	23 And the city does not have need of the sun nor of the moon in order that they might give light in it, for the glory of God illumined it, and its lamp is the Lamb.
ἵνα φαίνωσιν αὐτῇ, in order that they might give light in it,				
ἡ γὰρ δόξα τοῦ θεοῦ ἐφώτισεν αὐτήν, for the glory of God illumined it,				
καὶ ὁ λύχνος αὐτῆς τὸ ἀρνίον. and its lamp [is] the Lamb.				
21:24 καὶ περιπατήσουσιν τὰ ἔθνη διὰ τοῦ φωτὸς αὐτῆς, And the nations will walk by its light,	24 And the nations will walk by its light, and the kings of the earth will bring their glory into it,	24 And the nations will walk by its light, and the kings of the earth will bring their glory into it,	24 And the nations will walk by its light, and the kings of the earth will bring their glory into it (so the church will be composed of Gentile Christians from every country throughout the history of the church),	24 And the (converted) nations will walk by its light, and the kings of the earth will bring their glory into it,
καὶ οἱ βασιλεῖς τῆς γῆς φέρουσιν τὴν δόξαν αὐτῶν εἰς αὐτήν, and the kings of the earth will bring their glory into it,				

Column 1 — Greek / English

21:25 καὶ οἱ πυλῶνες αὐτῆς οὐ μὴ κλεισθῶσιν ἡμέρας,
and its gates may never ever be shut by day,

νὺξ γὰρ οὐκ ἔσται ἐκεῖ,
for there will be no night there,

21:26 καὶ οἴσουσιν τὴν δόξαν
and they will bring the glory

καὶ τὴν τιμὴν τῶν ἐθνῶν εἰς αὐτήν.
and the honor of the nations into it.

21:27 καὶ οὐ μὴ εἰσέλθῃ εἰς αὐτὴν πᾶν κοινὸν
And there will never ever enter into it any profane thing

καὶ [ὁ] ποιῶν βδέλυγμα καὶ ψεῦδος
and the one making abomination and a lie

εἰ μὴ οἱ γεγραμμένοι ἐν τῷ βιβλίῳ τῆς ζωῆς τοῦ ἀρνίου.
except the ones having been written in the Book of Life of the Lamb.

Column 2

25 and its gates may never ever be shut by day, for there will be no night there,

26 and they will bring the glory and the honor of the nations into it.

27 And there will never ever enter into it any profane thing and the one making abomination and a lie, except the ones having been written in the Book of Life of the Lamb. Those in the church through faith in Christ enjoy the blessings of the new covenant (purity, honor, glory), while those outside the church, especially old Israel, experience the curses of the old covenant (impurity, dishonor, darkness).

(**Editor's note:** Those [few] preterists who believe that Christ will still return at the end of history also believe in a literal eternal state; compare the other three perspectives to one degree or another [historicist, futurist, and idealist].)

Column 3

25 and its gates may never ever be shut by day, for there will be no night there,

26 and they will bring the glory and the honor of the nations into it.

27 And there will never ever enter into it any profane thing and the one making abomination and a lie, except the ones having been written in the Book of Life of the Lamb. Only those who believe in Christ alone for salvation are in the Lamb's Book of Life. And the true church now is the new Jerusalem, and at the second coming of Christ that church will enter into the eternal state to enjoy forever the presence of God and Christ. Not so the counterfeit, apostate church of Roman Catholicism.

Column 4

25 and its gates may never ever be shut by day, for there will be no night there,

26 and they will bring the glory and the honor of the nations into it.

27 And there will never ever enter into it any profane thing and the one making abomination and a lie, except the ones having been written in the Book of Life of the Lamb. Even though the two peoples of God will live in the new heaven and new earth, the new Jerusalem, they both are Christians because they believed in Christ. There is no room here for a two-covenant approach (which says that Israel will be saved by keeping the Mosaic law [not by faith in Christ], while the church will be saved by believing in Christ [not by keeping the Mosaic law]). Rather, both Israel and the church believe in Jesus and on that basis are in the Lamb's Book of Life.

Column 5

25 and its gates may never ever be shut by day, for there will be no night there,

26 and they will bring the glory and the honor of the nations into it.

27 And there will never ever enter into it any profane thing and the one making abomination and a lie, except the ones having been written in the Book of Life of the Lamb. The key to being in the church and not outside of it is faith in Christ. These blessings and honors belong to the church now because of its union with Christ in heaven but will be made visible and finalized at his second coming (cf. Col. 3:1–4), which will begin the eternal state.

Greek Text and English Translation	Preterist View	Historicist View	Futurist View	Idealist View
22:1 Καὶ ἔδειξέν μοι ποταμὸν ὕδατος ζωῆς λαμπρὸν ὡς κρύσταλλον, And he showed me a river, water of life bright like crystal, ἐκπορευόμενον ἐκ τοῦ θρόνου τοῦ θεοῦ καὶ τοῦ ἀρνίου. flowing from the throne of God and the Lamb.	1 (A vision of the church, the new creation/paradise regained) And he showed me a river, the water of life bright like crystal, flowing from the throne of God and the Lamb.	1 (A vision of the church, the new creation now and in the eternal state) And he showed me a river, the water of life bright like crystal, flowing from the throne of God and the Lamb.	1 (A vision of the new Jerusalem in the eternal state) And he showed me a river, the water of life bright like crystal, flowing from the throne of God and the Lamb.	1 (A vision of the church, the new creation now and in the eternal state) And he showed me a river, the water of life bright like crystal, flowing from the throne of God and the Lamb.
22:2 ἐν μέσῳ τῆς πλατείας αὐτῆς In the middle of its street καὶ τοῦ ποταμοῦ ἐντεῦθεν καὶ ἐκεῖθεν ξύλον ζωῆς and on this side and that side of the river [was] the Tree of Life ποιοῦν καρποὺς δώδεκα, κατὰ μῆνα making twelve fruits, according to the month ἕκαστον ἀποδιδοῦν τὸν καρπὸν αὐτοῦ, each giving its fruit, καὶ τὰ φύλλα τοῦ ξύλου εἰς θεραπείαν τῶν ἐθνῶν. and the leaves of the tree [were] for healing of the nations.	2 In the middle of its street and on this side and that side of the river was the Tree of Life making twelve fruits, according to the month each giving its fruit, and the leaves of the tree were for the healing of the nations.	2 In the middle of its street and on this side and that side of the river was the Tree of Life making twelve fruits, according to the month each giving its fruit, and the leaves of the tree were for the healing of the nations.	2 In the middle of its street and on this side and that side of the river was the Tree of Life making twelve fruits, according to the month each giving its fruit, and the leaves of the tree were for the healing of the nations.	2 In the middle of its street and on this side and that side of the river was the Tree of Life making twelve fruits, according to the month each giving its fruit, and the leaves of the tree were for the healing of the nations.
22:3 καὶ πᾶν κατάθεμα οὐκ ἔσται ἔτι. And any curse is no longer [there]. καὶ ὁ θρόνος τοῦ θεοῦ καὶ τοῦ ἀρνίου ἐν αὐτῇ ἔσται, And the throne of God and the Lamb will be in it, καὶ οἱ δοῦλοι αὐτοῦ λατρεύσουσιν αὐτῷ and his servants will do service to him,	3 And any curse is no longer there. And the throne of God and the Lamb will be in it, and his servants will do service to him,	3 And any curse is no longer there. And the throne of God and the Lamb will be in it, and his servants will do service to him,	3 And any curse is no longer there. And the throne of God and the Lamb will be in it, and his servants will do service to him,	3 And any curse is no longer there. And the throne of God and the Lamb will be in it, and his servants will do service to him,

22:4 καὶ ὄψονται τὸ πρόσωπον αὐτοῦ, and they will see his face,	4 and they will see his face, and his name will be upon their foreheads.	4 and they will see his face, and his name will be upon their foreheads.	4 and they will see his face, and his name will be upon their foreheads.	4 and they will see his face, and his name will be upon their foreheads.
καὶ τὸ ὄνομα αὐτοῦ ἐπὶ τῶν μετώπων αὐτῶν. and his name [will be] upon their foreheads.				
22:5 καὶ νὺξ οὐκ ἔσται ἔτι And night will not be any longer,	5 And night will not be any longer, and they have no need for a light of a lamp and light of the sun, because the Lord God will give light upon them, and they will rule forever. Thus, the church already participates in Christ, the second Adam (see Rom. 5:12–21), who has removed from them the curse of the First Adam (see vv. 2–3), exile from the presence of God (v. 4), and subjection to sin (v. 5). Roman Catholicism, however, remains in the first Adam.	5 And night will not be any longer, and they have no need for a light of a lamp and light of the sun, because the Lord God will give light upon them, and they will rule forever. Thus, the church already participates in Christ the second Adam, who has removed for them the curse of the First Adam (vv. 2–3), exile from the presence of God (v. 4), and subjugation to sin (v. 5). Roman Catholicism, however, remains in the first Adam. In the eternal state after the Parousia, the church will be fully exempt from Adam's sin and paradise will be completely restored.	5 And night will not be any longer, and they have no need for a light of a lamp and light of the sun, because the Lord God will give light upon them, and they will rule forever. In the eternal state, after the temporary Millennium, the new Jerusalem will be free of the first Adam's curse (vv. 2–3), exile (v. 4), and sin (v. 5), because it is in Christ the second Adam. The new Jerusalem will literally be paradise restored in the new heaven and new earth.	5 And night will not be any longer, and they have no need for a light of a lamp and light of the sun, because the Lord God will give light upon them, and they will rule forever. Thus, the church already participates in Christ the second Adam, who has removed for them the curse of the first Adam (vv. 2–3), exile from the presence of God (v. 4), and subjugation to sin (v. 5). The pagan world and the apostate church, however, remain in the first Adam. In the eternal state after the Parousia, the church will be fully exempt from Adam's sin, and paradise will be completely restored.
καὶ οὐκ ἔχουσιν χρείαν φωτὸς λύχνου καὶ φωτὸς ἡλίου, and they have no need for a light of a lamp and light of the sun,				
ὅτι κύριος ὁ θεὸς φωτίσει ἐπ᾿ αὐτούς, because the Lord God will give light upon them,				
καὶ βασιλεύσουσιν εἰς τοὺς αἰῶνας τῶν αἰώνων. and they will rule forever.				
22:6 Καὶ εἶπέν μοι· οὗτοι οἱ λόγοι πιστοὶ καὶ ἀληθινοί, And he said to me, "These words [are] faithful and true,	6 And he said to me, "These words are faithful and true, and the Lord God of the spirits of the prophets (of the NT) sent his angel to show to his servants what things must happen soon at the fall of Jerusalem.	6 And he said to me, "These words are faithful and true, and the Lord God of the spirits of the prophets (the Protestant Reformation) sent his angel to show to his servants what things happen soon beginning with the Rapture.	6 And he said to me, "These words are faithful and true, and the Lord God of the spirits of the prophets sent his angel to show to his servants what things must happen soon at the second coming.	6 And he said to me, "These words are faithful and true, and the Lord God of the spirits of the prophets sent his angel to show to his servants what things must happen soon at the second coming.

Greek Text and English Translation	Preterist View	Historicist View	Futurist View	Idealist View
καὶ ὁ κύριος ὁ θεὸς τῶν πνευμάτων τῶν προφητῶν ἀπέστειλεν τὸν ἄγγελον αὐτοῦ and the Lord God of the spirits of the prophets sent his angel				
δεῖξαι τοῖς δούλοις αὐτοῦ ἃ δεῖ γενέσθαι ἐν τάχει. to show to his servants what things must happen soon.		must happen soon at the second coming.		
22:7 καὶ ἰδοὺ ἔρχομαι ταχύ. "And behold, I come quickly. μακάριος ὁ τηρῶν τοὺς λόγους τῆς προφητείας τοῦ βιβλίου τούτου. Blessed [is] the one who keeps the words of the prophecies of this book."	7 "And behold, I come quickly to judge Israel and Jerusalem in A.D. 70. Blessed is the one who keeps the words of the prophecies of this book."	7 "And behold, I come quickly at the second coming. Blessed is the one who keeps the words of the prophecies (of the Protestant Reformation) of this book."	7 "And behold, I come quickly at the Rapture for the church before the Great Tribulation is unleashed on earth. Blessed is the one who keeps the words of the prophecies of this book, which deal with the prophecy of the book of Revelation."	7 "And behold, I come quickly. Blessed is the one who keeps the words of the prophecies of this book."
22:8 Κἀγὼ Ἰωάννης ὁ ἀκούων καὶ βλέπων ταῦτα. And I, John, [am] the one who hears and sees these things. καὶ ὅτε ἤκουσα καὶ ἔβλεψα, ἔπεσα προσκυνῆσαι And when I heard and saw, I fell to worship ἔμπροσθεν τῶν ποδῶν τοῦ ἀγγέλου τοῦ δεικνύοντός μοι ταῦτα. before the feet of the angel showing to me these things.	8 And I, John, am the one who hears and sees these things. And when I heard and saw, I fell to worship before the feet of the angel showing to me these things.	8 And I, John, am the one who hears and sees these things. And when I heard and saw, I fell to worship before the feet of the angel showing to me these things.	8 And I, John, am the one who hears and sees these things. And when I heard and saw, I fell to worship before the feet of the angel showing to me these things.	8 And I, John, am the one who hears and sees these things. And when I heard and saw, I fell to worship before the feet of the angel showing to me these things.

Greek / Literal	Interpretation 1	Interpretation 2	Interpretation 3	Interpretation 4
22:9 καὶ λέγει μοι· ὅρα μή· σύνδουλός σού εἰμι — And he says to me, "See [that you do] not [do this]! I am your fellow servant / καὶ τῶν ἀδελφῶν σου τῶν προφητῶν — and [one] of the brothers of the prophets / καὶ τῶν τηρούντων τοὺς λόγους τοῦ βιβλίου τούτου· — and of the ones keeping the words of this book. / τῷ θεῷ προσκύνησον. — Worship God!	9 And he says to me, "See that you do not do it! I am your fellow servant and one of the brothers of the prophets and of the ones keeping the words of this book. Worship God (not the ceremonial laws of the old covenant)!"	9 And he says to me, "See that you do not do it! I am your fellow servant and one of the brothers of the prophets and of the ones keeping the words of this book. Worship God (not the papacy or anyone or anything associated with it)!"	9 And he says to me, "See that you do not do it! I am your fellow servant and one of the brothers of the prophets and of the ones keeping the words of this book. Worship God (not the Antichrist)!"	9 And he says to me, "See that you do not do it! I am your fellow servant and one of the brothers of the prophets and of the ones keeping the words of this book. Worship God (not the world system)!"
22:10 Καὶ λέγει μοι· μὴ σφραγίσῃς τοὺς λόγους — And he says to me, "Do not seal the words / τῆς προφητείας τοῦ βιβλίου τούτου, — of the prophecies of this book, / ὁ καιρὸς γὰρ ἐγγύς ἐστιν. — for the time is near.	10 And he says to me, "Do not seal the words of the prophecies of this book of the replacement of the old covenant by the new covenant, for the time is near (A.D. 70, the fall of Jerusalem).	10 And he says to me, "Do not seal the words of the prophecies of this book regarding the triumph of the Protestant Reformation over the Roman Catholic "Church," for the time is near for the second coming of Christ, at the end of history.	10 And he says to me, "Do not seal the words of the prophecies of this book regarding the end times, for the time is near. This is so because there are no signs of the times that will precede the rapture of the church; thus the Rapture can happen at anytime.	10 And he says to me, "Do not seal the prophecies of this book regarding the church and the kingdom, for the time is near in the sense that the kingdom of God has already dawned through the church and one day will be made complete at the second coming of Christ, at the end of history.
22:11 ὁ ἀδικῶν ἀδικησάτω ἔτι — The one who is unrighteous, let him be unrighteous still; / καὶ ὁ ῥυπαρὸς ῥυπανθήτω ἔτι, — and the one who is unclean, let him be unclean still; / καὶ ὁ δίκαιος δικαιοσύνην ποιησάτω ἔτι — and the one who is righteous, let him do righteousness still;	11 The one who is unrighteous, let him be unrighteous still; and the one who is unclean, let him be unclean still; and the one who is righteous, let him do righteousness still; and the one who is holy, let him be holy still! These commands pertain to two categories: the Jew and the Christian.	11 The one who is unrighteous, let him be unrighteous still; and the one who is unclean, let him be unclean still; and the one who is righteous, let him do righteousness still; and the one who is holy, let him be holy still (because	11 The one who is unrighteous, let him be unrighteous still; and the one who is unclean, let him be unclean still (because he trusts in his own works of righteousness); and the one who is righteous, let him do righteousness still; and the one who is holy, let him be holy still by worshipping Christ!	11 The one who is unrighteous, let him be unrighteous still; and the one who is unclean, let him be unclean still by aligning with the anti-God, anti-Christian world system; and the one who is righteous, let him do righteousness still; and the one who is holy, let him be holy still.

Greek Text and English Translation	Preterist View	Historicist View	Futurist View	Idealist View
καὶ ὁ ἅγιος ἁγιασθήτω ἔτι. and the one who is holy, let him be holy still!		he trusts in Christ alone for salvation)!		be holy still by being faithful to Christ!
22:12 Ἰδοὺ ἔρχομαι ταχύ, καὶ ὁ μισθός μου μετ᾽ ἐμοῦ Behold, I am coming quickly, and my reward [is] with me ἀποδοῦναι ἑκάστῳ ὡς τὸ ἔργον ἐστὶν αὐτοῦ. to give to each one as is his work.	12 Behold, I am coming quickly (in A.D. 70), and my reward is with me to give each one as is his work.	12 Behold, I am coming quickly at the second coming, and my reward is with me to give each one as is his work (but based solely on faith in Christ).	12 Behold, I am coming quickly at any moment, and my reward is with me to give each one as is his work.	12 Behold, I am coming quickly (even though the kingdom of God is not yet complete, its dawning in history assures the church that the second coming of Christ will come), and my reward is with me to give each one as is his work.
22:13 ἐγὼ τὸ ἄλφα καὶ τὸ ὦ, I [am] the Alpha and the Omega, ὁ πρῶτος καὶ ὁ ἔσχατος, ἡ ἀρχὴ καὶ τὸ τέλος. the first and the last, the beginning and the end.	13 I am the Alpha and the Omega, the first and the last, the beginning and the end.	13 I am the Alpha and the Omega, the first and the last, the beginning and the end.	13 I am the Alpha and the Omega, the first and the last, the beginning and the end.	13 I am the Alpha and the Omega, the first and the last, the beginning and the end.
22:14 Μακάριοι οἱ πλύνοντες τὰς στολὰς αὐτῶν, Blessed [are] the ones who wash their robes, ἵνα ἔσται ἡ ἐξουσία αὐτῶν ἐπὶ τὸ ξύλον τῆς ζωῆς in order that their authority will be over the Tree of Life καὶ τοῖς πυλῶσιν εἰσέλθωσιν εἰς τὴν πόλιν. and that they may enter by the gates into the city.	14 Blessed are the ones who wash their robes, in order that their authority will be over the Tree of Life and that they may enter by the gates into the city. This is the blessing of the new covenant that belongs to the church through faith in Christ.	14 Blessed are the ones who wash their robes in the substitutionary death of Christ, not in the Catholic concept of the "imitation of Christ," in order that their authority will be over the Tree of Life and that they may enter by the gates into the city.	14 Blessed are the ones who wash their robes in the blood of the Lamb, in order that their authority will be over the Tree of Life and that they may enter by the gates into the city of the new Jerusalem (of Rev. 21–22).	14 Blessed are the ones who wash their robes, in order that their authority will be over the Tree of Life and that they may enter by the gates into the city (the church now and the eternal state later).
22:15 ἔξω οἱ κύνες καὶ οἱ φάρμακοι Outside [are] the dogs and the sorcerers	15 Outside are the dogs and the sorcerers and the fornicators and the murderers and the idolaters	15 Outside are the dogs and the sorcerers and the fornicators and the murderers and the idolaters	15 Outside are the sorcerers and the fornicators and the murderers and the	15 Outside are the dogs and the sorcerers and the fornicators and the murderers and the idolaters

καὶ οἱ πόρνοι καὶ οἱ φονεῖς and the fornicators and the murderers καὶ οἱ εἰδωλολάτραι καὶ πᾶς φιλῶν καὶ ποιῶν ψεῦδος, and the idolaters and everyone loving and making a lie. 22:16 Ἐγὼ Ἰησοῦς ἔπεμψα τὸν ἄγγελόν μου I Jesus sent my angel μαρτυρῆσαι ὑμῖν ταῦτα ἐπὶ ταῖς ἐκκλησίαις, to witness to you these things regarding the churches. ἐγώ εἰμι ἡ ῥίζα καὶ τὸ γένος Δαυίδ, I am the root and the offspring of David, ὁ ἀστὴρ ὁ λαμπρὸς ὁ πρωϊνός. the bright morning star." 22:17 Καὶ τὸ πνεῦμα καὶ ἡ νύμφη λέγουσιν· ἔρχου. And the Spirit and the bride say, "Come!" καὶ ὁ ἀκούων εἰπάτω· ἔρχου. And the one who hears, let him say, "Come!" καὶ ὁ διψῶν ἐρχέσθω, ὁ θέλων λαβέτω ὕδωρ ζωῆς δωρεάν. And the one who is thirsting, let him come; the one who is willing, let him receive the water of life freely. 22:18 Μαρτυρῶ ἐγὼ παντὶ τῷ ἀκούοντι I myself witness to everyone hearing	and everyone loving and making a lie. This is the curse of the old covenant that belongs to those outside Christ, non-believing Jews especially. 16 I, Jesus, sent my angel to witness to you these things regarding the churches. I am the root and the offspring of David, the bright morning star." 17 And the Spirit and the bride (the church, the new Jerusalem, not Israel) say, "Come!" And the one who hears, let him say, "Come!" And the one who is thirsting, let him come; the one who is willing, let him receive the water of life freely. Let Israel repent and receive Christ before judgment comes in A.D. 70. 18 I myself (John the apostle) witness to everyone hearing the words of the prophecy of this book. If anyone adds	and everyone loving and making a lie—sins that characterize the papacy. 16 I, Jesus, sent my angel to witness to you these things regarding the churches (the seven churches that correspond to the church throughout its history). I am the root and the offspring of David, the bright morning star." 17 And the Spirit and the bride (the true church, not Catholicism) say, "Come!" And the one who hears, let him say, "Come!" And the one who is thirsting, let him come; the one who is willing, let him receive the water of life freely—that is, the message of justification by faith apart from works. 18 I myself witness to everyone hearing the words of the prophecy of this book. If anyone adds upon these things (such	idolaters and everyone loving and making a lie; that is, those who do not receive Christ. 16 I, Jesus, sent my angel to witness to you these things regarding the churches. I am the root and the offspring of David, the bright morning star; that is, Jesus the Messiah, who will restore Jerusalem and the OT law." 17 And the Spirit and the bride (the church and converted Israel) say, "Come!" And the one who hears, let him say, "Come!" And the one who is thirsting, let him come; the one who is willing, let him receive the water of life freely. 18 I myself witness to everyone hearing the words of the prophecy of this book. If anyone adds (false prophecies)	and everyone loving and making a lie. This pertains to those who are not faithful to Christ. 16 I, Jesus, sent my angel to witness to you these things regarding the churches. I am the root and the offspring of David, the bright morning star." 17 And the Spirit and the bride (the true church) say, "Come!" And the one who hears, let him say, "Come!" And the one who is thirsting, let him come; the one who is willing, let him receive the water of life freely. 18 I myself witness to hearing hearing the words of the prophecy of this book. If anyone adds upon these things—the

Greek Text and English Translation	Preterist View	Historicist View	Futurist View	Idealist View
τοὺς λόγους τῆς προφητείας τοῦ βιβλίου τούτου· the words of the prophecy of this book. ἐάν τις ἐπιθῇ ἐπ᾽ αὐτά, If anyone adds upon these things, ἐπιθήσει ὁ θεὸς ἐπ᾽ αὐτὸν τὰς πληγὰς τὰς γεγραμμένας ἐν τῷ βιβλίῳ τούτῳ, God will add upon him the plagues having been written in this book,	upon these things (for example, adding the Jewish law to God's grace, see v. 21), God will add upon him the plagues (the curses of the old covenant) having been written in this book,	as the OT Apocrypha, church tradition, papal doctrine, Mariology, seven sacraments), God will add upon him the plagues having been written in this book,	upon these things, God will add upon him the plagues having been written in this book,	Word of God—God will add upon him the plagues having been written in this book,
22:19 καὶ ἐάν τις ἀφέλῃ ἀπὸ τῶν λόγων and if anyone takes away from the words τοῦ βιβλίου τῆς προφητείας ταύτης, of the book of this prophecy, ἀφελεῖ ὁ θεὸς τὸ μέρος αὐτοῦ God will take away his part ἀπὸ τοῦ ξύλου τῆς ζωῆς καὶ ἐκ τῆς πόλεως τῆς ἁγίας from the Tree of Life and from the Holy City,	19 and if anyone takes away from the words of the book of this prophecy (that is, removes the message that salvation comes through faith in Christ alone apart from works), God will take away his part from the Tree of Life and from the Holy City (the church, the new Jerusalem), of which has been written in this book.	19 and if anyone takes away from the words of the book of this prophecy by expunging the message of justification by faith from the Bible, God will take away his part from the Tree of Life and from the Holy City (the church, the new Jerusalem), of which has been written in this book.	19 and if anyone takes away from the words of this prophecy by downplaying the end-time prophecies of Revelation, God will take away his part from the Tree of Life (paradise restored) and from the Holy City (the new Jerusalem), of which has been written in this book.	19 and if anyone takes away from the words of the book of this prophecy of the Word of God, God will take away his part from the Tree of Life and from the Holy City, of which has been written in this book.
τῶν γεγραμμένων ἐν τῷ βιβλίῳ τούτῳ. of the ones having been written in this book.				
22:20 Λέγει ὁ μαρτυρῶν ταῦτα· The one who witnesses these things says, ναί, ἔρχομαι ταχύ. Ἀμήν, ἔρχου κύριε Ἰησοῦ. "Indeed, I am coming quickly. Amen! Come, Lord Jesus!"	20 The one who witnesses these things says, "Indeed, I am coming quickly. Amen! Come, Lord Jesus!" (No more	20 The one who witnesses these things says, "Indeed, I am coming quickly. Amen! Come, Lord Jesus!"	20 The one who witnesses these things says, "Indeed, I am coming quickly. Amen! Come, Lord Jesus!"	20 The one who witnesses these things says, "Indeed, I am coming quickly. Amen! Come, Lord Jesus!"

than one to two years will transpire before I will come to judge Jerusalem.)

22:21 Ἡ χάρις τοῦ κυρίου Ἰησοῦ μετὰ πάντων.
The grace of the Lord Jesus [be] with all [of you].

21 The grace of the Lord Jesus be with all of you.

21 The grace of the Lord Jesus, which is received by faith alone, be with all of you.

21 The grace of the Lord Jesus be with all of you.

21 The grace of the Lord Jesus be with all of you.

MORE TOOLS

TO HELP YOU UNDERSTAND
THE NEW TESTAMENT

A NEW READER'S LEXICON OF THE GREEK NEW TESTAMENT

OF THE GREEK NEW TESTAMENT

Michael H. Burer and Jeffrey E. Miller

FOREWORD BY DANIEL B. WALLACE

READ THE GREEK NEW TESTAMENT

A New Reader's Lexicon of the Greek New Testament
Michael H. Burer and Jeffrey E. Miller

IMPROVING ON EARLIER LEXICAL WORKS, *A New Reader's Lexicon of the Greek New Testament* incorporates all words that occur fewer than fifty times in the New Testament. In canonical order, it catalogs a word's frequency in each book, in each author's writings, and in the entire New Testament. References to rare or noteworthy word usages are included, allowing the reader to quickly identify words of special significance.

"What Kubo did for the last generation, Burer and Miller's *A New Reader's Lexicon* will do for the next."
—from the foreword by Daniel B. Wallace

"Very usable, exceedingly helpful, and a fine contribution to any student of the Word interested in serious reading of the Greek New Testament." —Grant Osborne, Professor of the New Testament, Trinity Evangelical Divinity School

"*A New Reader's Lexicon* is a step forward for the student of Greek and is sure to be of benefit to those who teach Greek. . . . The use of *A Greek-English Lexicon of the New Testament and Other Early Christian Literature* (*BDAG*) is a great touch." —Darrell L. Bock, Research Professor of New Testament Studies, Dallas Theological Seminary

"This lexicon . . . has overcome the noticeable shortcomings of Kubo and should well serve the person who wants to keep up their Greek by daily reading, but gets frustrated by having to spend so much time looking up words." —Gordon D. Fee, Professor of New Testament Studies, Regent College

Michael H. Burer is assistant professor of New Testament studies at Dallas Theological Seminary, where he received his Ph.D. He has published a number of scholarly works and contributed as an editor to the *New English Translation—Novum Testamentum Graece New Testament.*

Jeffrey E. Miller earned his Th.M. from Dallas Theological Seminary and is senior pastor at Trinity Bible Church in Richardson, Texas. He has published both scholarly and popular works.

978-0-8254-2009-2 | 512 pages | Hardcover

A WORKBOOK FOR INTERMEDIATE GREEK

π

Grammar, Exegesis, and Commentary on 1–3 John

HERBERT W. BATEMAN IV

KOINE GREEK READER

π

Selections from the New Testament, Septuagint, and Early Christian Writers

RODNEY J. DECKER

UNDERSTAND THE GREEK LANGUAGE

A Workbook for Intermediate Greek
Grammar, Exegesis, and Commentary on 1–3 John
Herbert W. Bateman IV

THIS THOROUGH SUPPLEMENTAL WORKBOOK LEAVES NO stone unturned! Presenting a twelve-step process for analyzing the Greek text of 1–3 John, this new resource will be especially welcomed by students in either their first year (second semester) or second year. Professor Bateman, a veteran instructor, guides students with well-crafted questions throughout. Though the book's focus is on syntax, it offers plenty of grammar review, as well as many historical, exegetical, and grammatical comments. Referenced to six intermediate grammars and five beginning grammars, it can be easily used in conjunction with many standard textbooks.

Herbert W. Bateman IV has taught beginning and intermediate Greek for more than twenty years on the college and graduate level. He is the editor of *Four Views on the Warning Passages in Hebrews, Three Central Issues in Contemporary Dispensationalism*, and *Authentic Worship*.

978-0-8254-2149-5 | 614 pages | Paperback

Koine Greek Reader
Selections from the New Testament,
Septuagint, and Early Christian Writers
Rodney Decker

PROVIDING GRADED READINGS IN KOINE GREEK from the New Testament, Septuagint, Apostolic Fathers, and early creeds, this unique text integrates the full range of materials needed by intermediate Greek students. Its many features include four helpful vocabulary lists, numerous references to other resources, assorted translation helps, a review of basic grammar and syntax, and an introduction to *BDAG*—the standard Greek lexicon.

Rodney J. Decker, who has a Th.D. from Central Baptist Theological Seminary, is professor of Greek and New Testament at Baptist Bible Seminary in Clarks Summit, Pennsylvania. He is the author of numerous journal articles and a highly respected monograph on the Gospel of Mark published in the Studies in Biblical Greek series edited by D. A. Carson.

978-0-8254-2442-7 | 312 pages | Paperback

iVocab
Biblical Greek

Version 2.0

θεός, -οῦ, ὁ

See and Hear Flashcards on Your MP3 Player, Cell Phone, and Computer

David M. Hoffeditz | J. Michael Thigpen

iVocab
Biblical Greek

Advanced Vocabulary by Frequency

David M. Hoffeditz | J. Michael Thigpen

BUILD UP YOUR GREEK VOCABULARY

iVocab Biblical Greek 2.0
Vocabulary for Six Beginning Grammars
David M. Hoffeditz and J. Michael Thigpen

THIS HELP COMPREHENSIVELY UPDATES AND EXPANDS the widely successful *iVocab Biblical Greek*. Version 2.0 continues to move beyond traditional ink-and-paper flashcards, allowing users to see and hear chapter vocabulary followed by the translation. A powerful, portable learning tool, it includes more than eight hundred audiovisual flashcards for your iPod®, other MP3 player, cell phone, or computer. Coordinated with six leading Greek grammars—Mounce, Duff, Black, Croy, Machen-McCartney, and Wenham—*iVocab Biblical Greek 2.0* features will maximize vocabulary learning for students!

978-0-8254-2745-9 | CD-ROM

iVocab Biblical Greek: Advanced Vocabulary by Frequency
David M. Hoffeditz and J. Michael Thigpen

THIS AID SIGNIFICANTLY COMPLEMENTS THE EXISTING iVocab Biblical Greek series by providing the next logical step for vocabulary acquisition and retention needs of students and pastors who no longer require vocabulary from an elementary grammar. Aiding intermediate and advanced undergraduate students, graduate students, and pastors who need to learn and retain vocabulary down to a specific frequency, either as a course requirement or for reading fluency, *iVocab Biblical Greek: Advanced Vocabulary by Frequency* includes Greek words that occur ten times or more, inflected forms that occur a hundred times or more, and irregular tense verbs.

978-0-8254-2774-9 | CD-ROM

David M. Hoffeditz, Ph.D., University of Aberdeen, is an associate pastor at Rocky Point Chapel in Springfield, Ohio, and served as an associate professor of Bible and Greek at the collegiate level for seven years. He is also an active guest speaker and lecturer.

J. Michael Thigpen is the executive director of the Evangelical Theological Society. He holds a M.Phil. in Hebraic and Cognate Studies and is currently completing his Ph.D. dissertation at Hebrew Union College. He has taught Hebrew on both the undergraduate and graduate levels.

Available wherever books are sold
www.kregel.com

What the New Testament Authors Really Cared About

A SURVEY OF THEIR WRITINGS

KENNETH BERDING
MATT WILLIAMS

EDITORS

The Historical Origins of the Gospels

WHY FOUR GOSPELS?

DAVID ALAN BLACK

FIND TEACHING RESOURCES

What the New Testament Authors Really Cared About
A Survey of Their Writings
Kenneth Berding and Matt Williams

FIFTEEN TOP-RATED PROFESSORS FROM TWELVE LEADING Christian colleges and universities have collaborated to write this compact, accessible New Testament survey. Introductory issues (Who? When? Where? Why?) are condensed to a one-page snapshot of all the most pertinent information. In addition, more than one hundred applications are highlighted in sidebars to clarify how the New Testament authors might apply their writings to Christians living in the twenty-first century. The book's uncomplicated structure and creative format make it a perfect tool for Christian education programs in church and college New Testament courses.

Kenneth Berding, Ph.D., is associate professor of New Testament at Biola University. His books include *Polycarp and Paul* and *What Are Spiritual Gifts? Rethinking the Conventional View*.

Matt Williams, Ph.D., is associate professor of New Testament at Biola University. His publications include *Two Gospels from One* and contributions to the Deeper Connections DVD Bible studies.

978-0-8254-2539-4 | 240 pages | Paperback

Why Four Gospels?
The Historical Origins of the Gospels
David Alan Black

THIS SUCCINCT TREATMENT OF THE SYNOPTIC Problem explains the "fourfold gospel hypothesis." By taking into account data within the gospels themselves and evidence from the early church fathers, Dr. Black affirms the traditional view that Matthew was the first gospel written, and suggests that Luke was written as its Gentile counterpart. Peter, whose recollections form the basis of Mark, provided the apostolic stamp of approval for Luke's gospel by drawing from both prior sources and bridging the gap between the two books.

David Alan Black, D. Theol., University of Basel, is professor of New Testament and Greek at Southeastern Baptist Theological Seminary in Wake Forest, North Carolina. He is the author of numerous books, including *Learn to Read New Testament Greek* and *Interpreting the New Testament*.

978-0-8254-2070-2 | 118 pages | Paperback

Available wherever books are sold
www.kregel.com

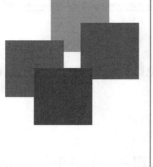

FOUR VIEWS ON THE WARNING PASSAGES IN HEBREWS

HERBERT W. BATEMAN IV
GENERAL EDITOR

GARETH L. COCKERILL • BUIST M. FANNING
RANDALL C. GLEASON • GRANT R. OSBORNE
CONCLUSION BY
GEORGE H. GUTHRIE

KREGEL
CHARTS OF THE BIBLE
AND THEOLOGY

"I know of no better collection of materials that illuminates Revelation than these resources."—Ben Witherington

Charts on the Book of Revelation

Literary, Historical, and Theological Perspectives

Mark Wilson

FIND TEACHING RESOURCES

Four Views on the Warning Passages in Hebrews
Herbert W. Bateman IV

USING THE POPULAR FOUR-VIEWS FORMAT, this volume explores the meaning of the five warning passages in the book of Hebrews to both the original readers and us today. Each of the four New Testament scholars present and defend their view and critique the view of the others. This unique volume will help readers better understand some of the most difficult passages in all of Scripture. Contributors include Grant R. Osborne, Buist M. Fanning, Gareth L. Cockerill, and Randall C. Gleason.

Herbert W. Bateman IV has taught beginning and intermediate Greek for more than twenty years on the college and graduate level. He is the editor of *Four Views on the Warning Passages in Hebrews*, *Three Central Issues in Contemporary Dispensationalism*, and *Authentic Worship*.

978-0-8254-2132-7 | 480 pages | Paperback

Charts on the Book of Revelation
Literary, Historical, and Theological Perspectives
Mark Wilson

THIS IS A CHARTS BOOK that does not seek to support specific interpretations of end-times prophecies. Instead, it depicts the literary, historical, and theological backgrounds of Revelation, arguably the New Testament's most challenging book. With seventy-nine charts, timelines, and maps (developed especially for this volume), this unique guide promises to help all Bible readers, especially students, teachers, and preachers, regardless of their theological background. All charts are reproducible for classroom use.

Mark Wilson is director of the Asia Minor Research Center, Izmir, Turkey, and has taught as an adjunct professor of New Testament at several universities and seminaries. Dr. Wilson wrote the commentary on Revelation in the *Zondervan Illustrated Bible Backgrounds Commentary*. His other titles include *Mastering New Testament Greek Vocabulary Through Semantic Domains* and *St. Paul the Traveler and Roman Citizen*.

978-0-8254-3939-1 | 136 pages | Paperback

DEFEND THE REAL JESUS

Putting Jesus in His Place
The Case for the Deity of Christ
Robert M. Bowman Jr. and J. Ed Komoszewski

THE CENTRAL THEOLOGICAL DISTINCTIVE OF CHRISTIANITY—that Jesus is God incarnate—has repeatedly come under fire from adherents to other religions and scholars who interpret Jesus as a prophet, angel, or guru. *Putting Jesus in His Place* is designed to introduce Christians to the wealth of biblical teaching on the deity of Christ.

978-0-8254-2983-5 | 392 pages | Paperback

Reinventing Jesus
How Contemporary Skeptics Miss the Real Jesus and Mislead Popular Culture
J. Ed Komoszewski, M. James Sawyer, and Daniel B. Wallace

FROM THE WORLDWIDE PHENOMENON OF *The Da Vinci Code* to the national best-seller *Misquoting Jesus*, popular culture is being bombarded with radical skepticism about the uniqueness of Christ and the reliability of the New Testament. *Reinventing Jesus* cuts through the rhetoric of extreme doubt expressed by these and several other contemporary voices to reveal the profound credibility of historic Christianity. Meticulously researched, thoroughly documented, yet eminently readable, this book invites a wide audience to take a firsthand look at the solid, reasonable, and clearly defensible evidence for Christianity's origins.

978-0-8254-2982-8 | 352 pages | Paperback

Who's Tampering with the Trinity?
An Assessment of the Subordination Debate
Millard J. Erickson

THEOLOGIAN MILLARD J. ERICKSON EXAMINES the various views concerning subordination within the Trinity and also looks at the discussion throughout the history of the church. In addition to providing rigorous theological analysis of the subject, Erickson exposes flaws in familial implications derived from the Trinity. This increasingly debated topic has finally received a thorough, careful, and objective treatment in *Who's Tampering with the Trinity?*

978-0-8254-2589-9 | 272 pages | Paperback

Available wherever books are sold
■■■■ **www.kregel.com** ■■■■